MONEY AND FINANCE IN THE TRANSITION TO A MARKET ECONOMY

Money and Finance in the Transition to a Market Economy

István Ábel
Professor of Economics, Budapest University of Economics, Hungary

Pierre L. Siklos
Professor of Economics, Wilfrid Laurier University, Canada

István P. Székely
Director of the Research Department, National Bank of Hungary

Edward Elgar
Cheltenham, UK • Northampton, MA, USA

Published by
Edward Elgar Publishing Limited
8 Lansdown Place
Cheltenham
Glos GL50 2HU
UK

Edward Elgar Publishing, Inc.
6 Market Street
Northampton
Massachusetts 01060
USA

A catalogue record for this book
is available from the British Library

Library of Congress Cataloguing in Publication Data

Money and finance in the transition to a market economy / István Ábel,
    Pierre L. Siklos, István P. Székely.
    Includes bibliographical references and index.
    1. Monetary policy—Europe, Eastern. 2. Monetary policy—Europe,
Central. 3. Banks and banking—Europe, Eastern. 4. Banks and
banking—Europe, Central. I. Ábel, István. II. Siklos, Pierre L.,
1955–   . III. Székely, István P., 1959–   .
HG930.7.M665 1998
332.4'947—dc21   97–43508
                                                                            CIP

ISBN 1 85898 228 6

Printed and bound in Great Britain by
Biddles Ltd, Guildford and King's Lynn

Contents

List of Figures

List of Tables

List of Contributors

István Ábel, Budapest University of Economics

John P. Bonin, Wesleyan University

Konstantine Gatsios, Athens University of Economics and Business

Pierre L. Siklos, Wilfrid Laurier University

István Székely, National Bank of Hungary

Preface

We are fast approaching the milestone of a decade since several of the economies in Central and Eastern Europe began to dismantle the structure of central planning and permitted their economies to be governed instead by market forces. The adoption of democratic political institutions would come later although it is still unclear how firmly entrenched these are in several of the countries which have since been labelled 'transitional economies'.

So much has been written on various aspects of the transaction process that it is difficult for an outsider interested in these developments to know where to begin, what were the important economic issues, and what has become of some of them.

This book makes a modest claim to be among the first to collect a series of articles which focus on the key questions and problems facing the transitional economies in the sphere of monetary policy and the financial sector. Our objective is to provide interested readers with a compendium of the types of reforms that were considered, why these proved necessary, and the implications of the actual developments in the initial stages of the transition.

As will become apparent, the book focuses on four major themes: the effect of state desertion on liquidity and the availability of credit in the economy; the failure of credit markets and the implications for corporate finance; the role of property rights and the importance of bankruptcy procedures in a well-functioning market economy; and the far-reaching effects of the separation of the central banking and commercial lending functions as well as the consequences on the overall operation of monetary policy in a transitional economy.

Each chapter begins with a Prologue which sets the stage for the material covered by the chapter, and its relationship to the other themes covered by the book, where appropriate. Each chapter also ends with a Postscript which very briefly explains subsequent developments and whether one can argue that the transitional phase has been completed.

Five of the chapters have been reprinted, with revisions, from previously published work. Three chapters represent new material not previously published (chapters 4, 7, and 8) while two other chapters (2 and 9) have undergone major revisions. However, with the addition of the Prologues and Postscripts, we have compiled a unified package which provides policy makers and interested academics with a coherent set of papers dealing with financial reforms in transitional economies. In addition, the list of references, which has been updated, provides we believe for the first time a good source for the vast literature on the subject which should prove especially useful for those individuals wishing to explore in greater detail the myriad of questions raised by the chapters in this volume.

The authors are grateful to the contributors for agreeing to include some of their previously published works, and to the various publishers for permission to reprint the articles in this volume. Finally, thanks are also due to Elsie Grogan for her usual efficient and speedy word processing.

Budapest, Hungary   István Ábel
Waterloo, Canada   Pierre L. Siklos
Budapest, Hungary   István Székely

1. State Desertion and Credit Market Failure in the Transition*

PROLOGUE

Although Hungary is credited with having begun the transition to market earlier than other centrally planned economies the sheer speed with which the government sector attempted to shrink in size relative to the economy as a whole is perhaps one of the distinguishing characteristics of the early experience of all socialist economies seeking to remake themselves into market economies. This chapter assesses the immediate impact of so-called state desertion which, it can be fairly said, is an essential catalyst of the economic transformation process.

1. INTRODUCTION: THE ROLE OF THE STATE IN THE TRANSITION

For the first two to three years of the transition, all of the Central East European (CEE) countries in transition experienced deep recessions. The austerity programmes pursued to stabilize these economies reduced private sector demand significantly. Liberalization of both prices and external trade added an inflationary shock to which the policy response was increased austerity. As the recession deepened, the tax base was eroded and transfer payments increased, plunging the fiscal budget into serious deficit. The budget deficit soaked up private savings that would have been better channelled into financing the business expansion necessary to initiate and nurture the supply response to price liberalization. Given this vicious cycle, determining the proper role for the state to play during the transition in the CEE countries is crucial.

Owing to its predominant, almost all-embracing, past role in the socialist bureaucratically managed economy, the state obviously must reduce substantially its economic activity in order to facilitate a successful transition to a mixed market economy. At the same time, the state must orchestrate the evolution and development of the environmental infrastructure necessary to support the growth of the market economy. According to Chang and Rowthorn (1994), the state must be involved whenever a new economic coordination

1

structure is established. As it withdraws from micro-managing the economic sphere in the CEE countries, the state must accept responsibility for nurturing, but not smothering, the maturing market economy.

That the state should be involved in developing the appropriate legislative support for the market economy is self-evident. It is equally important for the state to be an institution builder, i.e., an economic enabler as well as a legal enabler. In the CEE countries, system-specific legacies work against state intervention. The perception is strong that a continuing planner's mentality will perpetuate the petty tutelage of the earlier period. Such an attitude is a natural response to the overcentralization of the planning period. However, preventing state intervention may lead to state desertion and impede the transition to the market economy.

To conceptualize state desertion, we define two types. Type 1 state desertion is a rapid and continual decrease in the state's involvement in the aggregate economy. Such state withdrawal from macroeconomic activity could well be a contributing factor to the deep recessions observed in all CEE countries. Type 2 state desertion is an abrupt and discontinuous withdrawal of the state from the economic infrastructure that supports the allocational mechanism. Since the institutional and behavioural preconditions for a well-functioning markets are underdeveloped in CEE countries, state intervention (not state desertion) is required to fill the void. The state must create and nurture the economic institutions necessary to support the fledgling market economy. In this context, the major policy issue facing CEE governments is a lack of any historical precedence for such a radical restructuring of the state's role in so short a period of time. Hence the appropriate mix of state withdrawal and state support is difficult to ascertain.

The transition to a market economy requires the state to withdraw from directing the allocation of resources and leave this task to markets. At the same time, financial support is necessary if state-owned enterprises (SOE) are to be restructured so that they can perform efficiently in the new market setting. Financing is also required to allow new ventures to become strong enough to introduce much needed competition to nascent domestic markets. While relinquishing its role in the direct allocation of capital, the state must support the creation of a market-based alternative, i.e., a healthy independent banking sector. Commercial banks should take over the intermediation of savings and investment. However, CEE governments did not grant the newly created commercial banks sufficient autonomy nor did they provide them with a strong enough capital base to carry out intermediation efficiently. Rather, the CEE states left a financial black hole in which a credit market crunch threatens the macroeconomic stability attained at an already high cost.

The present chapter uses Hungary's experiences to illustrate the problems and issues to be dealt with in all transforming countries. In the next section, we identify type 1 state desertion in Hungary even though the macroeconomic data turn out to be potentially misleading. In section 3, we characterize type 2 state desertion of the Hungarian financial sector and conclude that the state acted irresponsibly in creating semi-independent commercial banks burdened with distorted loan portfolios of dubious quality. In section 4, we analyze the severely dysfunctional financial distress resulting from credit market failure in Hungary. In section 5, we evaluate several proposals for resolving the bad loans problem in CEE countries. Section 6 is a concluding one in which we recommend strong and decisive state intervention to strengthen commercial banks so that they may play their crucial intermediary role in the emerging financial markets in the CEE countries. As the following chapters make clear, this is advice not always heeded by these governments.

Table 1.1   General Government Operations: International Comparison (as percentage of GDP)

Country	Revenues	Expenditures	Deficit (-) or Surplus (+)
Hungary (1987)	**61.0**	**63.0**	**-2.0**
Hungary (1989)	**58.7**	**61.4**	**-2.7**
Hungary (1991)	**57.7**	**59.7**	**-2.0**
Hungary (1992)[1]	**56.5**	**63.6**	**-7.1**
Hungary (1993)[2]	**55.9**	**62.6**	**-6.7**
Netherlands (1989)	51.1	56.6	-5.5
Sweden (1988)	59.1	56.9	2.2
Denmark (1989)	59.6	59.4	0.2
Belgium (1987)	47.8	54.7	-6.9
Austria (1989)	46.9	49.7	-2.8
France (1989)	46.2	47.8	-1.6
Germany (1987)	46.0	47.9	-1.9
Poland (1987)	47.4	47.6	-0.3
Romania (1987)	52.8	45.5	7.3
Canada (1987)	40.3	44.7	-4.4
UK (1987)	42.7	44.0	-1.3
Finland (1987)	42.7	43.9	-1.2
Spain (1987)	35.0	38.6	-3.6
USA (1987)	34.9	36.9	-2.0

[1] Expected for 1992 as of February 1993.
[2] Planned for 1993.
Source: Kornai (1992, p.5) and Muraközi (1992, p.1051,1053) for the data for countries other than Hungary. For Hungary, data are revised and corrected by László Borbély of the Ministry of Finance.

2. STATE DESERTION IN HUNGARY: MYTH OR REALITY?

János Kornai (1992) measures the predominance of the state in economic activity in Hungary by the ratio of general government budget operations to GDP. As Table 1.1 indicates, until 1993, the Hungarian government was directly involved in about 60% of Gross Domestic Product (GDP). The typical proportion in market economies is between 40 and 50% (in the US economy, it is significantly below 40%). In Table 1.2, consolidated general government

Table 1.2   Consolidated General Government in Hungary, 1985-93 (as percentage of GDP)

Year	Total Expend- itures	Total Rev- enues	Enter- prise Sub- sidies[1]	Con- sumer Price Subsidy	Health and Educa- tion	Unemploy- ment Compensa- tion	Total Expendi- tures for Households[2]
1985	60.9	60.3	13.2	4.8	10.2	-	28.3
1986	64.6	61.5	14.0	5.5	9.9	-	29.6
1987	63.0	61.0	13.5	5.4	9.5	-	28.5
1988	61.6	61.5	11.3	3.1	8.6	-	31.1
1989	61.4	58.7	7.7	2.6	10.1	-	34.9
1990	56.4	57.6	6.2	1.8	11.8	0.1	35.9
1990[3]	(54.4)	(55.6)	(5.9)	(1.7)	(11.3)	(0.1)	(34.6)
1991	59.7	57.7	4.8	1.8	13.2	0.8	40.6
1991	(50.8)	(48.1)	(4.0)	(1.6)	(11.2)	(0.7)	(34.5)
1992[4]	63.6	56.5	4.4	0.7	12.8	3.1	39.9
1992	(51.4)	(45.6)	(3.6)	(0.6)	(10.3)	(2.5)	(32.2)
1993[5]	35.1	29.4	1.7	0.6	9.2	9.0	39.2
1994	34.7	27.2	2.3	0.6	9.4	8.6[7]	N/A
1995[6]	31.6	28.5	1.7	0.6	N/A	7.7[7]	N/A

[1] Includes subsidies received from Central Government, Extra-budgetary Funds and Municipalities.
[2] In addition to the categories mentioned in the table, includes expenditures on culture, sports, pensions, dependent care benefits and sick benefits.
[3] Data in parentheses are ratios calculated by assuming no change in GDP from 1989 to 1992.
[4] Expected for 1992 as of February 1993.
[5] Target for 1993 in the budget plan.
[6] Based on preliminary GDP data.
[7] Based on preliminary unemployment compensation expenditures data.
Source: Ministry of Finance Hungary. Consolidated data are revised and corrected by László Borbély.
Notes: For the years 1990-92 we adjusted the data for the effect of the recession.

expenditures and revenues as a percentage of GDP are recorded for Hungary from 1985 to 1995. Until 1992, both ratios are inordinately high by international standards. Moreover, expenditures as a percentage of GDP had been increasing since 1990 in Hungary. In 1992, this ratio was higher than it had been in all but one of the pre-transition years. Does the data indicate that type 1 state desertion is a myth in Hungary? A satisfactory answer requires consideration of the economic situation at the beginning of the transition.

After having stagnated with low real growth in the second half of the eighties, the Hungarian economy slid into a recession in 1990 with real GDP falling by 3.5%. The recession deepened in 1991 and continued in 1992 as real GDP declined by 12% and 5% respectively so that the cumulative drop over the three-year period exceeded 20%. Might this recession explain why the ratio of government expenditures to GDP in Hungary rose while the state was withdrawing from macroeconomic activity? To adjust the data for the effect of the Hungarian recession, we calculate the expenditure and revenue ratios for 1990, 1991, and 1992 as if GDP had remained constant at its 1989 level.[1] Then, a starkly different picture emerges. As Table 1.2 records, expenditures as a percentage of 1989 GDP are 54.4, 50.8, and 51.4 for 1990, 1991, and 1992 respectively. For the same years, the ratio of revenues to 1989 GDP becomes 55.6, 48.1, and 45.6. Therefore, after adjusting for the recession, the aggregate figures do indicate type 1 state desertion. The adjusted ratio of expenditures to non-recessionary GDP fell by ten points (or almost 18%) from 1989 to 1992. Currently at about 51%, this ratio places Hungary in the upper tier of Western market economies.

Even if GDP is not adjusted for the recession, the state's withdrawal from micro-managing the aggregate economy is evident. From Table 1.2, subsidies to enterprises declined from 13.5% of GDP in 1987 to 4.4% of GDP in 1992. The decline would continue in subsequent years. Consumer price subsidies as a percentage of GDP fell from 2.57 in 1989 to 0.73 in 1992. Table 1.2 also provides information on the changing composition of support for households. Support for health and education remain almost constant if GDP is adjusted. Unemployment compensation, which was nonexistent in 1989, grew to 2.5% of adjusted GDP in 1992 (and was forecast to reach almost 5% of actual GDP in 1993). Nonetheless, total support to households adjusted for the recession decreased from 34.87 in 1989 to 32.21 in 1992 for a decline of 2.66 percentage points. Consequently, aggregate state support of households was smaller by the end of the period owing mainly to the decrease in direct subsidies. The composition of state support changed to reflect the new and growing social safety net.

Reducing the state's interference with markets by decreasing direct subsidies to consumers and firms is a necessary condition for the emergence of markets. However, reductions in overall government expenditures decrease aggregate demand and exacerbate the decline in GDP. When adjusted for the effect of the recession, the ratio of aggregate government expenditure to GDP fell by ten points over a three-year period in Hungary. Thus, type 1 state desertion is discernible in the Hungarian macroeconomic data and it was partly responsible for postponing economic recovery. By 1993, the looming general elections, together with growing international pressure, combined to reduce the size of the public sector (e.g., see chapter 8), with rather dramatic results. The size of government shrank dramatically and the deficit became negligible by 1995. Subsidies to enterprises became relatively less important in relation to total government expenditures, as noted earlier, while the costs associated with providing unemployment compensation rose as a share of total government spending. Type 1 state desertion was essentially completed. In what follows, we focus on the early years of the transition and argue that irresponsible state withdrawal from the financial sector definitely impeded the progress of the transition in all CEE countries.

3. STATE DESERTION OF THE FINANCIAL SECTOR

The severe decline in real output experienced in the CEE countries since 1990 has its roots in a credit market failure caused by state desertion of the financial sector. During the planning period, household and business money circuits were institutionally separate. The fiscal budget provided the necessary intermediation by transferring liquidity from the household or external sector to the production sector. Institutionally, the Central Bank extended the credit for business expansion designated by the plan and administered company accounts. Interenterprise transactions were recorded as debits or credits at the Central Bank; no separate payments clearing system outside of the monobank system existed. Credit policy was subordinated to planning as enterprise officials negotiated with bureaucrats to obtain funds for investment. Monetary policy as practised in a market economy using indirect instruments did not exist.

Hungary moved in the direction of market reform earlier than other CEE countries by dismantling the institutions of annual physical planning in 1968. However, the dominant role of the state in financial intermediation persisted. Ábel and Székely (1992b) show that government money was the only causal explanation for liquidity in the business sector from 1974 to 1986. Monetized fiscal deficits provided overall liquidity to the economy prior to the restructuring of the banking system in 1987. Subservient to the state bureaucracy, the National Bank of Hungary played no major role in intermediating savings and investment. Until the banking reform in 1987, changes in the fiscal budget position and changes in interenterprise credit were inversely related (Ábel and Bonin, 1992a). The business sector responded to any decrease in fiscal liquidity by increasing the length of the credit queue. Hence, the fiscal budget position drove credit market behaviour up to the time when the banking system was demonopolized.

As a precursor to (or as an essential first step in) the transition, all CEE countries created two-tier decentralized commercial banking systems from their central (monopoly) banks by breaking off entire credit divisions. In Hungary, the separation occurred in 1987 along sectoral lines.[2] The four newly created commercial banks, in descending order of assets, are Hungarian Credit Bank, Commercial and Credit Bank, Budapest Bank, and Hungarian Foreign Trade Bank. The largest Hungarian bank in terms of assets is the National Savings Bank which is the primary collector of household deposits.

In all CEE countries, commercial banks are primarily state-owned (directly and also indirectly through ownership participation by state-owned client companies).[3] Their initial portfolios were saddled with nonperforming (bad) debt. As newly created commercial banks, they held virtually no loan-loss reserves. The CEE states accepted no responsibility for the distorted portfolios inherited from discredited political regimes. For example, the three largest Hungarian commercial banks were insolvent according to international accounting standards from their conception. Consequently, CEE banks were bequeathed weak loan portfolios without any compensating government support. As such, they are all victims of type 2 state desertion.

The loan portfolios of these banks continued to deteriorate with the recessions. Such financial distress is not without precedence; financial systems all over the world have experienced problems in the last fifteen years (World Bank 1989). However, CEE banks have particular characteristics that demand special attention when designing financial policy. The abrupt withdrawal of the state from the process of credit allocation left the newly created commercial banks as the primary conduits of credit in the economy. In particular, banks were expected to provide new capital to promising projects and ventures. However, by leaving them financially weak, the state abdicated its responsibility for the obligations that were incurred under the old regime. Type 2 state desertion makes it impossible for the banks to intermediate savings and investment efficiently.

In Hungary, the dilemma for the newly created banks was exacerbated by the New Banking Act, which became effective on 1 December, 1991. This act introduced specific categories for rating the loan portfolios of the banks, mandated the accumulation of provisions (loan-loss reserves) against the qualified loans in the portfolio, and specified a schedule for meeting international capital adequacy targets. Although this legislation was designed to make Hungarian banking standards more consistent with international ones, the provisions required against bad loans severely impacted the banks' ability to make new loans. The cost of services and interest spreads were maintained at levels high enough to allow banks to generate sufficient cash flow to accumulate the required loan-loss provisions. In essence, the New Banking Act imposed a flow solution on the (bad debt) stock problem.

The bad loans left on the books when the commercial banks were created became a burden on the healthy segment of the commercial sector. Companies that serviced their loan obligations did so at unusually high interest rates. High financing costs discouraged small-scale entrepreneurial activity, inhibited entry of new firms, and precluded the capital injections necessary to restructure potential profitable state-owned enterprises to prepare them properly for privatization. By pricing investors out of the market, the commercial banks promoted further stagnation. By refusing to accept responsibility for the legacies of the past, the state left the banks with no alternative. Type 2 state desertion of the financial sector seriously impaired the ability of the newly created commercial banks to carry out their primary function, namely to allocate credit on economically rational grounds.

In leaving commercial banks burdened with bad (inherited) loans, the state substituted its earlier transparent support of ailing companies through direct fiscal subsidies with nontransparent financial redistribution. Companies with nonperforming loans had their interest arrears capitalized by the banks. Furthermore, the banks continued to do business with their old clients, many of whom held ownership shares in the banks, even when these clients did not meet interest obligations. Consequently, the stock of bad debt increased. The healthy segment of the commercial sector supported ailing companies by paying high fees for financial services and high rates for loans. These financial transfers were less transparent than the earlier direct subsidies from the fiscal budget; moreover, as we develop in the next section, they were severely damaging to the health of the emerging market economy.

4. CREDIT MARKET FAILURE: THE CONSEQUENCES OF STATE DESERTION

Although the three largest Hungarian commercial banks were insolvent by international standards from inception, the banking system generated large cash flows from the beginning of the transition.[4] In 1991 and 1992, household deposits grew rapidly in Hungary. An interbank market transferred these deposits from the National Savings Bank to the commercial banks. Unsterilized injections of foreign exchange in accounts opened by foreign companies doing business in Hungary added further liquidity to the banking system. Although the supply of loanable funds increased substantially, interest rate spreads remained large. Even when inflation declined in 1992, nominal lending rates remained high.[5] The commercial banks used this increased liquidity to attend to solvency problems by accumulating the provisions required by the new banking legislation rather than to take an active role in providing credit to the emerging private sector.

The high spreads maintained throughout this period made borrowing from domestic banks unattractive to high-quality commercial costumers and led to credit market failure in Hungary.[6] On the demand side of the loanable funds market, the Hungarian production sector can be divided into three tiers consisting of good, struggling, and bad companies. The first tier consists of currently profitable companies that tend to operate either in export-oriented activities or in retail trade. These companies either generate sufficient internal funds to finance investment or, if they are joint ventures, they obtain credit from the mother company. Moreover, domestic companies exporting to Western markets have access to international capital markets at rates that can not matched by Hungarian banks. Hence, good companies tend to avoid the domestic credit market and the Hungarian banks are left with lending opportunities mainly in the second two tiers.

The third tier consists of companies that are already heavily indebted and, due to the nature of their markets, can not continue to exist in their present form (e.g., many Hungarian SOEs in heavy industry and the energy sector). These companies will ultimately either be forced to enter bankruptcy proceedings or become chronically dependent on subsidies from the state budget. In the former case, liquidation or reorganization will occur. Obviously, these are not good credit risks for a bank attempting to improve the quality of its portfolio. Hence, unless they are forced to do so by the state for political reasons, banks are no longer extending new credit to this tier.

The middle tier consists of companies that are currently struggling, due primarily to the deterioration in the domestic economy, even though they are potentially profitable under normal conditions. To become profitable, a company in this tier may need to change both its market outlook and its management and to introduce new products and new technology. An injection of new capital, financed either by a strategic partner (equity) or by long term bank credit, will be required to transform such a company into a profitable venture. The only strategic partner with sufficient equity and know how to accomplish the task in the near future is a foreign company. Until the nondiversifiable (macroeconomic and systemic) risk is reduced, foreign equity can not be attracted in sufficient quantities. However, the commercial banks are equally reluctant to take the risk involved with restructuring companies that have yet to prove their creditworthiness. Hence, the stagnation and the 'wait and see' attitude of creditors and potential equity holders.

Consequently, the Hungarian credit market exhibits an undesirable separating self-selection equilibrium in which the creditworthy borrowers are not interested in borrowing from the domestic banks and the riskier borrowers remain as the only available clients for these very banks. As a result, the increased supply of household savings observed in Hungary during the first three years of the transition is not directed toward the production sector because the commercial banks that were created to perform this intermediation are concerned about the quality of their portfolios. Instead of providing credit to the business sector, Hungarian banks have chosen to purchase government securities and channel domestic savings into financing a fiscal budget deficit which was above 7% of GDP in 1992 (Table 1.1). Hence, business investment is crowded out by fiscal expenditures because the banks find the risk-return bundle on government securities more attractive.

The brunt of the Hungarian credit crunch is born by potentially profitable but risky ventures (both creating new companies and restructuring middle-tier companies). Yet even though they are financially risky, new businesses must be encouraged to lead the country out of its recession and provide jobs for the workers being laid off as SOEs restructure. Owing to the provisioning requirements against bad loans, Hungarian banks are currently unable (and prudently unwilling) to intermediate savings and investment effectively. Hence, the production sector does not receive the new capital it requires and the end to the recession is brutally slow in coming. Neoclassical economic theory argues in favour of government intervention to redress market failure. The Hungarian state should take this lesson to heart and assume its responsibility for creating an undesirable outcome in the credit market when it dealt the banks a weak hand, i.e., the bad loans problem.

5. THE BAD LOANS LEGACY: AN EVALUATION OF PROPOSED SOLUTIONS

At the time that the commercial banks were created, the bad debt in CEE countries could have been recognized as inherited from the previous regime and removed from the balance sheets of the banks. The consolidated balance sheet of the state would have been unaffected since the state (either directly or indirectly) owned both the banks and the companies. Any decrease in state assets (loans on the banks' balance sheets) would have been matched by an equal decrease in state liabilities (the companies' debts). If it had had sufficient information to evaluate the loan portfolios when the banks were created, the state could have designed a credible once-and-for-all bad debt cancellation programme.[7] Then the newly created commercial banks would have started their life with cleansed balance sheets and would not have been burdened with the bad-debt albatross.

Although this argument is compelling, it would not have resolved the problem of inherited weak portfolios. Even if all the bad debt in the original portfolios had been removed, the situation of the commercial banks would still be financially fragile today. The deep recession and the loss of the Soviet market added significantly to the stock of nonperforming company debt in CEE banks. Long term loans made and long term obligations taken with clients during the previous regime turned bad because of these macroeconomic shocks. Hence, the portion of current bad loans that was actually inherited from the previous regime is difficult to identify. Furthermore, a forward-looking classification of the loan portfolios is difficult to accomplish. In some cases, debtor companies are antiquated with obsolete capital and no competitive market position. Evaluating such assets is a relatively simple task as it amounts to estimating scrap values. For most companies, the uncertainty of future profit streams makes a realistic 'market' value of the assets is difficult to establish.[8] In the intermediate stage of the transition, portfolio evaluation is still a difficult task.

To avoid the issue of identifying bad debt, Begg and Portes (1993) recommend removing all inherited loans from bank balance sheets. The state is then charged with the responsibility of 'marking these loans to their market values' and, thus, making transparent the actual condition of its consolidated balance sheet. Although such a proposal forces the state to take responsibility for decisions made by previous regimes, the removal of the entire stock of inherited debt from bank balance sheets would have undesirable consequences. From the bank's perspective, the balance sheet must balance so someone has to pay for debt cancellation. One possibility would be to reduce bank liabilities sufficiently to offset exactly the reduction in bank assets. Then debt removal would be financed by writing down the deposits of healthy profit-making companies and private households. Given the magnitude of the stock of inherited debt, the confiscation of such a significant portion of deposits would surely destroy confidence in commercial banks.

Recognizing this fact, Begg and Portes (1993) recommend issuing government bonds equal in face value to the loans removed.[9] They stress that the securities should earn a market rate of return and be sufficiently liquid to avoid having their value eroded by inflation. If all inherited debt is replaced in this fashion, the asset side of the banks' balance sheets would consist mainly of liquid government securities. If the banks are sufficiently independent from state control, they can expand their loans and investments subject to a fractional reserve requirement on deposit liabilities. The additional liquid bank reserves created by this exchange is potentially inflationary. To reduce commercial banks' free reserves, the central bank could increase the reserve requirement (temporarily) to attenuate the inflationary impact of the government issue.

When amended to recognize its potential inflationary consequence, the Begg-Portes proposal leaves the relationship between the central bank and the commercial banks in a rather primitive state. The central bank retains control over the aggregate level of credit while commercial banks are encouraged to take independent allocational decisions. However, reserve requirements are likely to be quite high. The banks would be making loans for which they would be held fully responsible. Yet with high reserve requirements, the cost of funds is likely to be high. As a result, the cost of credit would be high. Consequently, an infusion of liquid government securities accompanied with high reserve requirements to offset its inflationary potential is not likely to jump-start lending to businesses and unblock credit markets.

The proposal also presumes that the state has the resources and capabilities to manage the entire portfolio of inherited debt as effectively as the banks. However, the individual commercial banks are the best sources of information about their clients. As such, they are better able to monitor managerial malfeasance (e.g., asset stripping) and to work out the problem parts of their portfolios more successfully than a centralized government agency. Bonin and Mitchell (1992) develop a model in which the value of the state's assets will be higher if banks rather than a state agency work out the problem loans. Both moral hazard considerations and informational asymmetries make the centralized working out of bad loans suboptimal from the perspective of state wealth maximization.

More than likely, the government authorities in the CEE countries have understood that removing all inherited debt was infeasible.[10] Each state opted for some form of decentralized policy in which the banks were given the responsibility to work out their bad debt. At the same time, banks were required to accumulate reserves against the qualified part of the portfolio. However, this policy of bank self-reliance with its accompanying provisioning requirements is the primary cause of credit market failure in Hungary (as we argue above). The proper policy is for the state to avoid type 2 desertion of the financial sector and resolve the bad debt problem.

Since Hungarian commercial banks are required to evaluate their portfolios according to the requirements of the Banking Act, it would be possible for the state to remove only bad loans from bank balance sheets. Unless properly designed, this approach would penalize banks that have already accumulated significant provisions. To remove only the bad loans against which sufficient loan-loss reserve are held amounts to confiscating funds from healthier financial institutions. Thus, proper bank governance would be discouraged. An attractive alternative would be recapitalization of the banks using subordinated debt, either government-issued or government-guaranteed (private) debt. Bank net worth would increase and loan work out would be left in the hands of the commercial banks. These banks are in the best position to handle this task because of the information they have on their clients. This combination of decentralized bank work out (self-reliance) and government-assisted recapitalization is preferable to centralized schemes based on debt forgiveness alone.

6. CONCLUSION: STATE WITHDRAWAL VS. STATE DESERTION

The transition to a market economy requires state withdrawal in the aggregate sense of decreasing the role played by the state in overall economic activity and in the petty tutelage sense of eliminating direct interference with market activities. However, the state must not abdicate responsibility for the burdens that past decisions impose on evolving institutions. Rather, the state must become an economic enabler; it must build and strengthen the environmental underpinnings on the emerging market economy. In Hungary from 1990 on, the aggregate data on subsidies clearly indicates a rapid decline in the state's direct interference with production and distribution. By adjusting government expenditure to GDP ratios for the recession, we demonstrate a rapid and continual decline in the state's involvement in aggregate economic activity (type 1 state desertion). The level of support to the household sector is also declining even as unemployment compensation transfers increase rapidly. State desertion of this type has the potential to lengthen and deepen the recession in Hungary.

The Hungarian state's abrupt and discontinuous withdrawal from the process of credit allocation (type 2 state desertion of the financial sector) is unambiguously deleterious to the health of the nascent market economy. Inherited bad loans inhibit the newly formed commercial banks from performing effectively their intermediation function. Credit markets exhibit a separating self-selection equilibrium in which good risk clients are driven away from domestic banks by the high cost of funds and services. As a result, the commercial banks assist in the crowding out of private investment as they attempt to improve the quality of their portfolios. Hence, companies attempting to restructure and newly emerging entrepreneurs face a severe credit crunch. The state must intervene to break the gridlock and jump-start investment in the productive sector.

Why should the state be held responsible for the quality of the banks' portfolios? By reducing subsidies to companies, the state withdrew its direct fiscal support leaving these companies in a precarious financial condition. These loss-making companies were heavily indebted to the commercial banks. Furthermore, the recession and a more stringent bankruptcy act in Hungary combined to make more client's loans bad according to the classifications in the banking act. As a result, Hungarian commercial banks continue to support unhealthy companies with non-transparent subsidies (e.g., interest capitalization). The state not only deserted the financial sector; it continues to contribute to its distress.

How should the state walk the tightrope between helpful assistance and meddling interference? The objective is to provide the support necessary to nurture the development of credit markets. As a precondition, the state must assume responsibility for the bad loans problem. In doing so, it must not interfere directly with the lending activities of the commercial banks. Therefore, the Hungarian government should continue its self-reliance programme but at the same time it must inject fresh capital into the banking system. By using subordinate debt to recapitalize the banks, the state would both accept responsibility for the legacies of the past and maintain the necessary arm's-length relationship with the commercial banks.

State desertion (type 2) of the fledgling financial sector imposes too great a cost on the economy. The peculiar type of credit market failure that evolved in the CEE countries requires government intervention to assure the healthy development of market institutions. On the road to the mixed market economy, the state should withdraw from economic activity but not abdicate its responsibility to address market failures. State desertion has the potential to stall the transition indefinitely.

POSTSCRIPT

The extent to which state desertion influenced the costs of the transition is still very much open to debate. In both Poland and the Czech Republic economic growth has rebounded although the state involvement in the financial sector is greater than in the industrialized economies. In Hungary, state desertion from the financial sector proceeded somewhat slowly because of difficulties with the process of privatization. Improvements in the fiscal situation in some, but not all, of the transitional economies have also assisted the process of 'state desertion'. However, financial markets remain relatively immature and commercial banks still cannot be said to be well-functioning financial intermediaries in the sense understood in industrialized economies.

NOTES

* Originally published in *Acta Oeconomica*, 46 (1-2, 1994), 97-112, by I. Ábel and J.P. Bonin, and reprinted here with substantive revisions. The authors gratefully acknowledge the support provided by the National Council for Soviet and East European Research (grant number 807-07) and MTA OTKA Research Fund (grant number 681).

1. In market economies, recessions are accompanied by fiscal budget deterioration due to increased transfer payments and decreased taxable income. Although similar effects must be occurring in Hungary, we do not adjust the data to try to separate out cyclical from structural aspects of the fiscal budget.

2. In Czechoslovakia (separation in 1990) and Poland (separation in 1989), regional divisions were maintained.
3. The direct ownership share of the state in the four large commercial banks varies between 35% to 50% but the residual in all cases consists almost entirely of ownership shares held by state-owned companies. This arrangement creates the curious situation that company privatization increases the state's ownership share in the commercial banks because the company's share reverts to the state when it is privatized.
4. In 1990, profit margins were high enough for taxes and dividends from the financial sector to constitute 7.6% of fiscal receipts (Ábel and Bonin, 1992).
5. The spread in real interest rates was even greater due to the difference (about 9% in 1992) between CPI and PPI inflation. Historically, margins in the retail sector had averaged about 10%. As retail trade became increasingly privatized, margins increased to approach those in Western market sectors which average 30% to 40%. The difference between the ratio of tradeables to nontradeables also explains gaps in CPI and PPI inflation. Since real household deposit rates should be calculated using CPI while real commercial lending rates should use PPI, the spread of real rates was even larger than the spread of nominal rates.
6. See Thorne (1992) for a discussion of financial de-intermediation in Eastern Europe.
7. To avoid any incentive for banks to continue making bad loans because they expect subsequent bailouts, Caprio and Levine (1992) recommend linking debt forgiveness to bank privatization.
8. To avoid having to evaluate entire bank portfolios to determine how much debt should be removed, Scott and Levine (1992) have suggested forgiving bad debts only when the enterprise is privatized.
9. For Poland, Begg and Portes estimate the financing implications of this policy to be between 2% and 3% of GDP. Whether or not such an addition to the fiscal deficit is feasible or warranted can be argued.
10. In 1991, Czechoslovakia adopted a programme in which 20% of the existing commercial loans were transferred from the banks' balance sheets to the newly formed Consolidation Bank. Although this programme was the most adventurous among CEE countries with respect to debt removal, it still left Komercni Banka, the largest commercial bank in the Czech Republic, with a shortfall in loan loss reserves of 9 billion koruna (or about 5% of its remaining loan portfolio) for 1991. The Hungarian government negotiated with the banks to guarantee about 10 billion forints of doubtful loans purported to represent about half of the existing bad debt at the time that the commercial banks were created in 1987.

2. Constraints on Enterprise Liquidity and Their Impact on Monetary Policy*

PROLOGUE

One of the immediate effects of the transition (see Chapter 1) was the abandonment of a ready source of finance for both large and small firms, namely the state. Complicating matters further are the difficulties faced by the emerging private sector unable to access a well-functioning capital market. The reason is that the newly independent banking sector, saddled with bad debts, preferred to hold guaranteed state debt over risky private sector debt.

This chapter points out that an immature capital market produced two effects: a credit crunch (see also Chapter 3) and widespread resort to trade credit. The latter is a phenomenon that market economies faced, for example, during the 1950s and early 1960s.

1. INTRODUCTION

With the transition to a market economy comes a transition in the role and effectiveness of monetary policy. The adoption of market capitalism in Hungary, and in other Central and Eastern European countries, has led to the emergence and growth of a large number of privately-owned firms with risky future prospects because of difficulties in accessing capital markets. These events have also had an influence on the banking sector's own expectations of success. The ensuing difficulties are compounded by the stance of monetary policy as presently pursued by governments of the former socialist countries.

The macroeconomic environment facing Hungary during the period 1988-1992 was dominated by the collapse of the Soviet market, the impact of the introduction of market driven instruments and institutions, the deepening recession and growing protectionism of Western European countries. In addition, as the 1992 *Annual Report* of the National Bank of Hungary points out, new Bankruptcy, Accounting and Banking Laws were introduced that year (but debated in preceding years) which '*...launched far reaching changes not only in the way of thinking of economic agents, but also in their practical behaviour...*' (p.10, italics in original). Other transition economies (e.g., Poland) have tended to postpone the introduction of bankruptcy legislation in part to enable the large scale enterprises to reform themselves prior to facing the judgement of the marketplace and also because of perceived political consequences from the anticipated large number of prospective bankruptcies (see Mizsei, 1994; Siklos and Ábel, 1995 and Chapter 4 in this volume). Aggregate measures such as industrial output and the unemployment rate[1] reveal a steady deterioration in the overall performance in the transition economies, at least until 1993. In Hungary, for example, industrial output begins to rise in 1993 and the unemployment rate begins to trend downward.[2] By mid-1994, unemployment began to rise as higher world interest rates and political instability began to take their toll.

This chapter begins with an overview of monetary policy in the transitional phase. We then note the relationship between trade credit and inflation for an individual firm. While the implications of the relationship are well known, they seem to have been largely forgotten by policy makers who have adopted monetary policies consonant with those in western industrialized countries. We then demonstrate that the type of restrictive policy pursued by the central bank plays a critical role but one which is likely to reduce the chances of a successful transition to a market economy measured in terms of output and inflation. This is the subject of Section 4. Our findings contradict other studies (e.g., Dittus, 1994) which assign a relatively smaller role to the possibility of a credit crunch in the early stages of the transition (see Siklos and Ábel, 1995).

The separation of the government's budget deficit financing from monetary policy is at the heart of existing transition programmes. The independence of monetary policy is a feature of these programmes whose origins can be traced back to 1987 in Hungary's case. The most pressing issue at the beginning of the transition process is how to deal with the dubious quality of the debt held by state-owned enterprises, including inter-enterprise credit, and how it would be treated in a reformed banking system.[3] Section 5 deals with other issues relative to the debts accumulated by firms under the old centrally planned regime. The chapter concludes in Section 6 with a summary. Our focus is on Hungary though we comment also on the experience of other transition economies. The reason is not only that Hungary's reforms have, in a sense to be described below, been deeper and gone further than in most of the other transition economies but also because there exist relatively more pertinent data which can be used to buttress our arguments. Our objective, however, is not to discuss what can be done about the past conundrums faced by the transition economies.[4] Rather, we wish to highlight the problems for monetary policy of a nature which is less well known or understood by analysts or economists who study industrialized economies.

2. OVERVIEW OF MONETARY POLICY: WAS THERE A CREDIT CRUNCH?

With this backdrop in mind this chapter investigates the contribution of monetary policy to the seemingly high economic costs of the transition (also see Kolodko *et al.*, 1992). This chapter makes no claim that monetary policy actions were the *sole* determinant of macroeconomic performance in the transition economies, only that it is plausible to attribute a significant proportion of the poor Hungarian macroeconomic performance to monetary policy actions during the period under study.[5]

Generally, monetary policy has been characterized by high ex post real interest rates, ostensibly to stem credit growth.[6] This is the result of the National Bank of Hungary's avowed decision to implement a restrictive monetary policy. What is perhaps misunderstood in industrialized countries with sophisticated financial systems is that in Hungary, as elsewhere in Central and Eastern Europe, the transition to a market economy in the absence of well organized capital markets has meant a relatively greater reliance on trade credit as a financial vehicle. More importantly, applying prescriptions from industrialized countries, such as high interest rates to control credit growth, or other forms of non-price credit allocation, to reduce inflation may be frustrated or sidestepped in the transition economies and, indeed, may result in more not less future inflation. After all, the observed interest rate is but one element among others which explains the volume of credit generated by the financial system. Thus, firms seek credit from other sources, such as inter-enterprise credits, and there is the consequent danger that the central bank will monetize the debt in the future if these credits become in arrears. On the other hand, there is the possible deflationary impact stemming from real exchange depreciation, also a result of government policy. Based on Hungary's experience until the early 1990s, the former scenario is more likely as real effective exchange rates have risen over time in Hungary (as well as in Poland and Czechoslovakia; see Siklos and Ábel, 1995). Given the nature of exchange rate regimes in several of the transition economies, namely either a fixed exchange rate (e.g., the Czech Republic), a crawling peg (e.g., Poland), ad hoc exchange rate adjustments (e.g., Hungary), the continuing persistently high inflation rates in most of these countries relative to their major trading partners have led to a deterioration in the current account. Thus, for example, Hungary's balance of trade in its current account began to record deficits by late 1992 which have continued despite significant devaluations and interest rate increases into the summer of 1994.[7]

3. INFLATION AND FIRM FINANCING

One consequence of inflation is a reduction in the real value of the stock of outstanding debt denominated in the domestic currency. For indebted firms this, of course, is good news. But, in market-oriented economies, as inflation rises the nominal interest rate is also expected to rise and this can lead to serious financial difficulties. Consider Table 2.1 which shows a highly simplified income and expenditure statement for a firm and serves purely to illustrate some of the arguments in this chapter.[8] In the top panel zero inflation is assumed. A firm is assumed to have debts of 400 at a real interest rate of 5% per annum. Given the income and expenditures shown in the table this leaves a profit of 40. Now, let the inflation rate rise to an annual rate of 30%.[9]

Table 2.1 The Consequences of Inflation for Firm Profits

Case 1	Income and Expenditures with Zero Inflation			
	Income			200
	Expenditures:	Wages	100	
		Materials	40	
		Interest payments[a]	20	___
	Total			160
	Profit		40	
Case 2	Income and Expenditures with 30% Inflation			
	Income			260
	Expenditures:	Wages	130	
		Materials	52	
		Interest payments[b]	146	___
	Total			328
	Profit (Loss)		(68)	

Notes: a) Debt is 400 with nominal and real interest rates of 5% (i.e., 400x0.05=20).
b) Nominal interest rate is 36.5%; real interest rate is still 5%.

Assuming the same real interest rate, nominal interest rates would have to rise to 36.5% (1.05x1.30) in order to leave lenders with the same real interest rate.[10] Also, assume that all prices and costs also rise by 30% as a result of accommodating increases in the money supply.[11] The nominal interest cost of the debt would thus rise to 146 (=400x0.365). Thus, an otherwise profitable firm would now experience a loss of 68 as a result of inflation. Only firms with zero debt to begin with, who would earn the same profit in real terms as before,[12] or ones who reduce their debt to try to maintain the same level of profit in real terms as before (=52), would be unaffected by such a policy. In the latter case this would require a reduction in the outstanding debt to just over 71, that is, a reduction of over 82% in the debt outstanding. In this sense, a high interest rate policy is effective in reducing the debt of a particular firm. Notice also that the real interest rate is the same in both cases. Thus, inflation has created a loss for firms unable or unwilling to reduce their debt levels, necessitating a search for more debt to finance their loss thereby further exacerbating the problem of debt into a vicious circle as in the numerical example discussed above.[13] This result is important for, historically, the most important sources of finance for firms in industrialized countries have been retained earnings and bank loans. Therefore, an underdeveloped financial system combined with a chronically inflationary policy clearly has negative consequences for the economy as a whole and for monetary policy in particular. This outcome is also partly revealed by the relatively high fraction of non-performing loans generally in the transition economies. As Dittus (1994) points out, this perpetuates the 'symbiotic relationship between enterprises and banks'. Indeed, this type of relationship may lead to increased pressure on banks to increase their credits to the business sector even if sound banking practices would dictate otherwise.[14] Presumably, the policy also intends to raise, albeit perhaps only temporarily, the real interest cost of the debt to persuade firms, individuals, and foreigners, that the new monetary policy will be immediately reflected in nominal interest rates.[15] Notice that this result abstracts from the potential efficiencies that might influence a firm's behaviour under inflation. In other words, depending on the relative efficiency with which the firms in our scenario operate, the debt load may become larger as a consequence of inflation.

During the 1980s, industrialized countries engineered a high real interest rate policy to reduce inflationary expectations. It has been said, however, that the length of time necessary to achieve the credit constraining outcome is longer than in the past because well functioning capital markets have produced a large number of derivative financial products to overcome such constraints, at least temporarily (see Siklos, 1994a, Chapter 14). Such derivative products enable the necessary financial adjustments to take place without perhaps the large adjustments costs which would otherwise be expected. The difficulty in Central and Eastern Europe is that well developed capital markets are non-existent,[16] and that, for the time being, most governments are crowding out private borrowers because of the need to finance their deficits. In particular, creditworthy borrowers in Hungary look abroad for funds while other enterprises refrain from raising credit domestically. These developments are reflected in the fact that, by the end of 1993, the share of bank credit to the entrepreneurial sector fell to 51.9% from 73.8% at the beginning of 1992. Meanwhile, the share of lending to finance the government's budget deficit rose to 30.2%, again by November 1993, from 7.2% at the beginning of 1992.[17] Therefore trade credit continues to fulfil an essential function but, as Table 2.1 illustrates, some firms will not be able to sustain higher debt levels for long before going bankrupt. Unfortunately, it is not necessarily the least efficiently run firms which would fail. Instead, ones which happen to be saddled with the highest debt to begin with as the state begins to desert the formerly state-run enterprises via privatization are at risk.[18] The end result is inefficient and perhaps not that much different than in a command economy in the sense that, instead of market forces determining the successful from unsuccessful firms, artificial initial conditions may determine firms' success rates.

4. MONETARY POLICY AND THE ROLE OF INTEREST RATES

It is perhaps not surprising that the worldwide emphasis on the control of inflation, originating in the stagflation of the 1970s, would carry over to the newly independent central banks.[19] The overriding concern with inflation manifests itself as a restrictive monetary policy. Restrictive here means high real interest rates to stem credit growth. Together with other reforms aimed at converting the economy from a centrally planned one to a decentralized market system, it has been suggested that the transition period would be characterized by a type of J-curve effect (Brada and King, 1992). Thus, at the beginning of the transition, a sharp fall in output (viz., real GDP) would occur which would eventually be reversed some time in the future. The path then taken by real GDP would then be reminiscent of a J.[20]

Two pillars form the basis of a transition programme such as the one implemented in Hungary and in the other transition economies of Central and Eastern Europe. The first is that economic activity would henceforth be driven by consumer demand. By contrast, in a planned economy, the central planners decided what to produce, at what price to sell the commodities, and in what volume these commodities would be produced. The second pillar consists of permitting markets to freely set prices. Since prices conveys information about the value of a commodity, monetary policy plays a crucial role in the process or, rather, it can play a role in ensuring that price stability is maintained. Again, this is unlike a centrally planned economy in which monetary policy, as such, was non-existent since decisions about the money stock, for example, were set in advance according to output levels expected or set by the central planners.[21]

In order to understand the role of monetary policy as it influences economic activity let us consider the following illustration. Suppose the monetary authorities implement a restrictive monetary policy. Brechling and Lipsey (1963) revived an old debate when they suggested that firms can rely on trade credit to frustrate policy makers' attempts at reducing expenditures by the private sector.

One possible avenue is what Brechling and Lipsey call a quantity adjustment. Simply put, the quantity of trade credit in the private sector rises sufficiently to offset any restrictive monetary policy. Another possibility they consider is an interest rate effect. In this case, firms reallocate their financial portfolio to offset or neutralize the impact of monetary policy.

Thus, one reaction to the shortage of credit would be for firms to ensure that the wage bill, among other costs under its control, be reduced. If this is the principal impact of the restrictive policy then national income would eventually be reduced via a reduction in expenditures. Alternatively, firms could redirect some of their resources toward holding more financial instruments since these return more than available alternatives. To the extent that the higher yields are used to maintain the current wage bill there need not be any impact on labour income. Otherwise, the tight monetary policy will have an indirect effect on incomes.

The objective of any restrictive monetary policy is, of course, to influence economic activity whether or not this is accomplished directly or indirectly. Its influence is most felt if all firms adjust in such a way as to leave the labour force unaffected and by reducing other expenditures such as the reduction of imports, or through inventory adjustment. Alternatively, the full weight of the adjustment is made on the labour force while the remainder of a firm's portfolio is unaffected. It may also be pointed out that a restrictive policy via interest rates changes may only have temporary effects.[22]

In a centrally planned system firms typically were not permitted nor indeed did they need to make any of the types of adjustments normally made by firms in a market determined system. The reason is that the plan was centred on achieving a particular output target. Therefore output was largely an exogenously determined variable unlike a market determined system in which output is generated endogenously. It is thus unclear why the authorities in Hungary, during the reforms of the 1970s and 1980s, blamed firms for not displaying any reactions in their operations to interest rate changes.[23] The reason monetary policy at that time was ineffective was the inability of firms to modify their portfolio under the centrally planned system.

It is, however, an exaggeration to believe that monetary policy was completely ineffective under the centrally planned regime. It is more accurate to state, as Portes (1983, 1978, 1977) has shown, that while central plans can set output targets, it is doubtful that these exactly matched the needs of the economy. Under the separate monetary circuits characteristic of centrally planned economies (see Ábel and Székely, 1992b) strict control of the quantity of money in the households circuits provided an effective support to price regulatory measures in controlling CPI inflation while preventing desirable supply adjustments. Of course, even if monetary policy has some real economic effects under such a regime it can be damaging to the economy, an example being where an interest rate increase does not have the desired effect on output. For this reason, the sensitivity or elasticity of the effect of interest rate changes on firms' portfolio decisions is an important question. But this also requires that firms be able to freely adjust their portfolios.[24]

Let us now turn to the impact of the current monetary policy on inflation in the transition economies. While the objective of a restrictive policy is to reduce inflation, it is conceivable that inflation will follow from higher interest rates. One advocate of the latter possibility is Laffer (1970) who suggests that the definition of money should be altered to include a component for both the utilized and unutilized portions of trade credit.[25] Since trade credit represents purchasing power it should be reflected in any monetary policy decision meant to control spending and, therefore, inflation. Thus, any policy meant to control an M1 type definition of the money supply will amount to nothing if trade credit and government deficits are eventually monetized. In addition, of course, there is the question of the behaviour of velocity. In transition economies there are a number of forces at work influencing velocity. First, expected inflation was high in the early stages of the transition prompting velocity to rise. Then, as the banking system begins to develop along the lines of those in market economies, a kind of monetization of the economy takes place which, combined with a high (real) interest rate policy, would tend to produce a fall in velocity, especially when associated with lower expected inflation, as individuals choose to hold more money, a significant fraction of which returns near market rates (i.e., at yields attractive relative to those paid on government securities; Siklos, 1993; Siklos and Eckhold, 1997). If we examine a plot of income velocity levels for Hungary since 1987, based on a broad monetary aggregate (IMF definition), a rising trend is evident until 1991, consistent with the high expected inflation rates at the beginning of the transition (see also the following chapter). The subsequent fall in velocity is also consistent with the monetization process and, possibly, expectations of lower inflation. The behaviour of ex post real interest rates over the same period also conforms with the foregoing discussion. Indeed, by 1994 a conflict arose between the central bank and the government over high real interest rates both before and following the election of a new government in the Spring of that year. This led to concerns being raised in domestic and international financial markets about the independence of the National Bank of Hungary and the ability of the government to meet deficit targets set by the IMF. One particular worry is whether additional bailouts, which would amount to another form of credit to the business sector, would be necessary.[26] Finally, Table 2.2 provides annual data about the financial asset holdings of households in Hungary. Thus, we see a fall in cash holdings with a rise in the relative holdings of savings deposits and securities issued either by financial institutions or governments, especially in 1991, which is entirely consistent with Figures 2.1 and 2.2.[27] This trend continues through 1995.

Table 2.2 Financial Assets of Households in Hungary, 1990-93

Year	Cash		Savings Deposits		Securities	
(Dec)	HUF bn	% Tot.	HUF bn	% Tot.	HUF bn	% Tot.
1990	181.2	28.3	332.8	52.1	125.3	19.6
1991	204.9	24.1	432.0	50.8	213.8	25.1
1992	209.6	23.9	582.4	51.5	277.9	24.6
1993	322.2	24.1	696.1	52.1	317.7	23.8
1994	348.5	28.5	808.4	66.1	394.5	32.3
1995	386.1	22.8	1030.6	60.8	571.8	33.8

Note: National Bank of Hungary, *Monthly Report*, 6/1994, Table IV/1, p. 100, and *Annual Report*, 1995, Annex A/V/10.

Unfortunately, the literature on the role of trade credit in monetary policy applied to industrialized economies with private enterprises is diverse and the empirical evidence inconclusive or contradictory. Among the relevant studies are those of Bianchi *et al.* (1979), Brechling and Lipsey (1963, 1966), Coates (1967), Henderson (1959), Junk (1964), Meltzer (1960, 1964) who emphasize the significance of trade credit in monetary policy. See, however, White (1964) for criticisms of Brechling and Lipsey. Statistical studies which have attempted to provide empirical evidence about the role of trade credit include the noteworthy papers of Herbst (1974) and Nadiri (1969) which evaluate the evidence in light of the above analyses.[28] For example, Herbst relies on quarterly US data (1956-66) from the Lumber and Wood industry and finds that trade credit is largely determined by factors endogenous to the industry rather than originating from monetary policy actions. Nadiri, who also uses quarterly US data from the manufacturing sector as a whole, concludes that trade credit does increase significantly when monetary policy is tight but he finds little evidence of inflationary consequences. Meltzer points out that large firms (i.e., these would be the equivalent of the state-owned enterprises in the transition economies) are able to find credit in the non-bank sector (e.g., commercial paper; this is an idea recently revived by Kashyap *et al.*, 1993) and that smaller, less liquid, firms tend to rely more on trade credit when monetary policy is tight. As pointed out earlier, these non-bank sources are generally unavailable or the market for them is, as yet, very thin in the countries considered in this chapter. Brechling and Lipsey find that trade credit in the UK economy rises when there is a monetary contraction and that the impact is inflationary (as did the famous Radcliffe Committee on the working of the UK monetary system) while Coates and White do not concur with this conclusion.

5. TRADE CREDIT HYPOTHESES

5.1 The Determinants of Gross Trade Credit

Many would agree that inter-enterprise credit, whose growth may have been facilitated by credit constraints or by firms, decisions to rely on this type of credit, reduces the demand for money, that is, raises the velocity of circulation as measured in terms of conventional monetary aggregates. By implication, inter-enterprise credit is a means to circumvent a restrictive monetary policy. Thus, the impact of interest rate changes is also mitigated by the creation of this form of debt.

Theories of the determination of inter-enterprise credit can be divided into two categories: theories of gross and net trade credit. Essentially, the theory suggests that the stock of gross trade credit can grow independently of the restrictive stance of monetary policy.[29]

In a closed economy, of course, the quantity demanded and supplied of trade credit are identical. At the micro-level, however, there is an impact on firms which depends on how each one adjusts its portfolio. Thus, there may be firm, specific effects even if aggregate effects are nil. Brechling and Lipsey (1963) give one such example. Suppose firm A is indebted to firm B and that credit is restricted. Firm A could then maintain its debt with firm B by reducing its debt with, say, firm C. In other words, firms set up in essence what is a clearing arrangement amongst themselves. In this fashion restrictive credit policies can, in principle, be circumvented and, since the demand for money is unaffected, trade credit arrangements create an externality for the rest of the private sector. Some of the empirical evidence to be presented below is consistent with such an interpretation.[30] It should be remembered, however, that these are short-term remedies since sooner or later either the debt must be paid to the government or the central bank may be called upon to cover the losses. Hence, if trade credit can be inflationary in the short-run a reversal will take place given sufficient time.

5.2 The Determinants of Net Trade Credit

Attempts by some firms to increase their level of debt through trade credit implies a reduction for some other firms, other things being equal. We have so far ignored firms desired demand for cash. It may be that suppliers of credit may wish to hold less cash while holders of debt are willing to hold more cash. Therefore, in this case monetary policy restrictions can also be overcome. It is thus possible to overcome the restrictions on the net amount of trade credit outstanding. It is, of course, an empirical question to determine how firms react since, in theory at least, there are many possibilities of avoiding restrictive credit policies.

Brechling and Lipsey (1963) believe there are, in principle, three possibilities to avoid constraints on net trade credit. Firms could permit the use of any unused portion of trade credit to firms who wish or need to use it. Alternatively, one set of firms might be too weak relative to another group thereby limiting the sources of funds. A third possibility is that defaults spread through firms because of the refusal of some firms to advance credit or the unavailability of any credit.

5.3 Trade Credit: The Hungarian Experience

The Hungarian Institute for Economic Research prepared a report outlining the financing arrangements of enterprises (Gazdaságkutató Intézet, 1990). The 1988 sample consists of 4405 firms in the nascent phase of the transition, but excludes the banking sector. Unfortunately, the data have not since been updated. Below we focus on two aspects of the report, namely the correlation between trade credit and firm liquidity.

Liquidity

This refers to the firms' liquid assets which consist of cash and marketable assets.[31] On the liability side liquid liabilities consists of short-term loans extended by other enterprises and various other short-term loans.[32] Liquidity is then defined as the ratio of liquid assets to liquid liabilities. For 47% of firms, which represents 2091 firms in the sample, the ratio is less than 0.2, which suggests small receivables relative to payables. Therefore firms obtain goods from suppliers and tend to sell finished products for cash at the retail level. The difficulty is that, unlike in market economies where alternative sources of short-term liquidity are readily available, firms in transition economies tend to rely on trade credit which quickly fall into arrears (see below). As arrears grow the liquidity crunch facing firms worsens. According to this definition of liquidity, the firms in the sample can be grouped into 31 different classes. The classes were defined in such a way that class 1 consists of those firms with zero or negative liquid net worth. The remaining firms are thus classified into 30 different categories with equal numbers of firms in each category (there are thus 144 firms in each class). Receivables and payables were compared in each group and averages were computed for each class. Firms with the lowest liquidity ratios were also the ones for which receivables were substantially smaller than payables. For the average firm in the sample receivables were greater than payables. It is also noteworthy that, as the liquidity ratio rises, receivables display a tendency to fall. This is explained by the fact that as liquidity concerns increase, trade credit rises in a parallel fashion. The correlation between receivables and payables was also found to be positive.

Revenues

As one goes down the list of firms by class we find that, although receivables and payables are positively correlated, payables rise faster and receivables more slowly the worse the liquidity position of the firm. Thus profitability and liquidity, as measured in this study, appear to be positively correlated.

The role of trade credit in firm financing

The Hungarian Institute's most important finding may be summarized as follows. Internal financing played the most important role, turnover credit was the second most important source of financing, while receivables were placed third in 1987. In 1988, receivables became the second most important source, while internal financing maintained its position (Mérő, 1990, p.69). Since the data are for 1988 it is reasonable to ask whether there have been any changes in the ability of firms to call upon financing from the commercial banking sector. Nagy (1992) reports, based on aggregate commercial banking sector data, that lending to enterprises fell by the end of 1991, as a percentage of assets, to 58% from the 79% level reached in 1987. In 1992, credits to enterprises fell again by 1.7% from the 1991 level. It is only in 1993 that a recovery of sorts is apparent since credits to enterprises rose by 6.2% in 1993. However, the figure reflects the effect of the creation of the Loan Consolidation Bank.[33] The desire on the part of the banking sector to improve the quality of its portfolio, both to meet BIS capital-adequacy standards and to attract buyers in advance of imminent privatization, and the relative attractiveness of government securities combined to worsen the liquidity crunch, especially for the large enterprise sector. Pinto *et al.* (1993) found a similar result for Poland. One difficulty with the above evidence is that the data so far combine ordinary trade credit and arrears. Fortunately, Hungary is among the few transition economies for which there exist useful data on trade credit arrears.[34]

Table 2.3 shows the rising number of firms with arrears of HUF 25 m and above. The three largest commercial banks - the MHB (Hungarian Credit Bank), OKHB (National Credit Bank) and BB (Budapest Bank) - consider that 90% of this debt is unbacked. The MHB bank alone accounts for over 60% of these firms. Since the Loan Consolidation Programme and the introduction of a Bankruptcy law the data are no longer collected and, indeed, by definition are no longer relevant to the public sector, at least in theory. In practice, however, these arrears can still exist and create problems in monetary policy formulation particularly when large firms are involved and a kind of 'too big to fail' doctrine is followed by the government.

The Bankruptcy Law of 1992 (see also Chapter 4 in this volume), which became effective in April of the same year, represents a significant turning point as it hastened the rate of bankruptcies as expected (National Bank of Hungary, *Monthly Report,* 1/1993, p.23). The new bankruptcy law has conceivably had two effects which may give an inaccurate picture of the credit stance in the post January 1992 period. First, the number of firms reporting inter-enterprise credit fell. Second, all firms became more reticent in extending such credits since the risks associated with any losses are now significantly higher. Both of these developments are clear from the data shown in Table 2.3. This creates a potentially serious problem for monetary policy since the high level of enterprise arrears, relative to the situation at the beginning of the transition, can impinge on the independence of the National Bank of Hungary to pursue a monetary policy aimed at stabilizing inflation if the central bank is called upon to 'bail-out' bad debts. Data in Table 2.3 may be misleading because debt figures are expressed in nominal terms. Thus, Figure 2.1 plots inter-enterprise credit in real terms[35] as well as on a per firm basis.[36] Both series confirm the fall in debt outstanding relative to the pre-bankruptcy law period (the subdivision of the sample is shown in the Figure by a vertical bar at January 1992) though it is less noticeable in the per firm measure.[37]

After 1992 enterprise arrears essentially disappear due to the introduction of the Bankruptcy Act and subsequent loan consolidation schemes (e.g., see also Chapter 7). Any arrears simply become conventional trade credit which is not separately reported.

Table 2.3 Total Enterprise Arrears: 1987-92

Date	Total Debt*	Number of Firms
1987 January	14	82
1987 June	10	79
1987 December	14	82
1988 June	19	119
1988 December	46	208
1989 June	57	239
1989 December	73	314
1990 June	75	362
1990 December	90	432
1991 January	116	553
1991 February	115	586
1991 March	119	642
1991 April	129	616
1991 May	129	688
1991 June	131	695
1991 July	144	794
1991 August	137	856
1991 September	140	845
1991 October	149	965
1991 November	151	n.a.
1991 December	159	1021
1992 January	174	1113
1992 February	179	1157
1992 March	187	1152
1992 April	197	1143
1992 May	183	1078
1992 June	168	986
1992 July	154	877
1992 August	126	761
1992 September	106	617
1992 October	104	635
1992 November	107	667
1992 December	104	642

Sources: Sánta (1992), László and Szakadát (1992), and G. Láng from The National Bank of Hungary.
Note: * Firms with debts of HUF 25 m and above only. Total debt outstanding for remaining firms was in July 1991, for example, HUF 178 bn. After 1992 arrears data no longer recorded.

6. CONCLUSIONS

Although the focus of the chapter has been on the Hungarian situation, both because the data are relatively more ample and the transition to market was undertaken earlier than elsewhere in Central and Eastern Europe, the difficulties described above plague most of the transition economies. Hungary and the Czech Republic have opted for policies which combine the rationing of credit together with the resort to the interest rate instrument as an allocative device. Banks remain burdened by non-performing loans, often collude with enterprises and do not seem to be performing a constructive role in the transition to market (Dittus, 1994). But, in an underdeveloped financial system, this leaves banks as shaky pillars of reforms. Poland has a more moderate monetary policy and, consequently, experiences higher inflation than either Hungary or the Czech Republic. Russia and the Ukraine are at the other extreme. Their monetary policy is openly inflationary and the old 'soft-budget constraint' has yet to be effectively replaced.

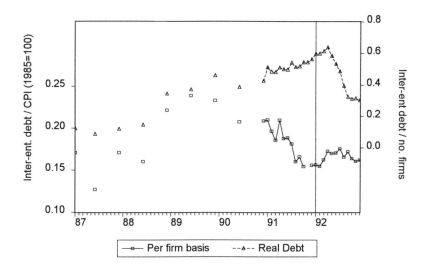

Sources: Table 2.2 and International Monetary Fund, International Financial Statistics, CPI, line 64.

Figure 2.1 Real and Per Firm Enterprise Arrears

The difficulty for enterprises in the transition to a market economy is that, after years of central planning, they still do not possess all the necessary means to adjust their portfolios in the face of a world which operates in a conventional monetary policy framework but does not give firms adequate access to capital markets. Moreover, when access to such markets is possible, it is often for short-term credits rather than the long-term financing that enterprises newly freed from central planning require to become competitive in the marketplace.[38]

We also illustrated a variety of ways in which the monetary policy in Hungary during the early 1990s, in particular, has more drawbacks than advantages. In essence this is because the types of efficiencies and rationalizations of enterprises which exist in a well-functioning market economy had not been achieved in the formerly centrally planned economies in advance of fundamental changes in the conduct of monetary policy. It is important to develop a well-functioning capital market in conjunction with the adjustments necessary to shift from centrally planned prices and quantities to market driven ones. In addition, decisions about financial adjustments require that firms be permitted to make independent financial decisions. However, the State still has a significant, if waning, influence on the economy and, unfortunately, reforms so far have been introduced in an inconsistent fashion (also see Siklos and Ábel, 1995).

POSTSCRIPT

Inflation remains a problem in most transitional economies with the exception perhaps of the Czech and Slovak Republics. What remains unclear since the article was originally prepared, and later revised, is how much of a hindrance 20% inflation, say, is to overall economic growth. Recent research suggests that the costs of reducing inflation to single digits may not yield any net output gains. Industrialized economies, however, have in the past few years required that monetary policy focus on very low inflation rates (3% or less). Yet, it cannot be said that capital markets function well. For example, the gap between lending and deposit rates remains high (e.g., 6 to 8% in Hungary in 1996), and real interest rates also remain high (in part because of exchange rate policy; see Chapter 9). The one bright spot is that banks in the transitional economies are today becoming better able and more willing to act as intermediaries in corporate finance but this has been facilitated by the gradual withdrawal of the government sector from capital markets.

NOTES

*   An earlier version of this chapter appeared under the title 'Constraints on Enterprise Liquidity and its Impact on the Monetary Sector in Hungary' published in *Comparative Economic Studies* 36, (Spring 1994), by I. Ábel and P.L. Siklos, and reprinted here by permission. The present chapter is a substantial revision of the earlier article.

1.   Industrial output in Hungary measures the volume of industrial production. Unemployment rates in Hungary measure the number of registered unemployed workers as a percentage of 'economically active' (i.e., employed and unemployed) persons. For more details on the definitions used see, for example, National Bank of Hungary, *Monthly Report*, 1/1994, Table I/13, p.46.

2. For a more detailed description of macroeconomic policies and performance during the transition in Hungary, Poland and the former Czechoslovakia, see Siklos and Ábel (1995). Suffice it to note that industrial production fell from 100 in January 1989 (1985=100) to approximately 60 by January 1993. See National Bank of Hungary, *Annual Report,* 1992, p.19. By contrast, the unemployment rate rose from 2% in January 1991 to a peak of 14% by the end of 1993 before falling to about 12% by the end of 1993. See National Bank of Hungary, *Monthly Report,* 1/1994, p.11.

3. Although the issues discussed in this chapter stem principally from the problems of state-owned enterprises, the lack of maturity of the financial system and monetary policy in general have a negative impact on emerging private enterprises as well. See below, Siklos and Ábel (1995), and Ábel *et al.* (1994).

4. On this issue see, for example, Begg and Portes (1993).

5. Indeed, some of the transition related output effects must be ascribed to the collapse of trading patterns *vis-à-vis* the USSR and the other former CMEA partner countries. See, for example, Balcerowicz (1994).

6. In Hungary, for example, real ex post interest rates, calculated as the difference between the central bank loan rate and inflation in the CPI, averaged approximately 15% during the second half of 1991. By comparison, similar rates were higher in Poland (29%) but much lower in Czechoslovakia (4%) over the same period. Monthly data were used from the International Monetary Fund's *International Financial Statistics.* Since the end of 1991, real ex post interest rates have fallen but, except in the Czech Republic, they remain high by western industrialized countries' standards. Also high by western industrialized countries' standards is the spread between borrowing and lending rates at commercial banks. But, as will be pointed out later in the chapter, high ex post real interest rates represent only one element in the monetary policy problems faced by some of the transition economies.

7. See National Bank of Hungary, *Monthly Report,* 6/1994, p.23. Poland too has experienced a similar fate (see Narodowy Bank Polski, *Information Bulletin,* 4-5/1994, Table 10). Only the Czech republic has maintained a current account surplus, though by the first quarter of 1994 it had fallen considerably from either 1992 or 1993 levels. See Czech National Bank, *Monthly Bulletin,* 5/1994, p.1.

8. See also Li and Pradhan (1990) who base their results on the theory outlined in Wadhwani (1986). The problems of inflation and trade credit are also considered in Gordon (1982).

9. One reason for a sudden jump in inflation is price liberalization combined with an (initially at least) accommodating monetary policy as a consequence of the legacy of debts carried over from the central planning era.

10. This is the result of the well known Fisher effect. The result assumed in Table 2.1 is the one expected in equilibrium which, in financial markets at least, is likely to be attained quickly, especially as inflation accelerates. The calculations assume a fixed rate debt and ignore the distinction between existing debt versus new borrowing.

11. This too is an equilibrium result best understood in terms of a quantity theory type relationship.

12. This would have been 60 in a world of zero inflation and 78 in a world of 30% inflation.

13. It was pointed out to us that under case 1 inflation implies a constant real debt, if fully reflected in interest rates, while under case 2 the real value of outstanding debt would decrease. Consequently, the value of the firm (i.e., of equity) is the same under the two scenarios. This, of course, is correct. However, leverage (i.e., the debt to equity ratio) is lower for the firm which incurs a loss than for the profitable firm. If the leverage ratios were the same, which seems an equally reasonable basis for comparison, then debt outstanding is still higher under case 2. Put differently, the firm under case 2 has an incentive to acquire more debt, which would leave it as leveraged as the profitable firm, which is also consistent with the outcome described in the text above.

14. Also, see Blommenstein and Spencer (1993) in this connection.

15. If there is a time lag between the purchase and sale of material inputs the loss calculated in case 2 of Table 2.1 is overstated since costs are typically reported on a historical costs basis and not the opportunity costs basis implicitly assumed in the calculations. See Schaffer (1992) for a discussion of this point in relation to the Polish experience.

16. Derivative markets exist in Hungary, for example, but these markets are, at present, very thin.

17. See National Bank of Hungary, *Monthly Report*, 2/1994, Table IV/2. Ábel, et al. (1994) provide empirical evidence to the effect that a combination of bank lending to the government as well as direct government borrowing from the public explains this outcome.

18. This outcome will, in part, be influenced by government policies *vis-à-vis* heavily indebted state-owned firms. Consolidation programmes can soften the transition but Hungary chose to implement such a programme in 1992 only (along with a Bankruptcy Law), that is, well into the transition from central planning to market, while in the case of Czechoslovakia the same policy was an instrumental part of its reforms.

19. Independent in the sense of legal or statutory independence. For a survey of the literature on central bank independence, see Cukierman (1992), and Johnson and Siklos (1996). For the case of the transition economies, see Chapter 7 in this volume.

20. Portes (1991) argues that an L-shaped path for real GDP is more likely for the emerging Eastern European economies. This suggests that the output effects of the transition might be permanent instead of transitory.

21. While it is true that price liberalization began earlier in Hungary than in the other former CPEs, price liberalization is not complete but perhaps is sufficient from a political perspective.

22. If interest rates are changed infrequently. Alternatively, frequent interest rate changes could also lead to temporary effects because the costs of reacting to each one of them rise with the frequency of interest rate changes. In other words, interest rate volatility can make it difficult to distinguish temporary from permanent effects of interest rate changes.

23. While some firms had gained at least partial control over output and financial decisions after the reforms of 1968, the behaviour of firms in the financial sphere especially was still constrained for a considerable period of time following the start of the transition to market by the State via National Bank of Hungary credit and foreign exchange control policies.

24. It would be worthwhile, of course, to enquire how the restrictive monetary policy in the transition to market can be broken down into its output and interest rate components as defined above as this is critical to the success or failure of the present monetary policy. However, there is insufficient data at present to perform a serious statistical analysis of this question.

25. Friedman (1983) also finds that our understanding of the effect of monetary policy is enhanced by the reliance on the broadest monetary aggregates available.

26. At the time of writing, two loan consolidation schemes had already been introduced in Hungary. See Siklos and Ábel (1995) and Várhegyi (1994). The Czech Republic too has had to infuse its Loan Consolidation Bank with additional funds on more than one occasion. See e.g., Hrnčíř (1994a, 1994b). In Romania too, there several bailout schemes of this kind, see Rădulescu (1995).

27. The situation is comparable in Poland in the sense that velocity since 1992 appears to be rising due to higher inflation fears combined with slow reforms in the banking sector (after an initial fall due to the end of hyperinflation) while velocity is stable or falling in the Czech Republic precisely because the situation is the opposite of Poland's experience.

28. There have also been mathematical models proposed to analyze the importance of trade credit such as Schwartz (1974), Schwartz and Whitcomb (1979), as well as Wrightsman (1969).

29. There exists a separate literature which focuses on the transmission mechanism from credit (created by banks in particular) to economic activity. We shall leave this question aside in this chapter. For a recent survey of the relevant issues see, however, Kliesen and Tatom (1992).

30. It was pointed out to us that this scenario assumes that credit is quantity-rationed. Even if market interest rates are more or less clearing, banks in Hungary do effectively also ration credit to enterprises (of all kinds and not just state-owned ones) for three reasons. First, there is a crowding-out effect stemming from the relative attractiveness of holding government debt over commercial lending in their asset portfolios. For example, in 1993, banks in Hungary held approximately 38% of their assets in the form of government securities. Second, banks in Hungary are legally obliged to adhere to Bank for International Settlements capital adequacy standards. As a result, loans to enterprises would qualify as relatively high risk assets thereby reducing Hungarian banks' ability to meet the standards. Third, because commercial lending is perceived as being a highly risky proposition and the expertise in evaluating levels of risk from such activities is deficient, Hungarian banks are loath to lend to enterprises. The situation is broadly similar in the other transition

economies.

31. Lines I.05 and I.12d in the balance sheet of firms as reported to the Ministry of Finance.

32. Lines I.36 to I.47d as defined above.

33. See National Bank of Hungary, *Monthly Report,* 2/1994, p.23. By contrast, credits to 'small entrepreneurs' grew by 24.1% and 22.4% in 1992 and 1993, respectively. However, credits to this sector represent approximately only 12% of total credits to enterprises.

34. Other complications with the interpretation of the trade credit data arise because loan consolidation programmes can also mask the true magnitude of the arrears problem. See, for example, Calvo and Coricelli (1993) for available data on Poland, Romania, the former Czechoslovakia and Russia. Hungary's first loan consolidation programme began in March 1993. A second loan programme was announced in 1994. Moreover, the speed with which privatization takes place also has an influence on arrears.

35. Nominal debt figures were deflated by the Consumer Price Index from the International Monetary Fund's International Financial Statistics.

36. By deflating total debt by the number of firms.

37. One aspect of bankruptcy legislation not revealed in the figures is the impact of liquidations as a percentage of GDP. Blommenstein and Spencer (1993) report the findings of a study for Hungary which suggests that, by the end of 1992, liquidations represented 33% of GDP, an astonishingly high number.

38. See Hilbers (1993) for a discussion of the broader issues concerning monetary and credit instruments in the transition economies.

3. Fiscal and Monetary Policies in the Transition: Searching for the Credit Crunch*

PROLOGUE

An immature capital market raises the possibility of a credit crunch. While the previous chapter presumes such an outcome and analyses some of its implications, the present chapter attempts to determine its actual significance and impact on fiscal and monetary policies for Hungary, Poland, and the former Czechoslovakia.

The evidence for the existence of a credit crunch in the early stages of the transition is mixed and very much a function of the initial conditions facing each of these economies. The impact of economy-wide liquidity constraints has been among the most neglected issues in transitional economics.

1. INTRODUCTION

The experience of fundamental economic transformation currently sweeping Central and Eastern Europe provides economists with a unique opportunity to study the role and impact of monetary and fiscal policies. The former command economies have chosen to adopt some of the macroeconomic tools routinely applied in the industrialized world. Nevertheless, as both the speed and nature of the existing reforms differ across the transforming economies, the opportunity also presents itself to explore whether one road to market has, so far, resulted in better macroeconomic performance than another path to market liberalization. There exist many dimensions, of course, along which 'success' or 'failure' in macroeconomic terms can be examined and assessed. This paper suggests, however, that one determinant of the success of the transition, in terms of delivering rising living standards over time via rising output and low and stable inflation, is dependent on financial sector reforms as well as developments in monetary and fiscal policies. What follows then is a progress report on the role played by the financial sector in the transition process, and the ability of this sector to finance the needs of a market-oriented economy. As Phelps et al. (1993) have argued: 'if history is any guide, periods of extraordinary demands for investible funds have often brought forth large and sophisticated commercial banks providing large amounts of outside finance to firms over which they receive in return certain rights to control' (op. cit., p.40).

One of the most pressing macroeconomic issues facing the transitional economies is the financing of reforms to permit or facilitate the transition from central planning toward market-driven outcomes. At the outset of the transition the need for monetary and fiscal reforms was great. On the fiscal side there is the legacy of large deficits, owing to the need to finance inefficient state-owned enterprises, as well as the large scale subsidization of everything from foodstuffs to housing in the social sector. On the revenue side the absence of an efficient and modern tax collection apparatus places severe limitations on the government's budget constraint.

In the realm of monetary policy, an immature financial system, in a sense to be defined later in the paper, combined with the absence of monetary policy tools or the wherewithal to manage them poses serious economic threats. Moreover, the large scale price liberalization and the devolution of commercial banking operations from the government to, at least initially, quasi-governmental institutions also influences monetary and fiscal policies.

Although Hungary, Poland, and the former Czechoslovakia, broadly speaking, faced more or less the same initial macroeconomic conditions, their monetary and fiscal policy responses have differed along many lines, as we shall see. Nevertheless, one common element in the transitional experience perhaps is the role of the reforms in generating a shortage of liquidity and the persistence of such a shortage over time. In the initial stages of the transition constraints on liquidity, often referred to as the credit crunch, could have been triggered by the fear of, say, high inflation following price liberalization. If, as several authors have already pointed out (Calvo and Coricelli (1992), Ábel and Bonin (1992a)), a credit crunch leads to a stalling of the transition to market then the question which seems to have occupied much of the literature, namely whether the big bang approach is preferable to a gradualist transition in economic reforms, is misdirected. Instead, the problem is the credit crunch and its potential impact on economic performance. What is of interest too, however, is whether the crunch is a manifestation of some of the legacies of central planning alone or is coupled with the conduct of monetary and fiscal policies once in the transition phase. It is this distinction, usually ignored in the literature, to which this chapter is directed. While a credit crunch is a standard feature of recessions in industrialized countries we argue that there are, in addition, institutional characteristics in the transitional economies which can either exacerbate or ease the shortage of liquidity over time relative to what could be expected from a market economy in the recessionary phase of the business cycle.

The purpose then of this chapter is two-fold. First, to summarize the institutional changes implemented in the financial sphere in selected transforming economies. Second, to provisionally determine whether the chosen style of financial reforms have produced a shortage of credit, usually referred to as a 'credit crunch'. This is an important question because, as several authors have suggested (see the following sections) that its existence threatens the success of the transition to market.

Our analysis is restricted to Hungary, Poland, and Czechoslovakia (prior to becoming the Czech and Slovak Republics) for obvious reasons. These three countries are furthest along the path of transition to market and there exists now a sufficiently long historical and economic record to at least attempt some preliminary conclusions about their progress in the financial sphere so far.

The chapter is organized as follows. Section 2 provides a very brief overview of current macroeconomic performance in the three countries. Section 3 provides a brief comparative survey of the principal financial sector reforms in Hungary, Poland, and Czechoslovakia since approximately 1987. Section 4 asks whether, in light of existing macroeconomic issues, a credit crunch can be said to exist or have existed in any of the countries under study. Section 5 concludes and summarizes what we can learn so far about the macroeconomic transition to market in these three countries.

2. THE MACROECONOMIC SITUATION: A BRIEF OVERVIEW

Reforms aimed at lessening the role of central planning began much earlier in Hungary than in any other Central European country. Beginning in 1968, prices of selected commodities were liberalized and limited forms of private enterprise were permitted. Nevertheless, 1989 was the watershed year when the central planning concept was dismissed and market-oriented reforms began to be instituted. The transition phase has been marked by negative rates of growth in GDP from 1990 to 1993 – though, as 1994 began, there were forecasts of a turnaround and the resumption of positive economic growth. At the same time, a surge in consumer prices also delineated the old from the new regime and this paper is motivated in part by the monetary and fiscal policies implemented in the attempt to disinflate. As Montias (1994) points out, the central planning regime did not provide a viable institutional framework within which to conduct the 'stabilization' policies required in the transition to a fully market determined economy. As a consequence, central governments in all three countries experienced growing budgetary problems, at least until 1993. Finally, the legacy of international debts accumulated under the central planning regime and the constraints it imposed for financing the transition posed a serious threat. Table 3.1 summarizes a few key economic indicators for Hungary, Poland, and Czechoslovakia. They clearly show an acceleration in negative GDP growth beginning in 1989 or 1990 in all three countries. Of the three countries, Czechoslovakia has been most successful at avoiding a high inflation trap but all were able to sharply reduce inflation by 1992. In contrast, and with the exception of the Czech Republic, government deficits have risen sharply as a percent of GDP, especially in Hungary. Finally, international debt, evaluated in US dollars, has generally remained stagnant though it has grown sharply in the last two years in the Czech Republic.

Table 3.1 Macroeconomic Performance Indicators

| | | COUNTRY | | |
Indicator	Year	Hungary	Poland	Czechoslovakia/ Czech Republic
		% Change		
GDP Growth	1987	4.1	2.0	2.1
	1988	-0.1	4.1	2.3
	1989	-0.2	0.2	0.7
	1990	-4.3	-11.6	-0.4
	1991	-10.2	-7.2	-15.9
	1992	-5.0	-1.0	-5.0
	1993	-0.8	3.8	-0.9
	1994	2.9	5.2	2.6
	1995	1.5	6.5	4.8
CPI Inflation	1987	8.6	25.2	0.1
	1988	14.8	60.2	0.2
	1989	18.9	251.1	1.4
	1990	33.4	585.8	10.8
	1991	32.2	70.3	58.7
	1992	22.0	45.6	10.2
	1993	22.5	35.3	20.8
	1994	18.8	32.2	10.0
	1995	28.2	27.8	9.1
		% of GDP		
General Govt. Bal.	1987	-3.5	-0.8	-0.7
	1988	NA	NA	-1.5
	1989	-1.3	-7.4	-2.4
	1990	0.4	3.1	0.1
	1991	-3.3	-5.6	-2.0
	1992	-10.6	-7.2	-4.4
	1993	-5.6	-2.8	0.1
	1994	-7.4	-2.8	1.0
	1995	-2.9	-2.6	0.6

| Indicator | Year | COUNTRY | | Czechoslovakia/ |
		Hungary	Poland	Czech Republic
				Billions of US Dollars
International Debt	1987	19.6	33.5	6.7
	1988	19.6	39.1	7.3
	1989	20.4	40.8	7.9
	1990	21.3	49.0	8.2
	1991	21.0	48.4	9.6
	1992	20.8	48.6	9.9
	1993	24.6	47.2	8.5
	1994	28.5	42.2	10.7
	1995	31.7	44.0	16.5

Sources: Calvo and Kumar (1993, Table 1). Data for 1992 are estimates. GDP for Czechoslovakia until 1989 is Real Net Material Product. Data after 1992 are from National Bank of Hungary, *Annual Reports* (1994, 1995), and Austrian National Bank, *Focus on Transition* (various issues).

The chapter is organized as follows. Section 2 provides a very brief overview of current macroeconomic performance in the three countries. Section 3 provides a brief comparative survey of the principal financial sector reforms in Hungary, Poland, and Czechoslovakia since approximately 1987. Section 4 asks whether, in light of existing macroeconomic issues, a credit crunch can be said to exist or have existed in any of the countries under study. Section 5 concludes and summarizes what we can learn so far about the macroeconomic transition to market in these three countries.

As will be explained below, the key determinants of macroeconomic performance so far across the three countries lie in large measure with differences in monetary and fiscal actions during the first few years of the transition.[1]

Hungary and Poland both shared a common difficulty in obtaining IMF support. However, Poland's political system is in considerably greater turmoil than in the other two countries. Both Poland and Czechoslovakia experienced a 'big bang' approach to price and exchange rate liberalization while Hungary's approach has been more gradual in this respect. Also, privatization schemes seem to have preoccupied various Polish governments more than in Hungary. In Czechoslovakia even the process of privatization was subjected to a type of big bang. Finally, Poland has benefited from external financial support to a greater extent than either Hungary or Czechoslovakia.

As noted previously, several authors have commented on the dangers of a credit crunch during the transition to market. What we have in mind in this study is the credit crunch created by public borrowing requirements which displace private borrowing, or simply crowding-out. For the purposes of what follows we make no distinction between direct lending by governments, Consolidation Banks or other financial institutions which, as argued above, remain creatures of the State.

3. A REVIEW OF INITIAL FINANCIAL SECTOR REFORMS, 1987-1992

It is also helpful to briefly consider when and how financial reforms in Hungary, Poland, and Czechoslovakia, were implemented. As financial reforms began earliest in Hungary we begin with a description of that country's experience. Moreover, with reforms in the three countries covered in this study parallelling each other, much of the emphasis in what follows will be about the Hungarian situation. For Poland and Czechoslovakia we shall only discuss the differences vis-à-vis Hungary in their approach to financial reforms. While there now exists a vast literature on the overall reform or transformation process[2] few authors have provided a comparative review of the financial reforms (see, however, Calvo and Kumar (1993), and Borensztein and Masson (1993a, 1993b) and the volume edited by Bonin and Székely (1994)).

3.1 Hungary[3]

Although the reform process is said to have begun in 1968, for our purposes, the year 1987 marks the beginning of the relevant reforms since this is when Hungary introduced a two-tier banking system. Commercial banking type operations were transferred from the National Bank of Hungary (NBH) to newly created commercial banks. Specialist (i.e., merchant or investment banks) and savings banks were also created and these, for the most part, follow the German-Austrian universal banking model. Nevertheless, the State retains a controlling interest in the commercial banking sector. It is only toward the end of 1993 that privatization was expected to permit the government to divest itself of the commercial banking sector.[4] Significantly, the New Banking Act (NBA) stipulates that financial institutions comply with the proposals of the Basle Committee on Banking Supervision to achieve a risk-weighted asset-reserve ratio of 8% by 1 January, 1993 (for the details, see Siklos (1994a, ch. 10)). Escape clauses are built-in so that exemptions may be granted but ostensibly only until 31 December, 1994 and only on an individual basis (*New Banking Act* **II,** p.33; Ábel and Székely (1992)). Although meeting these standards is not itself an issue[5] (Ábel and Bonin (1992a, p.15) show that by 1990 these standards were well on their way to being met), the necessary portfolio reallocations no doubt have had significant macroeconomic implications (see section 4 below).

Complementing the banking reforms were reforms aimed at introducing a central bank with modern policy tools. Nevertheless, the reformed central bank continues to be hampered by the legacies of the past (Ábel et al. (1994)). For example, the NBH continues to be involved in the refinancing of enterprise bad debts in part because commercial banks have no incentive, under the present 'rules of the game', to provide long-term financing. Instead, the current incentive structure is entirely skewed toward the shorter end of the maturity structure.[6] This creates a mismatch between the needs of enterprises and the supply of loanable funds. The present state of affairs is akin to that of segmented markets in the sense that while enterprises prefer long-term financing commercial banks are largely constrained to supply short-term liquidity. Similarly, domestic and foreign investors have no wish to hold long-term government bonds preferring instead to hold short-term Treasury bills. And since sources of capital are primarily foreign,[7] the aforementioned mismatch problem is exacerbated. Moreover, as in the other previously centrally planned economies, Hungary's state-owned sector is saddled with significant inter-enterprise credit, a legacy of the central plan's rationing of crmedit but is especially the result of the imposition of tight 'western style' monetary policies (Ábel and Siklos (1994), Ábel et al. (1994), and see below). Thus, for example, by 1989, inter-enterprise credit represented over one-third of available short-term credit (34.6%; see Ábel et al. (1994, Table 3), up from 14% in 1982.

While the central banking and commercial banking sectors were reformed in line with existing European models, most notably that of Germany, no substantial reforms of fiscal operations have been implemented except for attempts to privatize state-owned companies.[8] Thus, by 1992, public debt as a percentage of GDP was 79.8% and only 65.3% a year earlier (Jaksity (1993, Table V). These figures would give Hungary the fourth highest debt/GDP ratio among the 12 OECD countries behind only Belgium, Italy, and Canada.[9] This raises the question of whether the current rate of growth in the public debt is sustainable.[10] Moreover, the current statutes of the central bank (see Act on the NBH, 1991, par. 19) permit the granting of credits to the State amounting to up to 3% of 'planned revenues of the central budget in that year'.

As is true elsewhere in Central Europe, a nascent money market[11] and an inefficient payments system (e.g., Ábel and Bonin (1992a)), combined with the effective absence of competition in the wholesale and retail banking sectors, imply that the functions of the present banking system are narrow by the standards of western industrialized countries. This problem is further exacerbated by other policies which have had major repercussions on commercial banks' balance sheets skewing their asset holdings toward liquid and low risk government debt and away from commercial lending (see Szabó (1991), Nyers and Lutz (1992), National Bank of Hungary (1993, various issues).[12]

A second problem with the reformed banking system has been the imposition of high reserve requirements, at least by western standards. Thus, the mandatory reserve ratio was originally set at 16% of deposits to be met on a daily basis (Balassa (1992, p.23); the reserve ratio was lowered to 14% in January 1993).[13] However, banks will earn interest on such deposits at 50% of the NBH's base rate while foreign exchange reserves will earn the market rate. The NBH argues (see NBH (1992, p.111)) that such high reserve requirements are justified on two grounds. First, the balance sheets of the corporate sector continue to deteriorate, necessitating the write-off of bad loans.[14] Second, the growing pressure on commercial banks to finance government expenditures, via relatively low risk loans, provides an incentive to skew lending toward the government. As in Italy, until very recently, high reserve requirements thus provide seigniorage income to the government.

Finally, the NBH has a specific exchange rate policy.[15] The domestic currency, the forint, was, until 1995, pegged to a basket of foreign currencies. Nevertheless, it is primarily driven by fluctuations in the US dollar and the NBH is actively involved in influencing the forint's course. Thus, the 'NBH implements its monetary policy..., by influencing or determining exchange rates...' (Act on the NBH, par. 8). Moreover, 'the NBH quotes and publishes the exchange rates serving to convert foreign currencies into forint and the forint into foreign currencies. The order of fixing and/or influencing the exchange rate is determined by the Government in agreement with the NBH' (par 13, Act on the NBH). Nevertheless, there are relatively few capital controls for large scale investors although some controls remain at the private level. Because of the desire and need for large capital inflows to finance necessary reconstruction and modernization of the infrastructure and formerly state-owned enterprises, failure to sterilize foreign exchange transactions produces significant monetary growth (Kemme (1992)).

3.2 Poland[16]

A two-tier banking system was introduced in 1989. The National Bank of Poland (NBP) became a traditional central bank by western standards but, as in the Hungarian example, the NBP automatically extends credits to the State up to a maximum of 2% of planned expenditures. Operations formerly conducted by the NBP were devolved into a newly created commercial banking sector which also assumed many of the existing bad debts of state-owned industries but, unlike Hungary or Czechoslovakia, no consolidation fund was created to assist in improving the viability of the commercial banking sector.[17] A distinguishing characteristic of the Polish financial experience has been its ability to obtain loan forgiveness from the US and European

Community (EC) countries. These same countries have been less generous toward Czechoslovakia and Hungary. Second, the IMF and western banks have been more directly involved in Polish financial affairs than in either of the other two countries in our sample. As in all the countries in this study, reserve requirements are steep. However, unlike Hungary, and more akin to the approach followed in western industrialized countries, reserve requirements vary by type of deposits (e.g., 30% on savings deposits and 10% on fixed-term deposits; see Kemme (1992)).

Until 1996, Poland retained strict capital controls so that the domestic currency, the zloty, was not a convertible currency to the same degree as was the forint.[18] However, Poland can be said to have been the first of the transitional economies to introduce a form of convertibility since the reforms were implemented at the same time that other financial and economic reforms were put in place – while the forint's convertibility came long after other financial and economic reforms were introduced.[19] Moreover, again unlike Hungary or Czechoslovakia (or later the Czech Republic), an exchange stabilization fund was set up in 1990. Both Hungary and Poland, following initial devaluations (see Borensztein and Masson (1993b, Chart I)), maintained a crawling peg. Having switched away from a dollar peg in 1991, the zloty's value is now more heavily influenced by the Deutschmark than is the forint. In the fiscal policy sphere, Poland's problems are similar to those experienced by Hungary, despite debt relief from international lenders.

3.3 Czechoslovakia and the Czech Republic[20]

At the central banking level, the principal distinguishing characteristic of the Czechoslovak financial reforms was the adoption of the Bundesbank model and the implicit acceptance of a programme of price stability, at least implicitly, following price liberalization on 1 January, 1991. Second, unlike the other two countries considered in this study, Czechoslovakia set up a Consolidation Fund as part of the initial package of reforms leading to the creation of a two-tier banking system. In addition, while banks formed after 1990 must adhere to the Basle capital-adequacy standards, existing banks' balance sheets need to attain this level only gradually (no target date currently exists).[21] In addition, reserve requirements for banks are considerably lower than in Hungary (8% for monthly deposits), a reflection perhaps that many bad loans are off the books of the newly formed Czechoslovak commercial banks. While Czechoslovakia did not have a stabilization fund of the kind created in Poland, a large stand-by arrangement with the IMF (of 105% of their quota) exists together with foreign exchange reserves (see below) to permit foreign exchange market interventions. The crown (koruny) is convertible on current account transactions and is pegged (with adjustments permitted) to a basket of currencies. Combined with a relatively low foreign debt load and a healthy budgetary situation,[22] Czechoslovakia's financial transition was, therefore, in appearance faster and perhaps less traumatic in economic terms than even the gradualist approach followed by Hungary (inter alia, Kemme (1992)). Czechoslovakia has also led the way in overall privatization schemes with the voucher system introduced in 1992 which also applied to former state-owned banking enterprises. While the Czech republic has continued that fast pace of reform since the break-up, Slovakia has lagged behind. Moreover, in the face of rising deficits, the Slovak Crown has depreciated relative to the Czech Crown. The Czech crown is pegged to a basket of currencies whose weight has been adjusted periodically. In June 1993, the basket is made up of the German Deutschmark (65% weight) and the US dollar (35% weight; see Hrnčíř (1993)).

Despite the apparent softness of the transition there are some disquieting signs of impending financial difficulties even in the Czech Republic. For example, Hrnčíř (1993) reports that between December 1991 and June 1993 there has been a large substitution in the ownership in shares of bank credit away from (former) state firms toward the 'private' sector.[23] But since the 'private' sector now includes former state-owned firms, which own most of these shares, the data give a misleading picture of the health of the Czech financial sector. We thus have a situation where the former state-run sector owns practically a majority stake in bank credits issued by commercial banks which advanced these credits to the former state-firm in the first place. This makes for an uncomfortable customer-client relationship since banks manage most of the funds which form a majority of the share issue and, consequently, face additional pressure to extend credits which are not backed in any real sense. Despite the creation of a Consolidation Bank the Czech government began preparing yet another bailout of the commercial banks as this study was written.

4. WAS THERE A CREDIT CRUNCH? THE STORY UNTIL 1992

The potential shortage of liquidity alluded to so far can be said to be akin to the credit crunch in that '... if firms have limited access to credit or if interest rates are high, the increase in production costs would lead to a credit crunch'. (Calvo and Coricelli (1992, p.71)). A credit crunch means that firms are only able to borrow with considerable difficulty or not at all (Sundararajan and Baliño (1991, p.2)). There has been considerable renewed interest in identifying credit crunches, particularly in the United States where the Savings and Loan scandal, combined with an overall tight monetary policy pursued by the Federal Reserve, has led some to argue that a new credit crunch emerged in the US during the early 1990s (see, for example, Bernanke and Lown (1991), Owens and Schreft (1992) and Peek and Rosengren (1993) for empirical evidence).

In industrialized countries with sophisticated money markets a tightening of monetary policy by the monetary authorities leads to higher nominal and real interest rates and thus to lower aggregate demand. Alternatively, the tightening of monetary policy can occur via non-price aspects of banking behaviour, such as regulatory changes. Hence, a credit crunch can still appear even when nominal interest rates are low. Banks may also contribute to a credit crunch through a contraction of their own as reflected in the asset side of their balance sheet.[24] Thus, for example, when the banks reduce the amount of commercial loans (large) enterprises in industrialized economies can offset the fall in liquidity by issuing more commercial paper.[25] This option, however, is not yet available to firms in the transitional economies due to the under- development of capital markets. Nor is self-financing much of an option as enterprise arrears grow (see below) and losses are the order of the day with relatively few enterprises able to consistently generate profits.[26]

Figure 3.1 plots real balances for narrow and broad monetary aggregates. A single vertical bar in each figure marks the date of the beginning of the transition in each country. Admittedly, dating the beginning of the transition has an element of arbitrariness. However, doing so permits some rough comparisons to be made between the 'old' and 'new' economic regimes. Except for Czechoslovakia, real balances are only moderately lower than before the transition began. However, for Poland, it could be argued that real balances simply reflect the elimination of the monetary overhang. The situation is quite different for Hungary where the monetary overhang problem had little practical relevance. Only recently has the steep decline in real balances been reversed, thereby raising the distinct possibility that Hungary alone has experienced a credit crunch. The data for Czechoslovakia may simply reflect the failure of the Czechoslovak National Bank to hold monetary growth in line with its stated targets.[27] If lower money demand in Hungary and Poland is associated with the output contraction and anticipations of higher future inflation then, as argued by Calvo and Coricelli (1993), this may lead to a 'bad' equilibrium in part because of the resulting impact on the government's budget. The public, expecting higher inflation despite the government's promise to lower inflation through a restrictive monetary policy, will reduce its holdings of money. In order to generate the necessary revenues the government could be prompted to rely increasingly on a combination of policies such as monetization of the deficit (including the deficit of existing

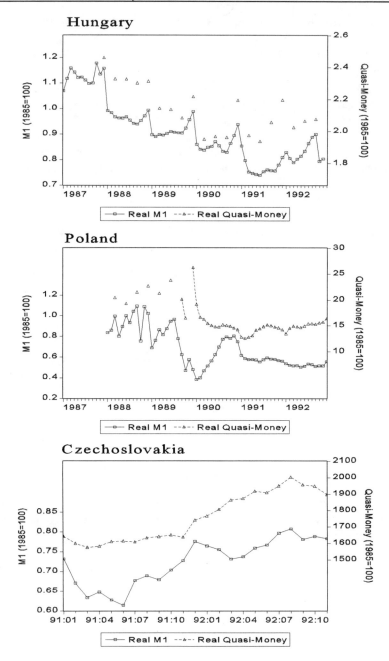

Figure 3.1 Money Supply

and former state enterprises) or a currency devaluation. The end result is more inflation and continuing reductions in money demand and a vicious circle leading to a 'bad' equilibrium.

Taken at face value then real balances in Figure 3.1 reveal no such likelihood of a bad equilibrium for Czechoslovakia but possibly one for Hungary and Poland. If the deficit financing scenario outlined above is a credible one then it will mean more crowding-out and the continuation of a credit crunch in these two countries. This is because it has been common for economies stabilizing in the aftermath of high inflation to ensure credibility via high real interest rates (see Siklos (1990), for a survey).

Another indicator of credit conditions is the currency-money ratio. Thus, if the banking sector can attract funds away from the holding of currency – the primary financial asset in a command economy – the currency-money ratio would fall. If, however, the banking system does not provide an attractive environment in which to place financial assets then this would be reflected in a currency-money ratio which is not falling. Figure 3.2 plots the currency-money (CM) ratio for Hungary and Poland, the two countries for which there were sufficient data. There is a downward trend in Poland's CM ratio

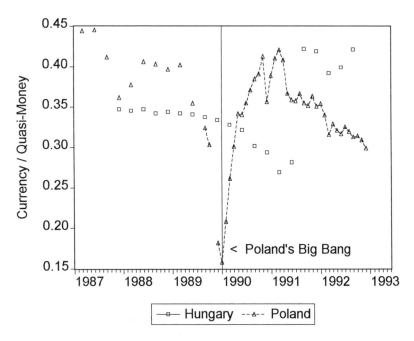

Figure 3.2 Currency-Money Ratio

following the 'big bang' and a small downward trend is also apparent in Hungarian data until the end of 1991.[28] Thereafter Hungary's CM ratio jumps to a higher level where it appears to remain stable.[29] One would have expected, other things being equal, portfolio reallocation to have resulted in shifts away from currency toward interest earning assets such as those included in a broad money measure. The behaviour of the CM ratio suggests then that banks are not acquiring the liquidity necessary to foster financial development as in the historical development of banking systems in western industrialized countries (Siklos (1997, Chapter 3)). Part of the reason may be that, on the basis of real ex post interest rates as seen in Figure 3.3, these have yet to be high enough to entice money holders to reallocate their liquidity toward the banking system.[30] While ex post real interest rates have often hovered around zero they have been volatile which is relevant considering the fact that much of the available liquidity is short-term in nature.[31,32] This outcome reflects the fact that the central banking authorities are caught in a difficult bind. To attract liquidity into the financial system sufficiently high real interest rates are necessary. But for the newly independent banking system to be profitable the implication is that enterprises would be discouraged from borrowing since real interest rates on loans would also be high. Thus, it could be argued that a new kind of subsidy has replaced the previous arrangement of granting credits to enterprises via state budgets. Or, using the terminology attributed to Cairn and used to describe financing under central planning, a different soft budget constraint has replaced the old soft budget constraint devised by the former Communist States. This approach is most apparent for Czechoslovakia and least evident for Hungary since, as noted above, nominal interest rates remain somewhat regulated whereas, for the most part, prices are more market determined.[33]

The real interest rate is, of course, in part a function of inflation performance. In this respect, it is interesting to compare the inflation performance of the three countries.[34] By 1992 inflation in Hungary stood at 20.3% while Poland's and Czechoslovakia's inflation rates were 37.7% and 11.0%, respectively. Czechoslovakia benefited from a combination of low foreign debt which, together with growing foreign exchange reserves (see below), meant that, in effect, the real value of the crown was relatively well backed in the 'real bills' doctrine sense of the term. By contrast, Hungary's high foreign debt load and deeply indebted banking system meant that low inflation credibility had to be gained via the credit crunch policy. Sharply rising foreign exchange reserves, however, assisted in backing the value of the Hungarian forint. Poland appears to represent an intermediate case with foreign loan forgiveness and rising foreign exchange reserves helping to dampen inflationary expectations following an inflationary peak of almost 600% reached in 1990 before falling as a consequence of these other events.

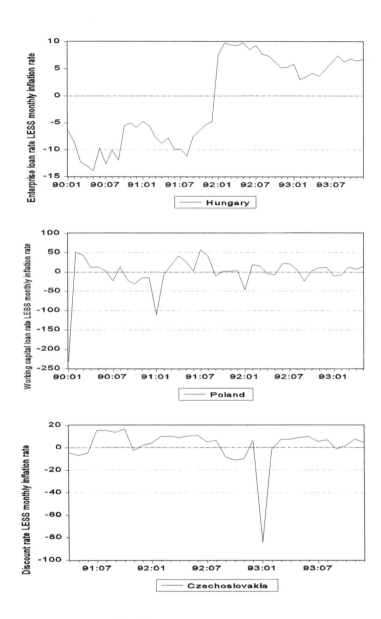

Figure 3.3 Real Ex Post Interest Rate Measures

Another useful indicator of credit conditions is the velocity of circulation shown in Figure 3.4. Other things being equal, a lesser reliance on cash to finance transactions would be reflected in a higher velocity of circulation (Bordo and Jonung (1987) and Siklos (1993)). Velocity does not appear to have risen in any of the three countries, except temporarily, as would be expected in a credit crunch. The release of the monetary overhang may simply have overcompensated for the monetary impact of the credit crunch.[35] Nevertheless, there is some evidence that the joint behaviour of velocity and the currency-money ratio is consistent with a model in which velocity is positively related to the currency-money ratio.[36] Thus, as commercial banking spreads, the CM ratio should fall to reflect a reduction in the public's reliance on currency and the growing volume of deposits and in the sophistication of the financial system. This would lessen the impact or likelihood of a credit crunch.

A few other broad indicators of the possibility of a credit crunch were also examined. For example, a credit or monetary crisis should significantly affect the money multiplier and the monetary base. Figure 3.5 plots the M2 money multiplier for Hungary and Poland only because there were too few observations available for Czechoslovakia. One would expect the multiplier to fall as banks reduce their assets and as the demand for currency rises (e.g.,

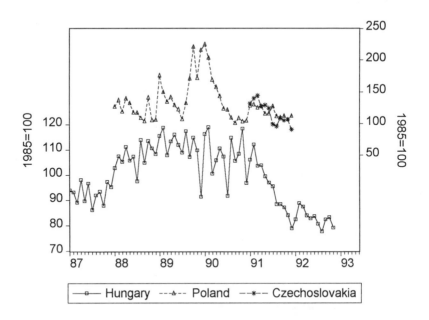

Figure 3.4 Income Velocity

see Sundararajan and Baliño (1991)). The latter occurs especially if the public is sceptical about the safety of the banking system. Figure 3.5 appears to show that, for Hungary at least, the behaviour of the multiplier is consistent with the existence of a credit crunch until the beginning of 1992 when the multiplier starts to rise.[37] By contrast, for Poland, the data suggest that the economic crisis may have led to a precipitous fall in the multiplier which suddenly reversed a few months after prices and exchange rate systems were liberalized. The rise in the multiplier continues through the months during which some of Poland's foreign debt is forgiven and a privatization scheme is announced (see Table 3.2). It may be then that the credit crunch is a purely Hungarian phenomenon. This might also help explain Hungary's better inflation record relative to Poland. Of course, differences in deficit and exchange rate behaviour between these two countries may also have been important.

So far our analysis has concentrated on the purely financial aspects of the transition. However, as noted in the introduction, the amplitude of the business cycle may be directly affected not only by monetary considerations but also by the behaviour of the banking sector.[38] To investigate the role of aggregate credit in influencing economic activity Figure 3.6 plots industrial production and real domestic credit for the three countries in our sample.[39] Note that the two series move roughly in tandem with each other in the three countries.

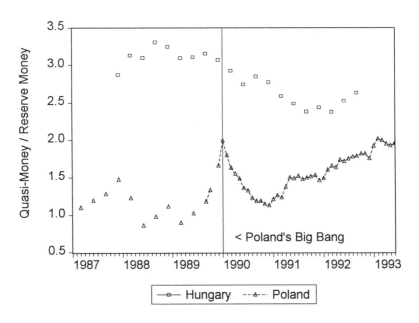

Figure 3.5 Money Multipliers

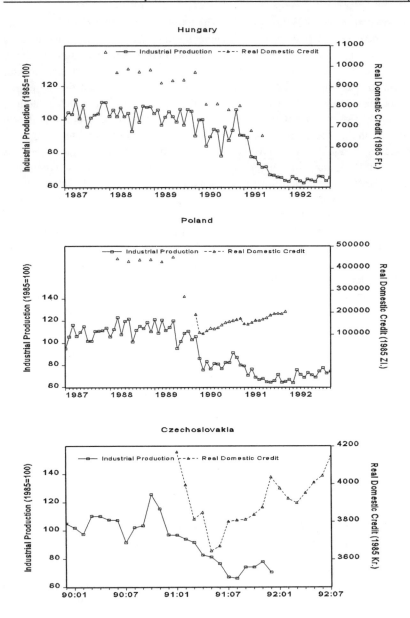

Figure 3.6 Industrial Production and Real Domestic Credit

Indeed, one striking difference between Hungary and both Poland or Czechoslovakia is that, in the latter two countries, real domestic credit rose after the transitional reforms were introduced whereas in Hungary, where no such big bang occurred, real domestic credit continued to fall until 1991. At the same time, industrial production in Poland and Czechoslovakia reversed their precipitous slide and stabilized. One way of analysing the connection between industrial production and real domestic credit is to test whether one series causes the other in a statistical sense. One such test, widely used and well-known, is Granger-causality testing. Table 3.2 presents Granger-causality tests between real domestic credit and industrial production. Note the differences in the test results between Hungary and the other two countries which is suggestive of the phenomenon described above. Real domestic credit is found to Granger-cause industrial production in the Hungarian data but the reverse appears to be true for Poland and Czechoslovakia as one cannot reject the null that industrial production is not Granger-caused by real domestic credit. By contrast, one is able to reject the null that real domestic credit is not Granger-caused by industrial production.[40] Consequently, the test results are suggestive of an output effect stemming from credit constraints; in other words, there exists a credit crunch for Hungary but not for Poland or Czechoslovakia.

Table 3.2 Granger-Causality Tests of Real Domestic Credit (RDC) and Industrial Production (IP)

Country	Null Hypothesis	F-Statistic	Significance Level
Hungary	RDC is **not** caused by IP	1.18	.32
	IP is **not** cause by RDC	10.02	.00
Poland	RDC is **not** caused by IP	2.59	.09
	IP is **not** caused by RDC	1.79	.19
Czechoslovakia	RDC is **not** caused by IP	.62	.45
	IP is **not** caused by RDC	4.40	.06

As noted previously, foreign sources of capital are vital in ensuring the liquidity and viability of the commercial banking sector and exchange rate policy has an important role to play in this regard. All three countries considered here chose to introduce an adjustable peg exchange rate system after an initial devaluation and fixing of exchange rates (see Borensztein and Masson (1993a, 1993b)). As Figure 3.7 reveals, foreign exchange reserves in all three countries rose sharply, particularly after 1990. For Poland this can be attributed to the reforms introduced that year (Sachs (1993)) and the same pattern holds for Czechoslovakia after its big bang of 1991. If the markets for these currencies were freely floating and operated as in the western industrialized countries – which of course they do not, strictly speaking – then this would be an indication of undervaluation in the respective currencies. As Figure 3.8 reveals, this appears to be the case since real exchange rates for Poland and Hungary have been steadily rising.[41] For Hungary, the real exchange rate rise has been steady since its banking reforms in 1987. For Poland, the rise in the real exchange rate of the zloty resumed a pattern which predated the big bang of 1990. Because these currencies appear to be undervalued, existing asset purchases, direct or indirect via the banking system, can be expected to be worth less in the future because revaluation is expected. But so long as the prospective capital gains are in the future this implies a tightening of credit flows thereby further exacerbating the severity of a credit crunch.[42]

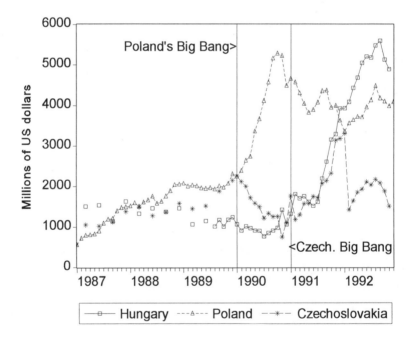

Figure 3.7 Foreign Exchange Reserves

Figure 3.8 Real Effective Exchange Rates

Finally, evidence about the existence of a credit crunch is also apparent from two other sources. As noted previously, a credit crunch can be signalled via firms attempting to obtain alternative sources of funds such as, for example, via inter-enterprise credits. Hungary's experience is illuminating in this respect. Between January 1987 and May 1992 total inter-enterprise debt rose 1300% while the number of firms engaged in such transactions also rose by over 1300% (Ábel and Siklos (1994, Table 2) and chapter 2, Table 2.2). There is, however, a sharp reversal in both trends beginning in April 1992. Thus, Hungarian monetary policy seems to have been instrumental in generating a credit crunch. The costs of such a policy would be reflected in the contraction of output whereas the principal benefits would be in the form of lower inflation and additional IMF support as well as a greater inflow of foreign investment. Hrnčíř (1993, Table 1) reveals that for Czechoslovakia inter-enterprise debt rose 948% between June 1989 and September 1992. The number of firms involved also rose by a similar proportion. There is no evidence of a sharp reversal and so it appears less likely that a credit crunch was engineered for Czechoslovakia.[43]

An additional source of credit constraints arises due to a consideration alluded to earlier, namely the inability to obtain long-term sources of funds from the commercial banking sector. Thus, in 1991, long-term corporate lending stood at less than 20% of total assets, which represents a 50% fall since 1988 (from data in Figure 3 in Ábel and Székely (1992a)). In the meantime, the spread between average deposit and loan rates in all three countries have risen sharply. In Hungary, for example, the spread at the short-term end of the maturity structure (i.e., one year or less) stood at less than 1% in 1988 and rose to over 8% by early 1992; (see Figure 6, Ábel and Székely (1992)) reaching levels of 12% by 1993 (NBH (1993, April), p.35). Similar outcomes are characteristic of the Polish and the current Czech Republic's experience. This may be taken as evidence of the growing risk premium on commercial loans. So far the data, broadly speaking, point to a credit crunch foremost in Hungary and, to a lesser extent, in Poland, and least evident in Czechoslovakia. Nevertheless, the data are not especially informative about the sources of the credit crunch which, as pointed out earlier, reflects a crowding-out phenomenon and confounds purely transitional factors with monetary and fiscal policies implemented since the transition began.

5. THE POST 1992 SITUATION IN BRIEF

Since 1992 the credit crunch described for Hungary has continued but the source of the problem has changed. As the deficit has shrunk (see Table 3.1), the problem is no longer government borrowing displacing private borrowing, but, rather, the imperative of reducing inflation, preferably to single digits. This has meant a continuation of high real interest rates. The need to reduce inflation is also a major consideration for Poland but less so for the Czech Republic. In both Poland and Hungary, relatively high real interest rates as well as economic recovery have attracted capital inflows with both countries experiencing substantial increases in international reserves. The Czech Republic too has been the beneficiary of increased capital inflows. All these countries have also experienced changes in their exchange rate regime. Poland's zloty now floats, Hungary's forint is devalued via a crawling peg mechanism, while the Czech Republic has considerably widened the fluctuation band for the koruny.

The poor fiscal situation which prompted the credit crunch in Hungary is now replaced with a persistent current account deficit, as shown in Table 3.3. However, unlike the situation until 1992, the current account threat is one shared by Poland and the Czech Republic, although the problem is receding quickly for Hungary. The role played by the current account is considered in Chapter 9.

Table 3.3 Current Account Balance

Year	Hungary	Poland	Czech Republic
		(millions of US dollars)	
1993	-3455	-2329	114.6
1994	-3911	-944	-49.7
1995	-2480	-2299	-1362.3
1996	-1678	-1352	-4475.8

Source: Austrian National Bank, *Focus on Transition* (various issues), Statistical Annex.

6. CONCLUSIONS

Taken together the evidence for the early years of the transition presented above suggests the possibility of a credit crunch in Hungary while this is less apparent in the other two countries considered. Because the crunch appears most severe in Hungary perhaps this raises a question about what the gradualist approach has accomplished for the Hungarian financial system.

To the extent that the data referred to in this chapter are faulty, it is possible that our interpretation of the credit crunch is misleading. For example, Sachs (1993) argues that industrial production data are biased since they do not reflect the growing importance of the nascent private sector. Second, since savings rates are high (unfortunately, the data in this respect are equally susceptible to being labelled as faulty) financing the transition may not be so problematic. While one cannot entirely dismiss these caveats we believe that the weight of the evidence is on our side. The lessons from Canada's own experience earlier this century serves to illustrate, even with relatively high savings rates, the importance for economic growth of capital inflows on a large scale, an efficient banking system, and few capital controls.[44] Moreover, so long as governments in the transitional economies considered in this paper, and Hungary and Poland especially come to mind here, continue constantly to draft new legislation, the resulting regulatory uncertainty can only contribute to prevent commercial banking from maturing and providing the intermediation services necessary to foster economic growth. In this connection, there are also lessons to be learned from neighbouring countries such as Austria. As Glück (1994) clearly points out, the Austrian experience is one of a slow and cautious road to full convertibility, credible inflation and financial liberalization over a twenty year span. While the transitional economies may not be able to afford the same amount of time as Austria had, a more systematic and orderly set of reforms is, at the very least, desirable.

POSTSCRIPT

The problem investigated in this chapter was an especially acute one in the first years of the transition. Capital controls have since been lifted in all three countries (that is in Hungary, Poland, and the Czech Republic, which succeeded the breakup of Czechoslovakia). However, as noted earlier, the lack of maturity in the financial system remains a problem throughout Central and Eastern Europe. On the whole, the transitional countries have managed the road to convertibility quite well with Poland and the Czech Republic fulfilling all of the International Monetary Fund's Article VIII requirements by 1996 (Hungary was the last of the three to do so during 1996). The next step remains the choice of the exchange rate regime for the next phase of the transition. We shall return to this final question again in the final chapter of this book. Also easing the credit crunch is the healthy rate of savings which continues, in the transitional economies considered here, to remain high relative to that recorded in industrial countries.

SOURCES OF DATA

National Bank of Hungary, *Monthly Report* (various issues).
National Bank of Poland, *Information Bulletin* (various issues).
Czech National Bank.
International Monetary Fund, *International Financial Statistics.*

NOTES

*   Originally published in *Establishing Monetary Stability in Emerging Market Economics,* edited by
       T.D. Willett, R.C.K. Burdekin, R.J. Sweeney and C. Wihlborg (Boulder, Col.: The Westview Press),
       pp.237-68, by P.L. Siklos and I. Ábel, and reprinted here by permission with substantive revisions.
       Siklos thanks Wilfrid Laurier and the Social Sciences and Humanities Research Council of Canada
       (grant 410-93-1409) for financial assistance. Ábel thanks MTA OTKA (Hungarian Academy of
       Sciences Research Funds, grant 681) for financial support. Versions of this paper were presented
       at the Austrian Institute of Economic Research (WIFO, Vienna) in June 1993 and at the International
       Monetary Fund in September 1993. The second author is grateful for the hospitality of the Fund
       where he was a Visiting Scholar in October 1993. Comments on earlier drafts by Andy Berg,
       Richard Burdekin, I. Székely, Carlos Végh, Tom Willett, and Georg Winckler were greatly
       appreciated.
1.   In the working paper version of this study, we compiled a chronology of economic and political
       events for the three countries which may be useful to some interested readers who are not familiar
       with the details of the transition process.
2.   See, inter alia, Ábel and Székely (1996), Hardy and Lahiri (1992), Duchatczek and Schubert (1992),
       Bruno (1992), Balassa (1992), Jindra (1992), Rudka (1992), Ábel and Székely (1992), Kemme
       (1992), Commission of the European Communities (1991), Székely (1990).
3.   See also Székely and Newberry (1993) for additional details about Hungary's transitional problems.
4.   See Chapter 8 for more recent details.

5. In part, because loan consolidation schemes help improve banks' balance sheets (Ábel and Bonin (1992a)). Also, much of the data discussed tends not to adjust for risk categories. When risk-adjusted weights are incorporated, Hungarian banks have not yet, strictly speaking, achieved the BIS standards. See *Bank Research Eastern Europe* (1991). The ratios referred to are percentage of adjusted capital which consists of the paid-in portion of registered capital, capital reserve, retained earnings, profit (loss) during a particular year, general provisions, and subordinated debt. See *New Banking Act in Hungary I* (1991, Annex, Appendix 2). Siklos (1994a, ch. 10) lists the principal risk-weights developed by the BIS.

6. For example, at the end of 1990, only .4% of loans of the Budapest Bank were long-term. Moreover, most of these loans were to companies in which the World Bank and the International Finance Corporation are also actively involved. See *Bank Research Eastern Europe* (1991).

7. Data for the Hungarian banking sector reveals that in 1991 almost 80% of funds were obtained from foreign sources. Except for 1989, when the same rate of foreign supply fell to 74%, the proportion of funds to the domestic banking sector coming from abroad has varied between 77% and 80%. See Nagy (1992).

8. The fiscal problems are not so much due to increases in spending but rather to problems with reducing the massive scale of subsidies and social programmes built up under the central planning regime as well as the slow pace of the reforms on the tax side of the budget equation. Centrally planned economies tended to rely on turnover style taxes, and the move toward ad valorem or value added style taxes, as well as the introduction of income taxes, has been hampered by an inefficient tax collection structure. Moreover, as taxes are relatively high, there exists an incentive for enterprises to avoid taxes by generating losses instead of profits. As Cukierman et al. (1992) have shown, countries with a poor tax collection infrastructure tend to resort to seigniorage which leads to persistently high rates of inflation.

9. Based on data from *OECD Main Economic Indicators*, various issues.

10. There is insufficient space here to discuss the separate question of the sustainability of public debt. See, however, Cohen (1991). Concern over this question is heightened by the fact that negative industrial productivity or real GDP growth combined with positive real interest rates have produced the 'unpleasant monetarist arithmetic' scenario. This also raises the question of central bank independence in Central Europe discussed in Siklos (1994b) and chapter 8.

11. In 1992, the NBH introduced two types of repurchase agreements. 'Passive' repurchase agreements are meant to be used as a conventional money market instrument, as in several western industrialized countries such as Canada. 'Active' repurchase agreements are meant to assist commercial banks with short-term liquidity problems.

12. Some of the data for the banking sector in Nagy (1992, Table 2) is instructive in this regard. Thus, between 1987 and 1991, commercial loans fell from 79% of total assets to 58% while holdings of securities rose from 1% to 12% of total assets over the same period.

13. There are a host of other prudential requirements which depend on whether outstanding loans are classified as 'bad' (see n.4 above for a definition) or otherwise. See *New Banking Act in Hungary I* (1991, par.28).

14. This is reflected in two different statistics. First, the passage into law of the Bankruptcy Act of 1992 has led to proceedings in the case of 2881 incorporated entities by July 31, 1993. Second, corporate tax revenues during the first seven months of 1993 were only one-quarter of the projected figure. See NBH (1993, July, p.21).

15. As argued in Siklos and Ábel (1997), the NBH acts as if it is implementing a real exchange target. One reason for pursuing such a policy is that, by 1993, the NBH was borrowing mainly from German and Japanese money markets. See NBH (1993, April, p.24).

16. A detailed account of the first year of the Polish attempt at stabilization is contained in Lane (1992). Wyczański (1993) points out that there have been many changes in the legislation affecting the banking system and the central bank since 1989.

17. This is partly reflected in the fact that, by the end of May 1993, 4950 enterprises were reported by commercial banks not to be creditworthy. This figure represents an increase of over 11% relative to the May 1992 figure. See Narodowy Bank Polski (1993, 5).

18. Capital controls can be viewed as a device, though not the only one, to ensure that a chosen exchange rate remain credible or stable. See Portes (1993) for a discussion of these questions as they apply to the European Monetary System. See also Kokoszczynski (1994).

19. This may also have been precipitated by the general belief that dollarization is a relatively more prominent feature in Poland than in either Hungary or Czechoslovakia.

20. See Aghlevi et al. (1992), Hrnčíř (1991), and Prust (1990) for additional details about the Czechoslovak transition programme.

21. One can speculate that, despite the Consolidation Fund, the balance sheet situation of Czechoslovak banks was even less favourable than for either Polish or Hungarian Banks. See Hrnčíř (1993).

22. According to Hrnčíř and Klacek (1991, Table 2), Czechoslovakia's foreign debt stood at 104% of exports in 1989. By contrast, Hungary's and Poland's external debt stood at 319% and 486% of exports, respectively, for the same year. By 1992, Czechoslovakia's external debt as a percentage of exports fell to an estimated 56.7% (Hrnčíř (1994b)).

23. From 66.89% of these credits at the end of 1992 to 42.53% at the end of June 1993. By contrast, the 'private' sector's share has risen from 9.78% to 40.10% over the same period (see Hrnčíř (1993, Table 1)).

24. This is called the credit channel effect of monetary policy (Bernanke and Blinder (1988)). Analyses which ignore the role of banks in the monetary transmission process are said to focus instead on the monetary channel of monetary policy. For our purposes, the terms credit or money crunches are used interchangeably.

25. Even in Hungary, where capital markets are relatively advanced compared with elsewhere in Central Europe, only 0.4% of corporate funding occurs via the bond market and an even smaller percentage of capital is raised via stock issues. All data are from Monthly Report of the National Bank of Hungary, October 1993, p.123.

26. Unless the effect is an output-induced one, in which case non-bank credit would also fall. See Kashyap et al. (1993). As Bruno (1992) points out, a credit crunch is not surprising in the aftermath of hyperinflation. Bolivia, Mexico, and Israel all experienced the same effect after their stabilizations.

27. This is certainly consistent with the evidence presented in Hrnčíř (1991).

28. More discussion about the behaviour of the CM ratio follows when we describe the behaviour of velocity. While it is plausible that the absence of deposit insurance, except in Hungary which introduced such a scheme in 1993, may have influenced the CM ratio, there is no evidence of such an independent effect stemming from the creation of deposit insurance in several of the industrialized economies unless it is viewed as being part and parcel of what is meant by financial development, broadly speaking (see Siklos (1993)).

29. We were not able to determine whether the jump is due to a change in the definition of either the currency or the quasi-money series. However, the jump does not appear to be due to some regulatory event.

30. Also, the data reveal the impact of interest rate ceilings on various bank deposits. See Kemme (1994) for a chronology of these ceilings for the three countries examined in this study.

31. Controls on interest rate levels are no longer in existence in these countries. They now appear to be adjusted to reflect market conditions over time but not necessarily on a month to month basis which is the data frequency used in generating estimates of ex post real interest rates shown in Figure 3.3. See Kemme (1994) for the current state of interest rate regulation in the transitional economies of Central Europe.

32. Subject to the caveat that ex post real interest rates need not be a good indicator of ex ante real rates.

33. This suggests that the so-called high real interest rate policy supposedly practised by the monetary authorities may not be entirely effective. One caveat to this interpretation is that our calculations may be sensitive to the choice of interest rate series. We did try a variety of definitions and our inferences appear to be robust. Alternatively, what may be signalling the severity of the credit crunch is the differential between borrowing and lending rates at the commercial banks. More about this possibility below.

34. All figures reported below are annualized monthly rates of change in the Consumer Price Index.

35. In a Quantity theory formulation, namely MV=Py, where M is the money supply, V is income velocity, and Py is aggregate nominal income (i.e., the price level (P) multiplied by real income (y)), if Py is stable then a release of the overhang should, other things being equal, signal a reduction in velocity. Thus, a monetary crunch could trigger a rise in velocity to offset its effects. Indeed, velocity in all three countries behaves as a random walk since tests fail to reject the null of a unit root in the logarithm of the levels at conventional significance levels. For Hungary the Dickey-Fuller test statistic is -1.442 (4 lags), -2.585 (4 lags) for Poland, and -0.864 (1 lag) for Czechoslovakia.

36. This is consistent with the institutionalist model of velocity's behaviour. See Siklos (1993) and references within. The regression of the logarithm of velocity (v), on a constant, the log of the CM ratio, and inflation (as a proxy for expected inflation) produced the following results:
for Hungary v=4.75+0.53CM+0.001π (R-squared=0.28; sample:1987.4-1991.2);
for Poland v=4.99+0.65CM+0.001π (R-squared=0.66; sample: 1990.01-1991.12).
There were too few observations to estimate a regression for Czechoslovak data, while the data for Hungary are quarterly because currency data were only available at this frequency. All coefficients were found to be statistically significant at the 1% level, except for Hungarian data.

37. Reserve requirements have begun to fall in the three countries considered in this chapter. Its effects would not, however, be apparent for the available data.

38. See Bernanke and Lown (1991) who provide empirical evidence to the effect that the most recent recession in the US (1990-92) was one of the few not directly caused by a credit crunch but rather by a weakness in the commercial banking sector's balance sheets. Given the discussion in section 3 above concerning the Basle guidelines applied to banks in the transitional economies, the parallels with the US situation are interesting.

39. Doubts have been expressed recently about both the quality of Industrial Production data and its relevance in analysing transitional issues. On this question see, for example, Sachs (1993).

40. While we have followed previous practice for such tests there is the possibility that Granger-causality test results can be overturned because of omitted variables bias.

41. The IFS CD-ROM did not contain the relevant series for Czechoslovakia. In 'Buy Now, While Currencies Last', *The Economist*, 20 June 1992, p.92, data for Czechoslovakia also reveals a rise in the real exchange rate of the crown since 1991. The undervaluation may, of course, have been a deliberate policy tool. It could be argued that such a policy acts as an insurance premium of sorts in light of the uncompetitiveness of the three countries considered here along the quality or technology dimensions of their exportable products.

42. This is purely a substitution effect for losses anticipated on foreign exchange transactions which can be offset by gains in production costs savings due primarily to relatively low real wages in all three countries. Other factors influencing the supply of funds include fiscal and monetary policies in western industrialized countries, notably those arising from the costs of German reunification as well as deficit financing needs in those countries. Another side-effect of a real appreciation, of course, is that the higher relative price of home goods leads to a reduction in aggregate demand. The resulting output loss makes investment in these countries still less attractive.

43. The data for Poland do not reflect inter-enterprise arrears but rather ordinary trade credit. Hence, discussion of these figures would be misleading.

44. There exists a vigorous debate, of course, about whether transitional economies should lift capital controls. The argument in favour of capital controls is the prevention of capital flight while those who oppose such restrictions view capital controls as necessary to ensure a commitment to market liberalization and low and stable inflation. Capital controls in all three countries have essentially since been lifted.

4. The Economics of Bankruptcy and the Transition to a Market Economy*

PROLOGUE

Property rights were limited in the former socialist economies. While home, land, and private company ownership did exist there were few, if any, economic consequences resulting from bankruptcies since the State effectively bailed out most failed concerns. Quite often privatization programmes were launched with little regard to the importance of bankruptcy procedures. This too was a neglected area of research in transitional economics. The result, in part, has been that far too many firms were allowed to go bankrupt. In addition, a kind of adverse selection took place in which arguably the wrong kinds of firms were permitted to go bankrupt. This chapter considers the relevant issues from the perspective of existing bankruptcy rules in selected industrialized economies.

1. INTRODUCTION

According to the often-repeated thesis of enterprise economics, the natural selection process resulting from the operation of market competition guarantees that in the long run only effectively productive enterprises survive. In other words, unprofitable enterprises, those whose resources could be used more efficiently in other activities, will be declared non-viable, and bankruptcy proceedings will be undertaken to liberate the society of this burden. The reorganization or dissolution of a firm is a specific, involuntary means for transferring ownership in the course of which the owner has only severely limited freedom to make certain decisions. However, it is not only the owner who is placed in a forced situation by such proceedings; nearly all participants of a market economy are made uncomfortable by such undertakings. Creditors, or certain groups of them, suffer losses of varying size, and clients are forced to seek out new suppliers. In other words, the question of who decides the fate of enterprises, and in what legal framework, is of considerable importance. Nor is it unimportant which costs are considered by the decision makers and on what their decisions are based.

The issue of bankruptcy, in spite of its eminent significance, has been largely overlooked in the initial phase of economic transformation. Privatization attracted a lot of attention, but the issue of appropriate handling of the potential problems elicited by the economics of bankruptcy has not.

In this chapter, we will first review the costs and decision-making regulations related to the liquidation of firms and examine the reorganization decisions in a similar manner. We will outline the general questions related to the proceedings involved and compare the practices that developed in market economies as well as those that are in progress in the transforming economies.

Bankruptcy proceedings are successful if the defunct enterprise's assets are utilized more productively in other areas. When reorganization, rather than liquidation, also solves the problems, then the firm's survival is justified, provided that another utilization does not offer better results. In working out the framework of the analysis, the writings of Meckling (1977), Miller (1977), Stiglitz (1972), and White (1984, 1989) are of primary significance. For the specific problems of the transforming economies, Mitchell (1990) and Mizsei (1993) are instructive.

2. THE LIQUIDATION OF AN ENTERPRISE

The liquidation of an enterprise does not have to be accomplished within bankruptcy proceedings: a firm may, without any specific legal proceedings, sell off its assets in order to pay off its debts from the proceeds thus accrued. However, if the income from such a sale is not sufficient to repay debts, then a legally qualified bankruptcy is unavoidable, and those who are not in the front ranks of creditors will inevitably suffer some losses. Still, it is less expensive to take this action than for each of the creditors individually to undertake legal action to enforce their claims. In other words, bankruptcy proceedings benefit both the enterprise in question and its creditors. Within bankruptcy proceedings, it is very important to define the parameters; after all, even if in the end a reorganization takes place, the negotiating terms required for mutual agreement are established by a comparison of the alternatives of the reorganization and the liquidation.

When a firm in the United States goes bankrupt, its liquidation is executed by a bankruptcy court. This is liquidation under the terms of so-called 'Chapter 7 of the bankruptcy law', as distinct from reorganization performed in accordance with ('Chapter 11'). While reorganization is under way, the regulations of Chapter 11 protect the firm against less patient creditors, who might flood the already drowning enterprise with lawsuits and thus seal its fate once and for all. Such protection is not only important for the enterprise but also benefits the creditors in that it creates an opportunity for the firm to regain its fiscal health, in which case creditors would have a better chance to press their claims successfully.

Thus the bankruptcy court supervises the dissolution of a firm and uses the income acquired from the sale of its assets to satisfy creditors in the order established by priority rules. Under this procedure, the creditors do not obtain proprietary rights to the firm.

Priority rights may be absolute or relative. Relative priority calls for creditors to bear the burden of losses in certain proportions. By contrast, absolute priority sets out a rank order: the claims of creditors thus ranked are satisfied in full as long as income from the sales makes this possible. First on the list are the costs of the liquidation proceedings (court and expert fees) as well as the loans that were extended – with the approval of the court – after the initiation of the bankruptcy proceedings. These are followed by obligations prescribed by law (taxes, consumer deposits, wages), even if they originate from times prior to the initiation of the bankruptcy.

Third are the non-guaranteed obligations, such as those put forward by the creditors and the owners of bonds issued by the firm. Regulations prescribe a certain rank order even for these. In the end come the shareholders, the owners of the enterprise. Moreover, even within the group of creditors, there could be certain individuals who could enjoy certain special claims on the firm's assets. These rights are agreed upon at the time of the loans' initiation, and the assets thus involved are specifically earmarked in the firm's credit reports. It may therefore happen that some creditors receive nothing from the income earned from the sale of the firm's assets, while those with special guarantees obtain the earmarked assets or equivalent values.

3. PRIORITY RULES AND EFFECTIVENESS

The initiation of bankruptcy proceedings in fact implies that not every creditor would receive what he or she demands: otherwise, the action taken by the bankruptcy court would be superfluous. Therefore, it must be decided who, on the basis of his claims, is entitled to how much of the outcome of the bankruptcy proceedings.

It is worth analyzing how the behaviour of all involved is influenced by the various ways in which the priority rules are set down. Using an analysis by White (1989), we may look at three different types of rules.

According to the first type of rule, older creditors enjoy an advantage over newer ones; that is, claims are satisfied in the order in which the loans were extended. Unless there are other exemptions, creditors are satisfied in full, as long as there is money for this. However, as soon as the money runs out, the next creditor, and all subsequent ones, receive nothing. The shareholders are at the end of the line.

The second type of rules sets up the exact reverse of the first; i.e., the creditors' ranking order starts with the most recent one, and priority is set up in chronological order backwards.

In the third case, creditors receive money in equal proportion; they are given an identical percentage of their claims.

The priority rules used in the United States contain elements from all three of these types. The first type of rule is used in setting up rank order among owners of enterprise bonds, if bonds were issued more than once and no special priority agreements were made. The third type (identical treatment) applies to creditors for whom the loan agreements did not contain priority guarantees for certain assets of the enterprise. And the second type of rule is, in fact, applicable to most of the recent creditors who were cautious enough to offer credit only with guarantees and special priority rights.

The rules of bankruptcy proceedings also influence economic effectiveness. In analyzing effectiveness, we first survey the process during which it is decided whether to liquidate or reorganize a given enterprise. In order to do this, we use a simple model: the sum of the enterprise's debts is denoted by D, of which the sum immediately due is D_1. The immediately realizable (liquidational) income, obtainable with immediate dissolution, is L_1. This is smaller than the bills to be urgently paid (D_1), otherwise there would be no need to consider liquidation. This also means that if the enterprise is dissolved, then all proceeds will go to the creditors according to the established priority rule and the shareholders (the previous owners) will receive nothing ($L_1 < D_1$). For the sake of simplicity, let us suppose that current earnings just cover expenses, so we do not have to take a producer surplus into consideration. Reorganization of the enterprise, however, is expected to generate some positive profits S in the next period. This is a natural assumption. If there were no such expectations there would be no reason at all to consider reorganization in the first place.

In order for the enterprise in question to avoid immediate liquidation, it needs credit or a new capital injection out of which it could pay off some of its overdue debts. Let us suppose that it issues bonds in the required amount and these are purchased by a bank. From the earnings, the firm pays off the loans that have just become overdue (D_1). Let the value of bonds thus issued be B, identical to the loans that have just become overdue ($B = D_1$). This can be interpreted as a bank guarantee that would assist the enterprise in overcoming its monetary insolvency, but only on condition that if the firm were to be dissolved the bank would have priority claims on getting paid. The bank would receive the bonds at a price below nominal value, since in exchange for the sum B, the firm accepted the $(1 + r) B$ obligation augmented by the bank interest of r percent.

Having settled in this way its immediate liquidity problems, the enterprise at the same time transformed its capital and debt structure. The market value of the enterprise has also changed, since transformation is associated with expected profits $(S > 0)$. The question now is whether it is worth weathering the first crisis by taking the above fiscal action, or do economic consideration dictate the firm's liquidation?

The alternatives are summed up in Table 4.1, which reveals that the shareholders (owners) gain by delaying the firm's dissolution if:

$$S > D_2 - L_2 \qquad\qquad (4.1)$$

where

S is the expected profit after reorganization,

D_2 is the firm's debt in the second period, and

L_2 is the liquidation value of the firm's assets in the second period.

Table 4.1 Comparing the Costs of Dissolution and Survival

In the event of dissolution:	
(a) Debt	D
(b) Resources usable for servicing debt	-
(c) Liquidation value of capital assets	L_1 $(L_1 < D_1)$
(d) Amount set aside for shareholders	- (since $L_1 < D_1 < D$)
(e) Creditors' loss	$D - L_1$
In the event of survival:	
(a) Debt	D_2 $[D_2 = (1 + r) D - D_1 + B]$
(b) Resources usable for servicing debt	S
(c) Earnings from bond issue	B
(d) SWAP of debts	D_1 $(D_1 = B)$
If firm is still dissolved after debt restructuring:	
(e) Liquidation value of assets	L_2 $[L_2 = (1 + r) L_1]$
(f) Amount set aside for shareholders	
- if $D_2 > L_2 + S$, then	-
- if $D_2 < L_2 + S$, then	$L_2 + S - D_2$
(g) Creditors' loss	
- if $D_2 > L_2 + S$, then	$D_2 - L_2 - S$
- if $D_2 < L_2 + S$, then	-

Legend:

r is interest rate (discount rate)

$D_2 = D (1 + r)$ is debt due in second period

$L_i (i = 1,2)$ is firm's liquidation value in period i

$B = D_1$ is bank assistance to settle debt coming due in first period

S is profit in second period

At the same time, the creditors' loss is reduced by delaying liquidation, if the profit (S) is greater than the difference in the liquidation value of the firm between the two periods, i.e.: $S > L_1 (1 + r) - L_2$. This is derived from comparing the discounted values of the loss accrued with the liquidation in the first period ($D - L_1$) and the loss accrued with the liquidation in the second period ($D_2 - L_2 - S$):

$$D - L_1 > \frac{1}{1+r} (D_2 - L_2 - S) \tag{4.2}$$

which directly leads us to the expression

$$S > (1 + r) L_1 - L_2 \tag{4.3}$$

Whether the enterprise can or cannot be helped is determined by the success of the bond issue, the concomitant offer of credit, or, as in the case above, the decision made by the bank. These, in turn, are influenced by the answer to the following question: if the bank offers assistance and the firm is still dissolved later, what kind of priority guarantees can the bank cite during the bankruptcy proceedings? Before we discuss these, let us examine another hypothetical case, namely, one in which the enterprise becomes entirely viable and avoids dissolution in the future. In such an instance, there will be no need to present the priority guarantees that have been instituted for bankruptcies. This becomes possible when, under a transformed debt structure, profit in itself is sufficient to satisfy the debts coming due, that is, if $S > D_2$. Although this condition ensures the enterprise's survival it is difficult to achieve it, since additional loans imply a cut to the size of profit by the amount necessary to service the debt.

Table 4.2 summarizes those earnings requirements (i.e., minimal demands towards S) – as shaped by the priority rights established by the bankruptcy proceedings – whose fulfilment enables the bank to offer assistance without the threat of loss, even if in the end the enterprise has to be dissolved. The most demanding effectiveness condition is established by the first and third types of priority ranking. The reason for this is that in these cases the only way for the bank to collect all of its money is for all creditors to be fully covered. This, of course, happens only when (with the firm surviving) the profit exceeds the difference between the value of the firm's remaining assets and its volume of debt. Otherwise, the bank will not offer assistance and the firm must be dissolved, even if this causes greater damage to the national economy than a reorganization of that firm.

If the bank, as the most recent creditor, enjoys priority rights, then the preconditions for offering assistance are less stringent. It may suffice for the profit achievable by a deferment to be greater than the difference between the firm's interim debt and its capital worth: $S > (1 + r) B - L_2$. Since a deferment reduces the loss of the other creditors only if the profit S and the remaining value L_2 together exceed the size of the payment $(1 + r) B$ to be made to the bank, it is inconceivable for the bank not to support any deferment that would cut the loss of the other creditors. However, it will still not be able to support cases in which the profit, while positive, would not equal the interest burden of guarantees extended by the bank.

Table 4.2 Priority Rules and Conditions for Bank Guarantee (Conditions for Delaying Liquidation)

	Type of rule		
	1.	2.	3.
	priority rights owned by		No distinction
	older	newer	
	bonds issued		
Bank suffers no loss	$D_2 < L_2 + S$ even the newest creditors suffer no loss	$B < L_2 + S$ at least newest creditor suffers no loss	$D_2 < L_2 + S$ no creditor suffers loss
Effectiveness criteria	$S > D_2 - L_2$	$S > (1 + r) D_1 - L_2$ $[S > (1 + r) B - L_2]$	$S > D_2 - L_2$

Remarks:

1. For the economy, it is advantageous to delay liquidation, if $S > 0$. Of the above requirements, the following is valid:

$$S > D_2 - L_2 > (1 + r) D_1 - L_2 > 0.$$

2. The value of bank guarantee (bond issue) equals the amount of debt immediately due $(B = D_1)$.

Legend:

r is interest rate (discount rate)
$D_2 = D (1 + r)$ is debt due in second period
$L_2 = (1 + r) L_1$ is firm's capital value in second period
$B = D_1$ is bank assistance to settle debt coming due in first period
S is profit in second period

To be sure, a deferment would reduce the national economy's losses (by the amount S), but the shareholders would still not receive anything, and the bank would lose some of its investment.

Regardless of the rule applied, all enterprises with a negative profit are to be dissolved. There are cases, however, in which firms are dissolved even though their survival would serve the demands of effectiveness. What this means is that none of the rules guarantees the rationality of bankruptcy proceedings. The reason for this is that neither the owner initiating the proceedings nor the bank evaluates the costs that have to be borne by the other creditors. They would be unlikely to choose deferment just to cut the other creditors' losses, unless this were also to benefit them.

4. REORGANIZATION

In the United States, firms that file for bankruptcy may choose between dissolution executed under the terms of Chapter 7 or reorganization under Chapter 11. Under a reorganization, company officers usually remain in their positions and the firm survives the crisis. It develops a programme of reorganization in order to settle its debts. Reorganization does not necessarily call for the sale of the enterprise or any parts thereof. In fact, reorganization is chosen as a substitute for such a sell-off. The plan must be approved by the creditors; after all, it is in their interest to avoid dissolution and see the firm survive.

There are several rules governing the acceptance of a reorganization plan. According to one of them, every creditor group must approve the plan (unanimous consent procedure). In such a case, the debtors frequently try to make the reorganization plan more appealing by overestimating the value of the firm's assets. The groups of creditors vote separately on whether to accept or reject the reorganization plan, and within every group a two-thirds majority is required for approval. To be more precise, at least half of the creditors must vote 'yes', and these 'yes' votes must represent at least two-thirds of the outstanding demands.

Another set of rules was designed to ease the pressure on the firm's managers. They prescribe, for example, that for the first six months votes may be cast only on proposals sponsored by the management. Thus, creditors may often do nothing more than observe actions undertaken by the firm's management.

If no acceptable plan is created in this manner, then another rule comes to be applied. According to this rule, the bankruptcy court may consider the plan approved if it is supported by at least one creditor group. However, this is an expensive alternative: the court tries to reinforce its decision with expert reports, which command their own price.

As we can see, reorganization has its own pitfalls, one of them being that enterprises may be reorganized even when it would be more desirable to dissolve them.

5. REORGANIZATION AND EFFECTIVENESS

In examining how priority rules of bankruptcy proceedings influence effectiveness, we have analyzed the case in which the enterprise overcomes its solvency problems by transforming its capital structure. Now we discuss the costs related to reorganization.

When it comes to reorganization, we have to use two kinds of costs in our evaluation. The first category is made up of costs associated with the plan's development and its realization: here we are talking about court costs, the wages of everyone dealing with the case, and all other costs arising in the course of reorganization. These costs are indicated by the letter T. In the other category belong other associated costs, which, due to rescheduling and deferments, arise on the side of creditors. We propose that these will be in proportion to the size of the debt, and their amount is indicated by sD $(0 < s < 1)$.

The result of reorganization is the profit it yields (S). *Society benefits from reorganization if this surplus exceeds earnings L (obtainable by dissolving the firm) by at least as much as the amount consumed by the process of reorganization:*

$$S - T > L \tag{4.4}$$

The enterprise is forced to liquidation if the burden remaining after debt forgiveness $(1 - s)\, D$, combined with the T cost of reorganization, is greater in size than the value of expected profit obtainable by reorganization:

$$S - T < (1 - s)\, D \tag{4.5}$$

A comparison of equations (4) and (5) yields a peculiar conclusion. *If $L > (1 - s)\, D$, then the enterprise benefits by choosing reorganization even if society would reap greater economic benefits from dissolving the firm.* What takes place in such cases is that by agreeing to the sD debt forgiveness, the creditors make an unnecessarily great sacrifice, which in fact implies assisting the shareholders. If the sum of debt forgiveness is established so that the remaining debt equals the firm's capital value, then no such assistance is implied. In such an instance, the firm's managers make their decision concerning reorganization or liquidation on the basis of considerations that match those of economic effectiveness:

$$S - T > L = (1 - s)\, D \tag{4.6}$$

In this case, the creditors jointly defer debts in the amount that they would not have been able to collect anyway.

If debt forgiveness is less than this amount, then the firm's management may still decide in favour of dissolution, even if reorganization would be economically more effective, i.e., when the following equation is valid:

$$(1 - s)\, D \;>\; S - T > L \tag{4.7}$$

6. BANKRUPTCY PROCEDURES IN MARKET ECONOMIES

The intention to provide legal protection to the bankrupt firms' employees, customers, and creditors is generally observable in all developed business environments. The manner and practice of how this intent is applied, however, vary widely. In Great Britain until quite recently the law made no distinction between dissolution and reorganization. A distinctive feature of the French law is that it grants an especially strong bargaining position to the employees of troubled enterprises (Simeon et al. 1987). German laws, similarly to those in Great Britain, regulate dissolution and reorganization jointly (Klasmeyer and Kubler 1983). Baird (1986) holds the view that if other market institutions provide mechanisms which guarantee the disappearance of firms ripe for such a fate and the survival of healthy ones, then there is no need for special bankruptcy laws.

In comparing the bankruptcy laws of five countries – Great Britain, the United States, France, Japan, and Germany – Mitchell (1990) points out interesting differences. As for the initial action, it is only in the United States that creditors have no right to initiate bankruptcy proceedings against enterprises. They can press their claims only through regular legal channels, and it is only the directorate of the debtor firm that can choose to file for bankruptcy. Regulations do not even prescribe when the directorate is obliged to take such action. French, German, and Japanese laws contain itemized definitions in this regard, while they also make it possible for creditors to initiate bankruptcy proceedings. The reason for spelling out these obligations is this: if the troubled firm's officers could conceal the situation, they could initiate excessively risky manoeuvres in the hope of escaping their predicament, thus jeopardizing the firm's remaining assets and the possibility of repaying its debts.

Possibilities for dissolution or reorganization are present in differing ways in various countries. France places the greatest emphasis on opportunities to reorganize. The primary aim of French regulations is to save debtor firms and the jobs they represent. In German regulations, dissolution is considered as practically the only solution, perhaps keeping in mind the risks arising from the differing criteria applied in discussing reorganization plans and those of economic effectiveness at the national level. In order for a debtor firm to execute a reorganization plan combined with a reduction in debts, it has to make cash settlements of at least 35 percent of its nonguaranteed debts. Regulations in Great Britain and Japan deal separately with dissolution and reorganization. In Japan reorganization can be initiated by the firm's directorate, a group of shareholders who own at least 10 percent of shares, or creditors, the latter in the event that their demands exceed 10 percent of the firm's capital assets. Reorganization may be transformed into dissolution if two-thirds of the creditors approve. In England, no such transformation is permitted.

Unquestionably, bankruptcy proceedings are relatively less frequent in smoothly operating market economies where capital markets are well functioning. The more institutional possibilities exist for transferring enterprise ownership, the less the system is forced to compel actions that are not proceeding naturally. In general, one finds a lack of fiscal discipline behind bankruptcies. True fiscal discipline, however, is not enforced by the threat of bankruptcy but by the effective operation of the capital markets.

This is demonstrated by the experience of the Hungarian economy, too, as discussed in the writings of Laki (1983), Papanek (1986), Tardos (1988), and Voszka (1986). Tardos (1988) observes that regardless of the economic system, bankruptcy proceedings by themselves are not enough to guarantee timely adaptabilitiy. In order for bankruptcy proceedings to serve society well, the capital, labour, and money markets must also perform in an orderly manner (Tardos 1988, p.274). Too stringent bankruptcy regulation in an economy which is in transition to a market economy may even cause serious problems instead of promoting such a transition.

7. BANKRUPTCY REFORMS IN EASTERN EUROPE: A TROUBLESOME DILEMMA

7.1 Bankruptcy Regulation Before the Changes

Although bankruptcy regulation appeared in the legal structure well before the changes of the 1990s – in Hungary it was introduced together with the new economic mechanism (NEM) in 1968 – it could not perform its role properly. The shortcomings of the previous regulation can not be blamed entirely on its legal structure which gave too much discretion to the authorities in influencing the final outcome. As the problem of bankruptcy is inherently rooted in the broader problem of property rights, its influence on economic decisions could not gain significance before changing property rights in the economy.

As Mizsei (1993) points out, financial rehabilitation was sometimes used to heal troubled enterprises in a non-transparent manner, and the interests of the ministries responsible for such enterprises were often completely dominating the interests of other parties involved (creditors). In the first half of the 1980s, only seven state enterprises were liquidated, and the analysis of Kuti and Móra (1989) suggests that their selection for such an action among the growing number of troubled state enterprises was totally random. The bankruptcy law which was introduced in 1986 had only a modest impact on actual bankruptcy proceedings. In a period of dramatic deterioration of financial conditions of the enterprises only in a few cases did the courts decide about the liquidation of a state enterprise. Without alternative owners other than the state itself liquidation seemed almost always more costly than reorganization (financial rehabilitation). The new rules, however, did enforce some financial discipline.

7.2 Bankruptcy Regulation of the Transition

The architects of the economic transformation in Hungary with the new bankruptcy regulation tried to solve two problems at once (Mizsei 1993). On the one hand they tried to establish a credible deterrent to the apparent lack of payment discipline by state-owned enterprises, and, on the other hand, they tried to eliminate the mounting chain of inter-enterprise indebtedness. To do so they introduced a draconian bankruptcy law with an automatic trigger which is not common even in the Western regulations. The law of 1992 obliges the executive of an enterprise to file for bankruptcy within eight days if its payment arrears exceed 90 days. Failing to do so the manager could be penalized under the civil code and would be held legally accountable with his personal wealth for the damage caused to the creditors by the delay in filing for bankruptcy.

The Hungarian law reflects the structure of the US Chapter 7 and Chapter 11 procedures for liquidation and reorganization, though the former is much more stringent and rigid than the latter in terms of requirements for achieving an agreement between debtors and creditors. The troubled enterprises have only 90 days to arrive at a restructuring agreement with their creditors who have to give their unanimous consent.

Although the law is an important step towards a functioning market economy, it is nonetheless insufficient on its own to bridge the gap between the need for a well functioning capital market and the mere reality of a very underdeveloped financial system unable to provide adequate financing for either new or old businesses.

7.3 The Consequences of a Stringent Bankruptcy Regulation in a Weak Market Environment

It is crucial for the success of the economic transformation that in designing new laws and regulations concerning bankruptcy procedures one takes into account their effect on the economy as a whole with its peculiarities. As discussed before, unfortunately the strategy followed by policymakers in the case of bankruptcy regulation in Hungary has been biased towards the monetary considerations of eliminating the inter-enterprise indebtednes. As a result they did not take into account in their calculations the impact of the transition itself on the variables represented by equation (4.7).

In particular, the liquidation value of enterprises (L) was depressed because the lack of capital markets, combined with the worldwide recession, implied an almost complete absence of demand for enterprises' assets.

At the same time, the debt forgiveness parameter (s) has fallen owing to banks' inability to forgive loans. especially in the process of the new capital adequacy requirements facing them. We therefore end up in a situation where the liquidation value of firms is smaller than the expected net surplus emerging from reorganization. On the basis of the decision rule reflected in equation (4.4), this in turn implies that the appropriate policy rule is reorganization rather than liquidation. However, due to the insufficiently small debt forgiveness, the net surplus from reorganization is usually smaller than the debt obligations of the firms, which implies that the firms should be liquidated. This is represented by equation (4.5).

Consequently the transforming economy finds itself caught in the dilemma represented by equation (4.7), namely, that a firm may be forced into liquidation even though reorganization may economically be a more efficient option for it and for the economy as a whole. Put differently, the economy may find itself trapped in a prisoner's dilemma situation: each indebted firm, by following what appears to be the only choice it has inflicts a negative externality on the economy. By way of a summary, Table 4.3 provides an overview of the costs and benefits of reorganization.

Table 4.3 Comparing the Costs and Benefits of Reorganization

(a) Debt before reorganization	D
(b) Deferred debt	sD
(c) Debt after reorganization	$(1 - s) D$
(d) Cost of reorganization	T
(e) Present value of production surplus	S
(f) Liquidation value of assets	L
(g) Amount set aside for shareholders	
- in event of immediate liquidation	- $(since\ L < D)$
- in event of reorganization	
if $S - (1 - s) D < T$	-
if $S - (1 - s) D > T$	$S - (1 - s) D - T$
- in event of liquidation after reorganization	
if $L < (1 - s) D$	-
if $L > (1 - s) D$	$L - (1 - s) D^1$
(h) Creditors' loss	
- in event of immediate liquidation	$D - L$
- in event of reorganization[2]	
if $sD > S - L - T$	$sD - (S - L - T)$
if $sD < S - L - T$	-

Remarks:
For economic efficiency, reorganization is advantageous if $S > L + T$. If the debt remaining after debt forgiveness is equal in size to the liquidation value of assets $(1 - s) D = L$, then, according to line (h) of the Table, the creditors' loss is smaller in the event of reorganization than in the event of liquidation, provided the condition $S > L + T$ materializes.
Notes:
1. We are setting aside the possibility that in this event the creditors may claim debts that have previously been forgiven, which would reduce the amount set aside for shareholders by another sD amount.
2. We are assuming that $S > L - T$, otherwise the criterion for economic effectiveness set up for reorganization $(S - L - T)$ would not be met.

POSTSCRIPT

Credits by the banking sector to government and large scale enterprises continue to grow while credits to households and small enterprises remain fairly stagnant, at least in Hungary. The situation is somewhat better in Poland and the Czech Republic. There continues to be a reluctance in the transitional economies to permit reorganization of firms. Therefore, the number of firms which declare bankruptcy and must be liquidated remains fairly high as banks are unwilling or unable to be flexible in their lending practices.

NOTE

* Originally appeared as CEPR Working Paper 878 (December 1993) by I. Ábel and K. Gatsios. Revisions have been made to the original draft.

5. Changing Structure of Household Portfolios in Emerging Market Economies*

PROLOGUE

In most market economies the household sector generates the bulk of economy-wide savings. In centrally planned economies with primitive financial markets and regulated prices there is little incentive to save. Consequently, one indication of the impact of the transition process consists in understanding the structure of household savings in the face of new financial instruments made available at more or less market rates. The case of Hungary is considered in this chapter since developments in the financial sector took place relatively quickly. The focus is on the early phases of the transition since it provides the best indications of the distance from central planning to market economies in the development of financial sophistication.

1. INTRODUCTION

Savings and portfolio allocation decisions of households are critical determinants of the transformation to a market economy. While private (personal) savings has attracted a great deal of attention (Portes and Winter, 1978; Hulyák, 1983; Nadrai et al., 1985; Riecke, 1985; Király, 1993; Mellár, 1990; Rappai, 1990), portfolio allocation has been until quite recently neglected. For Hungary, the only paper related to the portfolio allocation of households is Csunderlik (1985), who tried to analyse the interrelationship of private housing investment and personal savings. In this chapter we outline the basic characteristics of portfolio allocation of Hungarian households in the 1980s for which the data are most plentiful and detailed among the transitional economies. Special attention is paid to factors which will play an important role during the transformation, namely inflation, real interest rates, price and income uncertainties, changes in the financial markets, in the social security system and in housing finances. Many of these factors have so far not been candidates for explanatory variables in any analysis of savings and portfolio allocation in Hungary. This was understandable and acceptable in the period of relative economic and social stability; it is, however, no longer acceptable, as the economic transformation will increase both volatility and uncertainty.

Furthermore, one can say that these factors will become even more volatile soon, and thus that they will be even more important in explaining savings and portfolio allocation. This chapter, however, will not speculate about the future; rather we show that most of these structural elements were already present, and had a strong impact on the economy, well before the economic transformation of the late 1980s started. The data compiled here may require further econometric testing in the future but the information gained from the raw comparisons of the related time series is also instructive.

In section 2 we describe the effect of changes in interest rates on real and financial assets and debt instruments in the Hungarian households' portfolios since 1970. Sections 3 and 4 deal with the structure of household assets and section 5 gives an overview of the effects of financial reforms on their liquidity, riskiness and yield. Section 6 will summarize the results of raw comparisons and specify hypotheses for future empirical work as well as their implications for constructing a transformation policy.

2. INTEREST RATES AND THE ACCUMULATION OF FINANCIAL ASSETS

Until 1983 when bonds were reintroduced in Hungary, the structure of household financial assets was indeed extremely simple. It consisted of cash; time and saving deposits; saving notes; concessional and 'commercial'[1] loans (so-called 'bank loans'); housing loans (mortgages); and hire purchase and personal loans. Households were serviced exclusively by the National Savings Bank (OTP) and by the Savings Co-operatives (Takarékszövetkezet). Both institutions were under direct and stringent central control. Financial products were completely standardized and issuing conditions were set directly by the central authorities. The same applies to the debt instruments available to households. The amount of net credit these institutions could issue was centrally planned; this mechanism helped to keep the household sector in a net lending position.[2] Net personal savings were channelled directly to the National Bank of Hungary (NBH). Nominal interest rates on assets and liabilities given in Table 5.1 were centrally set by this bank and were kept practically unchanged until 1986. In fact, the central authorities regarded nominal interest rates as absolutely unimportant since, in their opinion, they had no impact whatsoever on personal savings.[3] The reasoning behind this viewpoint is simple. Households, having no other more attractive alternatives for investing their savings, were forced irrespective of the actual interest rate to put their unconsumed income into households' bank accounts. Had consumption been completely planned and controlled, and the (legal and illegal) private sector eliminated, this reasoning would have been correct. However, nothing was farther from reality than this assertion. As previous analyses clearly revealed, consumption plans were not *exogenously* set and were soft targets (Charemza and Király, 1988). Furthermore, the accumulation of financial wealth was quite strongly influenced by changes in the real *interest rates* on financial assets (see Figure 5.1)

Table 5.1   Interest Rates on Households' Deposits and Credits, 1981-90 (in percent)

	1981	1985	1986	1987	1988	1989	1990
Deposits[1]							
Sight deposits	2	2	2	2	2	8	8
Operating account	5	5	5	5	7	12	17
Time deposits							
1-year	5	5	5	9	13.5	13.5	19
2-year		6	6	10	14	14	19.5
3-year		8	8	12.5	15	15	20
Savings notes							
6-year	7	9	9	13.5	16.5	16.5	24
Young people's deposits							
5-year	6	6	6	8	14	14	18
7-year	6	8	8	11	18	18	25
CDS					18	16.8	20.8
6-month TBs					9	17.5	23
Credits[2]							
Housing loans							
Subsidized	0-3	0-3	0-3	0-3	0-3	19.5	25.5
Commercial		8	8	8	12	22	31
Hire purchase	6-8	5-9	5-9	12	13	24	35
Personal loans	8-10	8-12	8-12	13-15	15-17	24	35
Memorandum item							
Inflation (CPI)	4.6	7.0	5.3	8.6	15.5	17.0	28.9

Notes: 1. Interest rates on deposits and CDS as of 1988 are net rates (a 20 percent withholding tax is deducted).
       2. Interest rates on credits as of 1988 include fees.
Source: OECD, *Country Report on Hungary* (1991).

To get a more realistic picture one has to correct the stock of financial assets by the inflationary losses on *nominal* financial assets. In the corrected series the fluctuation in net financial accumulation is even more pronounced, as is shown in Figure 5.2 in billions of Hungarian forint (HUF). This observed fluctuation in real savings kept in financial assets may also be a result of changes in real incomes. We believe that real interest rates were as important as, or probably even more important than, real income in explaining portfolio behaviour in Hungary as early as the 1970s.

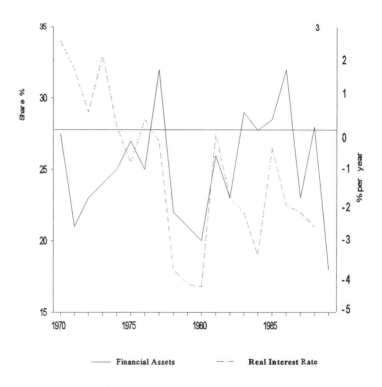

Figure 5.1 Savings: Share of Total, and the Real Interest Rate

3. STRUCTURE OF HOUSEHOLDS' ASSETS

The relatively low level of financial service industries in Hungary is reflected in the dominance of *cash* transactions.[4] The ratio between cash and deposits is fairly stable in Figure 5.3, and the share of cash holding is fairly high by international standards.

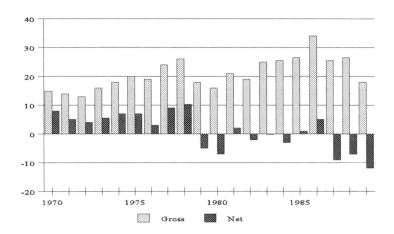

Figure 5.2 Real Annual Saving in Financial Assets, 1980 HUF (billions)

Bank *deposits* were absolutely free from any risk and were also absolutely liquid. They were guaranteed by the state. This was a mere formality, however, as the failure of the OTP was simply inconceivable; on the other hand, this guarantee was worth nothing against the state itself. In case of serious difficulties, a sudden freezing of deposits was by no means inconceivable: as recent events in the former USSR have shown, even cash is not immune to the confiscatory intentions of central authorities. Liquidity, however, was constrained only by the underdeveloped nature of the financial service industries. For quite a long period there was no chequebook accounts and deposits were accessible only at the branches where they were administered.

Mortgage instruments, like the other financial instruments available to households, were completely standardized and centrally controlled. A strictly limited amount of housing loan with a subsidized and fixed interest rate (the so-called 'concessional housing loan') was available to the purchasers (or prospective owners of newly built dwellings). For quite a while, the amount available under these conditions varied also according to the type of the dwelling, giving more finance to dwellings in large apartment houses. A larger family with more children also had preferential treatment in the form of larger allowances. Consequently, this sort of mortgage had to be rationed, which led to different restrictions. First, quite a large downpayment was required.[5]

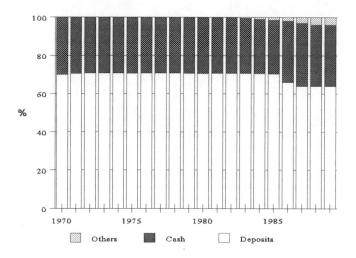

Figure 5.3 Structure of Real Financial Wealth, 1980 HUF (in percent)

Second, this type of mortgage was available only for newly built dwellings. The point of this restriction, apart from the apparent interest in increasing the number of residential units, was that the production and imports of building materials, as well as the capacity in the state-owned part of the residential building services' industry, was centrally planned.[6] For most of the 1970s the number of newly built houses (including owner-occupied ones) were effectively planned by central planners. The amounts of subsidized and any additional 'commercial' mortgage were consequently also kept under control.

Before 1988, a subsidized mortgage typically covered 45-50 percent of the total price (value). This was then supplemented with the 'commercial' housing loan (also called 'bank loan'), a standardized mortgage product with a higher and variable rate. The amount made available to a household was restricted by the downpayment requirements, and by the ratio between total money earnings and total debt service of the family. In addition, employers were entitled to provide interest-free credit facilities to their employees. The employer decided the amount given, but this type of credit was not eligible to be used as part of the downpayment. Finally, the state budget also provided a once-and-for-all capital transfer to first-time buyers (or builders) of new dwellings. The amount of this transfer increased with the number of children, and no money was given to childless families.[7] Altogether buying (or building) a newly built house or apartment was heavily subsidized, and after the changes in 1991 it is still subsidised, though much less so.

It is widely believed that as a result of the adverse impact of negative real interest rates and inflationary uncertainties, households gradually switched to real assets, abandoning financial ones. Another argument says that part of the financial wealth accumulation was a result of the persistent shortage in housing and reflected forced substitution between real and financial assets. In Figure 5.4 the structure of gross wealth accumulation (without corrections for depreciation in real assets and for inflationary losses in financial assets) does not seem to support this theory. Gross accumulation of financial assets fluctuated around 25 percent, with no clear trend in either direction. The other important observation demonstrated in Figures 5.4 and 5.8 is that the share of housing investment was more or less stable. This clearly points to a trade-off between consumer durables' investment and investment in financial assets.

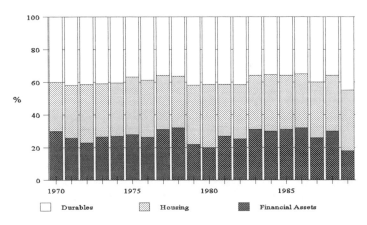

Figure 5.4 Breakdown of Annual Nominal Saving by Asset Type (in percent)

Calculating with real rather than with nominal values, the structure is somewhat different. Although total real wealth increased throughout the whole period, this is not the case for *real financial* assets. Real financial assets decreased first in 1980 and continuously and increasingly after 1986, as shown in Figure 5.5. The share of financial assets in total (gross) wealth steadily declined after 1978, the only exception being 1986.[8] These tendencies become even more apparent if *net real financial wealth* is considered (see Figure 5.6). This graph shows the cumulative impact of real net financial wealth accumulation already shown in Figure 5.2. It thus seems fair to say that the restructuring of households' portfolios of real and financial assets in the last twenty years has indeed been remarkable.

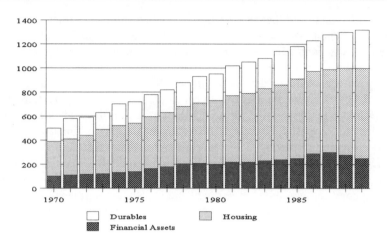

Figure 5.5 Real Wealth, 1980 HUF (billions)

4. FACTORS INFLUENCING REAL ASSET
   ACCUMULATION

The most important real asset of Hungarian households is their housing stock. The owner-occupation rate was high and increasing in Hungary throughout the whole period (see Figure 5.7). The number and the value of privately-owned dwellings (being almost exclusively owner-occupied) is fairly high. There is no official estimate for the value of this stock. The figures used here are our own estimates based on information on housing investments and costs.[9]

The lack of any more sophisticated estimate for the market value of the privately-owned housing stock can be explained by several facts. First, as the housing market in Hungary is very thin, very imperfect and, thus, very volatile, prevailing prices, even if they were precisely recorded (as they are not), would carry only a fairly limited amount of information on market values for those houses that never entered the secondary market. Furthermore, privately-owned houses are almost exclusively occupied by the owner, that is, there is no competitive rental market[10] which would determine some sort of market rate. Without market-determined rents, it is difficult to calculate the value of this asset derived from the yield it offers. Clearly, the centrally controlled and artificially low rents in the state-owned sector (the municipal apartments) are of no use for this purpose.

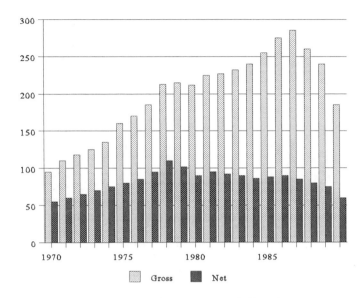

Figure 5.6 Real Financial Wealth, 1980 HUF (billions)

Subsidized rents in the state-owned apartment buildings and subsidisation of purchase (or building) newly built dwellings effectively killed the secondary market for housing. The supply in the state-owned rental sector, however, was rationed. The option to sell a privately-owned house and rent another one was therefore simply not readily available. The only option was to sell and buy a less expensive one, but in this case the transactions costs were extremely high. Furthermore, while this could still have been a way to withdraw equity for individuals, for households as a whole it was hardly possible, because the business sector was not allowed to invest in this market: it was strictly forbidden to convert residential houses to business offices. So the only way to reduce equity holdings in housing was to defer maintenance, and use the implicit income from this source for other purposes. Equity holding in housing was therefore a highly illiquid asset.

Supply was quite inelastic due to price controls and central planning of capacities and input materials. Excess demand was bound to emerge, and in fact in many periods could be detected using empirical techniques (Csunderlik, 1985). Building materials' imports, however, played an important role in mitigating the impact of excess demand; private supply of building services was also expanding at a rapid pace. Acute shortages were consequently not overwhelming in the market for relatively cheap apartments.

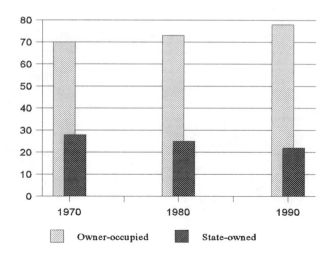

Figure 5.7 Changing Structure of Housing in Hungary, 1970-90 (in percent)

Investment in this asset was mostly motivated by demand for housing not met by the thin rental market. The pressure on families to go for owner-occupied housing increased in the 1980s. Figure 5.7 shows that the level of state provision in housing steadily declined; the number of state-owned rental apartments, as well as the newly built ones, decreased substantially after 1970. Furthermore, such rental apartments were not available in rural areas. In explaining private (personal) investment in housing one should thus also pay attention to demographic movements and other non-financial factors. Naturally, financial factors were important to moderate or encourage aspirations; nonetheless, to explain housing investment by financial factors only would probably be an ill-fated exercise.

Similar observations apply to *consumer durables*. The data for stocks are again our own estimates.[11] As shown in Figure 5.8, the share of investments in consumer durables, as well as the share of consumer durables in total wealth, has steadily increased. Purchase of consumer durables was the largest component in investment throughout the whole period, as shown in Figure 5.4. There is no evidence that for consumer durables as a whole there was a significant excess in demand. In one particular market, the car market, however, excess demand was clearly detectable throughout the whole period (Kapitány, 1989). Certain other goods were sometimes also in very short supply for shorter periods, but no disequilibrium analysis could establish the presence of overall excess demand for the consumer durable markets in any sub-periods in the period under investigation (Hulyák, 1983; Mellár, 1990; Rappai, 1990).

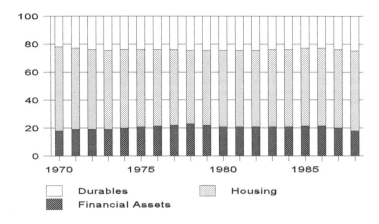

Figure 5.8 Structure of Real Wealth, 1980 HUF (in percent)

Liquidity of consumer durables is also very limited, and transaction costs are high in Hungary, comparable to the experience of other countries. Selling of used cars was the only exception, making the car market very liquid, with a fairly low level of transaction costs and high profits for dealers. Often as a result of rationed supply in new cars and excess demand, secondary (free) market prices of used cars exceeded the prices of new ones. Although for many people this appeared as a capital gain, in fact it is not clear whether it really was. To buy a new car one had to register for it with a heavy advance payment (50 percent of the prevailing purchase price). This advance payment was kept in a non-interest-bearing account which was not transferable. As the purchase prices at which the actual transaction took place were not fixed, and the waiting time on the average was two-three years, a substantial inflationary loss accrued in most cases for households. Approximately free market prices fluctuated around the present value of the purchaser's investment plus some premium depending on market conditions.

5. THE IMPACT OF FINANCIAL SYSTEM REFORMS

The first important financial innovation in the 1980s was the introduction of bonds in 1983. The first bonds issued to households appeared in 1984, when the secondary trade was also started; the introduction of bonds followed the segmented pattern of the financial sector. The bond market for households and for corporate investors developed in different ways. Until 1985, bonds issued to households could finance only community investment projects and they embodied contributions to these projects rather than financial investments. Accordingly, the amount of this sort of bond was negligible (1.1 percent of total household deposits). In 1986, these restrictions were lifted and bonds became financial assets heavily demanded by private investors. Until 1987, the market grew very fast and there was an excess demand on the market. Since, due to the excess demand, bonds were perfectly liquid and, due to the state guarantee, very safe, households regarded them as higher interest rate deposits. The only visible difference was that some minimal amount of investment was necessary. Yields, also set by the Ministry of Finance, were as much as 3 to 4 points higher (around 11 percent) than the then prevailing interest rates on deposits, or the inflation rate. Yields on bonds, like yields on other financial assets, were not subject to income tax. Not surprisingly, the market boomed, bonds issued in 1987 totalling HUF 12.7 billion (more than the increase in total household deposits), and the value of bonds in circulation reaching HUF 19.6 billion.

This situation changed dramatically in 1988, and there are several important conclusions to be drawn from what happened. Bonds issued to households suddenly lost all their advantages, while the risk attached to them became clear. Rates on household deposits were increased by 3 percent in October 1987 and by a further 2.5 percent in June 1988 (including premium). The interest rate on one-year deposits reached 13.5 percent net of tax (see Table 5.1). The state guarantee on bonds issued to households was terminated, and the bond market collapsed. Although underwriting banks (mainly the Budapest Bank) tried to preserve the liquidity of bonds by repurchase, the capital loss on bonds amounted to 10 percent. With the introduction of personal income tax, bond yields, like yields on other financial assets, became subject to a 20 percent, withholding tax, while the risk attached to the bond was not recognized by tax regulations.

As a consequence, the amount of new issues returned to the level of 1984 and secondary trading was almost exclusively confined to the repurchase by underwriting banks (holding 25 percent of bonds of this type by the end of 1988). Commercial banks took several steps to keep the secondary market alive but the inflationary expectations were (and still are) too high and volatile and yields on alternative short-term financial assets too high to make bonds competitive.

The next step in the development of the Hungarian financial markets was that commercial banks were allowed to issue certificates of deposits (CDs) to households, and by the end of 1988 the value of CDs in circulation reached HUF 5.6 billion (almost seven times more than the value of bonds issued to households and 28.6 percent of the increase in household deposits in savings institutions in 1988). In addition new and popular financial assets issued to households emerged (e.g., Treasury Bills, see below) while the households' propensity to save in domestic financial assets declined. In 1989, the value of new issues increased dynamically, while household deposits decreased.

A further important measure taken in January 1989 was to lift the restriction on commercial banks dealing with households. This step, however, did not mean that interest rate ceilings on household deposits were abolished immediately. They remained policy tools until 1992.

The next step in opening financial markets to households was the introduction of Treasury Bills (TBs) in March 1988. Due to liquidity and competitive rates (8, 9, 10 percent for three-, six- and nine-month TBs, see Table 5.1), TBs became quite popular. By the end of 1988, the value of TBs in circulation had reached HUF 4 billion (15 percent of accumulation of financial assets in 1988). By that time, interest rates on TBs had been substantially increased (to 16, 17.5 and 19 percent respectively), keeping the competitiveness of this form of investment.

It is important to notice that the financial instruments which became popular were all perfectly safe, highly liquid and artificially high-yield assets.[12] If any of these characteristics changed they were immediately abandoned: the best example is the history of bonds. Currently, households do not seem to be willing to buy long-term illiquid financial assets, but changes in inflationary expectations will probably bring about changes in this respect.

6. CONCLUSIONS

Transformation and restructuring in the Hungarian economy requires resources. Although an important but relatively small part of investment will undoubtedly be (direct) foreign investment, it is not likely that foreign investment will provide sufficient financing for the transformation. Domestic private savings will consequently play a crucial role, and saving and portfolio allocation decisions will be of foremost importance for monetary policies. This is even more the case if we take into consideration that the Hungarian economy inherited a distorted saving pattern and households' portfolio allocation mechanism. Starting in the late 1970s, inflation has accelerated and real interest rates on (time and saving) deposits (being centrally controlled) and also on concessional housing loans (and some other loans given to households) have become negative. This has had a strong impact on savings in general and on portfolio allocation in particular. The savings ratio dropped dramatically in 1979 and only slowly recovered during the first half of the 1980s. Households continuously restructured their portfolios, gradually abandoning financial instruments and favouring consumer durables and real estate.

The general belief that interest rates cannot play any role in the economy has rendered the problem of portfolio allocation irrelevant for Eastern European economies: this view, however, is not justified by empirical analysis and cannot any longer be supported. There is a vital need to investigate the impact of interest rate(s) on savings and portfolio allocation in transforming economies.

Economic transformation, at least in the short and medium run, will inevitably lead to increased uncertainty. There are potentially substantial uncertainties inherent in holding long-lived real assets and financial equity investments during the transformation period. Some of the real assets and financial equities may depreciate, or appreciate less than the overall rate of inflation. So the traditional assumption that inflation, depreciating money's purchasing power, makes it unwise to hold money or any other asset denominated in nominal terms, unnecessarily (beyond what is needed to finance current transactions), may not be operationally correct. Households and firms might react to higher expected inflation by increasing their demand to hold money and short- and long-term debt assets.

During the transformation debt assets may depreciate if the issuer goes bankrupt, or threatens to do so. All marketable debt assets will fall in nominal and real value if nominal interest rates rise (as is likely in the transformation). On the other side of the balance sheet, debt liabilities have their own dangers: the payments owed may become more burdensome than expected if inflation is less than expected. The somewhat unorthodox consequence is that risk-averse households and firms may respond to inflation by increasing their demands for money and debt assets over time.

For existing asset portfolios at any point of time, the conventional assumptions are plausible: higher expected inflation should encourage households and firms to hold more real assets and financial equity claims to real assets, while decreasing their holdings of long- and short-term debt assets and money, and increasing their indebtedness.

If expected inflation increases stock demands for real assets and equities, then the stock demands for debt assets and money must decrease. Within existing portfolios, households and firms cannot hedge the uncertainties of holding more real assets and financial equities by holding more debt assets and money. Savings flows alter this portfolio liquidity constraint over time as additional demand for real assets and equities can be satisfied without a concomitant decrease in the stock demand for additional debt and money. Households and firms may simultaneously decide to increase their demand to hold all components of their asset portfolios, provided that saving flows are positive.

This possibility, however, is not always advantageous. What will households and firms want to do with whatever saving flows there are? The answers to this question are very important in determining the outcome of the transformation process.

Alternative policies for reducing uncertainties and disadvantageous portfolio adjustments are an important – if not the most important – element of the transformation strategy, but most of these questions have remained unexplored until now.

POSTSCRIPT

Although financial markets remain relatively immature, the composition of financial wealth holdings has changed significantly since the data for this chapter were compiled. Thus, whereas bank deposits typically remain a dominant component of financial wealth, households now hold increasing quantities of cash, foreign exchange deposits and other assets such as life insurance and retirement funds. Financial assets, in general, are becoming a more significant component of overall wealth. Various share distributions, and other policies aimed at increasing the degree to which the general population is a stakeholder in the economy's success, no doubt hastened the speed with which financial wealth has grown in importance. Subsequent chapters revisit the issue with more recent data.

NOTES

*   Originally appeared as 'Changing Structure of Household Portfolios in Emerging Market Economies: The Case of Hungary, 1970-89' in *Hungary: An Economy in Transition*, edited by I. Székely and D. Newberry (Cambridge: Cambridge University Press, 1993), pp.163-80, by I. Ábel and I. Székely, reprinted by permission with minor revisions.

1.   We use the term 'commercial' loan to underline the difference between this type of loan and the concessional loan. The difference, however, was only minor. 'Commercial' loans carried a higher and variable interest rate but at the same time they were controlled in exactly the same way as any other loans earmarked to households.

2.   Partly because of the backward financial intermediation and also because of job and social security guaranteed by the state, the long-term savings motive was very weak and the net lending position of households was rather low in the 1960s and 1970s.

3.   Furthermore, personal savings were also considered unimportant. A surprising position, but explained by the fact that financial resources were mainly channelled to investors through non-market mechanisms.

4.   Chequebook accounts were introduced only in the 1980s, and the first ATM in Hungary was installed in 1989. It is notoriously difficult and slow to transfer money balances even inside the country.

5.   In the case of self-managed projects and/or houses built by the prospective owners – being the dominant case in the villages and smaller towns, but quite frequent in the larger towns as well – an own-cash contribution (upfront payment) had to be spent first before any money could be drawn on the credit line provided.

6.   The only affordable housing option for the majority of households in towns was to buy a cheaper (but consequently rationed) apartment in an apartment house built exclusively by large state-owned construction companies.

7.   Currently, the amounts involved are as follows. For a family with one child it is HUF 50,000, with two children 150,000, and with three children 400,000. Any additional child adds 100,000 to this amount. These amounts should be compared to the cost of approximately HUF 30,000-35,000 per square metre in an average Budapest apartment.

8.   This happened as a result of the combined impact of the change in the structure of nominal and real wealth accumulation and the inflationary losses on financial assets.

9.   The estimations were made as follows. The estimated cost of a square metre of dwelling in 1980 was taken as the base. A quality improvement of 2 percent a year was allowed for. This gave the constant value of one newly built square metre. This was multiplied by the amount of newly built square metres. The existing housing stock in 1950, from which year the recursive estimation started, was estimated to be equal to the real value of stock built between 1950 and 1960. The Hungarian CSO publishes figures on depreciation of private housing stock. The constant depreciation rate was set to match this figure for 1980. Parenthetically, this provides a fairly low real depreciation rate (around 1 percent a year), and even with this rate, the figures by the CSO for the recent years seem grossly under-estimated. This might be a very rough estimate, although nominal values per dwelling derived from this estimation and information on housing price index seemed quite realistic.

10.   There was a tiny market niche for foreigners, with soaring rents frequently denominated in hard currency. The segment, however, is highly distorted due to the nature of the housing market as a whole; it provides no reliable information on rents in general. In spite of the soaring rents, it was exceptional to build houses for rental purposes in this market; most of the apartments were rented out by people temporarily abroad.

11.   The initial stock of 1960 is assumed to be equal to four times the constant price purchases in that year. This assumption is based on information available for certain types of consumer durables per household and on the numbers of purchases of these goods in the same year. The depreciation rate is taken to be 10 percent in line with other estimates known in the literature. A consumer price index was used for deflating current price data.

12.   'Artificially high' in the sense that it was the state itself which offered (or entitled others to offer) rates, which were higher than the controlled rates on deposits.

6. Financial Intermediation and Industrial Restructuring in Central and Eastern Europe*

PROLOGUE

At the outset of the transitional process the division between central banking and commercial banking functions was non-existent. Once newly created commercial banks came into the picture the process of financial intermediation had to be developed. However, as explained in this chapter, this process was full of problems for the transitional economies for a number of reasons not the least of which was the crowding-out phenomenon (see also Chapter 3), the severe mismatch between assets and liabilities facing the emerging banks, as well as the inheritance of the bad loans of the past downloaded onto the new banking sector (see also Chapter 7). This chapter provides a general overview of all these issues.

1. INTRODUCTION

A relatively fast and substantial restructuring of the economies of Central and Eastern Europe (CEE) is necessary for a successful economic transformation and sustained growth in the longer run. It requires the restructuring of existing enterprises, the reallocation of capital to more profitable activities and enterprises, increased investments, and an economic environment within which successful private enterprises can expand their activities at a much faster pace than before. A necessary element of such an environment is a well-functioning and efficient financial system which can both collect savings and channel them to the most efficient uses, and provide high-quality, low-cost financial services for producers and financial investors. The availability of the latter to the newly emerging private sector consisting mainly of small and medium-sized producers is a vital prerequisite for a smooth and robust economic development. Financial institutions, in particular commercial banks, also have a central role in the restructuring of (formerly) state-owned enterprises (SOEs) and in imposing proper corporate governance on large (already or not yet privatized) enterprises.

This chapter investigates the possible roles that banks and other financial institutions can play in the process of industrial restructuring and also the impact of the problems financial systems in CEE face on this process.

The second section focuses on corporate finance during economic transformation. It investigates the reasons for the lack of and high costs of long-term investment finance. On the supply side, financial investors are reluctant to hold long-term assets owing to the high level of uncertainty inherent in the process of economic transformation. On the demand side, the typically large budget deficits,[1] reflecting the high social costs of economic transformation (e.g., unemployment) and the equally high costs of dealing with the legacies of central planning (such as bad loans), mop up most of the available long-term finance, crowding-out private business. The very limited access to private international capital markets is an additional reason for the scarcity of long-term finance. Regarding the commercial banks, their fairly limited capacity to assume risk and the newly introduced Western-style prudential regulations are the most important factors explaining why they tend to opt for rather conservative lending policies. Regarding the newly emerging private sector, the lack of a proper track record and collateral are further factors making banking finance a difficult to obtain source of long-term finance.

The third section is devoted to the role banks can play in imposing proper corporate governance on (former) SOEs and in enforcing and facilitating the restructuring of these enterprises. The fourth section focuses on the issue of 'bad loans'. The low and fast deteriorating quality of loan portfolios of banks is a natural consequence of economic transformation. Previously made long-term (investment) loans reflected the priorities of central planners and the strength of the different industrial and agrarian lobbies, rather than any sort of economic rationale. As previous chapters have shown, the simultaneous collapse of this system in CEE countries and the consequent collapse of trade among CEE countries changed the environment surrounding enterprises drastically. The different ways in which governments in CEE countries try to cope with bad loans have different consequences on the capital allocation mechanism. The section investigates the damaging repercussions of bad loans on capital allocation and industrial restructuring and the impact of the bad-loan schemes implemented so far.

Finally, the fifth section focuses on the degree of competition in the financial system. Competition has a direct and strong impact on allocative efficiency and on the quality and costs of capital and financial services for industry which is an important factor in international competitiveness. Though, currently, the international competitiveness of CEE countries is based on low wage costs, this advantage could well be offset by high costs of capital, and by the lack of access to proper financial services and the export credits.

2. FINANCING INDUSTRIAL RESTRUCTURING IN CENTRAL AND EASTERN EUROPE

Economic transformation inevitably leads to corporatization and a sudden and sizeable decrease in the extent to which the state is involved in the allocation of financial resources (see, e.g., Ábel and Bonin, 1992a): corporate finance then becomes an important issue. Therefore, when one thinks about industrial restructuring, trade reorientation, and export-led growth, it is important to pay attention to how new investments, among the most important elements and prerequisites, are (can be) financed at the enterprise level. In what follows, we shall investigate four main sources of corporate finance: banking (intermediated) finance, direct (bond and equity) finance, foreign direct finance, and retained earnings.

2.1 Bank (Intermediated) Finance for Investment

During economic transformation, long-term (investment) bank finance has been (and will be) available for industrial firms to a rather limited extent, for several reasons. The first of these concerns the limited supply of long-term loanable funds. Private financial investors are and in the foreseeable future will most likely be rather reluctant to hold long-term financial assets in large amounts, even in those countries where stabilisation policies have been relatively successful and private saving has increased (see, e.g., Ábel and Székely, 1993; Wyczański, 1993). Moreover, commercial banks have fairly limited capacities to carry out maturity conversion (converting shorter-term deposits into longer-term loans) owing to the newly introduced Western-type prudential regulations. Furthermore, banks have little experience with and knowledge of commercial lending (credit appraisal, monitoring), especially at massive scales and in granting longer-term loans (Golden, 1994; Wyczański, 1994).

Regarding the actual development so far, as a result of these factors, the share of long-term loans in new loans and the average maturity of bank loans decreased rapidly, while the share of short-term assets in banks' asset portfolios increased immensely (see, e.g., Ábel and Székely, 1994; Kokoszczyński, 1994). In general, with very few exceptions, the share of long-term financial instruments declined radically. Interbank deposits also became very short term (see, e.g., Dobrinsky, 1994; Kokosczcyński, 1994), long-term refinance credit from the central bank diminished (see, e.g., Ábel and Székely, 1994), and bonds other than government ones practically disappeared. Thus banks with weak deposit bases, in particular among households, had practically no access to long-term loanable funds.

Second, enterprises (will) have to compete with the government for long-term funds. Massive budget deficits characterizing economic transformation and costly rescue operations carried out by governments (such as the bad-loan schemes discussed below) create a strong demand for long-term funds on the part of the government.

While this is true in general for CEE countries, the extent to which these factors are present differs across countries and over time. Table 6.1 gives the figures for some of the CEE countries for the period 1990-93. It shows that in countries where macroeconomic stabilization was relatively successful, such as the Czech Republic (former Czechoslovakia), Hungary, and Poland (after

Table 6.1 Supply and Demand of Loanable Funds, 1990-93 (in percent)

		1990	1992	1992	1993
Bulgaria	personal saving[a]	1.4	10.8	23.0	15.9
	budget deficit[b]	4.9	3.4	6.0	11.5
	CPI inflation[c]	23.8	338.5	91.3	74.0
Czechoslovakia/	personal saving[a]	-0.1	5.9	5.3	N/A
Czech Republic	budget deficit[b]	-0.1	2.0	1.6	N/A
	CPI inflation[c]	9.9	57.9	10.8	20.8
Hungary	personal saving[a]	3.9	10.5	9.1	N/A
	budget deficit[b]	-0.9	4.6	7.2	5.6
	CPI inflation[c]	28.9	35.0	23.0	22.5
Poland	personal saving[a]	11.0	5.0	6.7	N/A
	budget deficit[b]	-3.5	6.2	7.2	N/A
	CPI inflation[c]	584.7	70.3	43.0	35.0

Notes:
[a] Personal net financial saving as a percentage of GDP; for Bulgaria, changes in household deposits with banks (end of the year over end of previous year). After 1992 or 1993, definitional changes and other data limitations prevent the calculation of comparable savings figures.
[b] Consolidated budget deficit expressed as share of GDP.
[c] Annual rate of CPI inflation.
[d] Czechoslovakia until 1992, the Czech Republic afterwards.
N/A means not available.
Sources: Figures for personal net financial saving and consolidated budget deficit for Czechoslovakia, Hungary, and Poland are from Dittus (1994). Data for 1993-95 are from National Bank of Hungary, *Annual Reports* (1994, 1995), Austrian National Bank, *Focus on Transition* (various issues). CPI inflation figures are from national sources. Figures for saving and budget deficit for Bulgaria are from personal communication.

1991), private saving increased significantly at the outset (as a share of both disposable income and of GDP, the latter being shown in Table 6.1). However, even in (former) Czechoslovakia, which is a very special case in this respect, a part of private saving was mopped up by the budget deficit. In Poland after 1990, the current budget deficit exceeded private saving, while in Hungary the positive gap between private saving and current budget deficit narrowed rapidly.[2]

But the current budget deficit does not fully reflect the finance requirement of the government. Since Table 6.1 suggests that the extent of the government's borrowing requirement was perhaps the largest in Hungary, in Table 6.2 we further investigate this issue for Hungary. As the figures in Table 6.2 suggest, the share of government borrowing (credit) in total domestic borrowing (credit) steadily increased during the economic transformation, from 43.6% in December 1990 to 57.3% in June 1993. This increase was much higher than current budget deficit figures for the same period would suggest. The two very substantial upward jumps in June 1991 and March 1993 shown in Table 6.2 are due to two loan consolidation schemes. The first one was related to the scheme that dealt with the concessional housing loans (for more details see Székely, 1994), while the second one was related to the scheme that dealt with a part of bad corporate loans (the latter will be discussed in more detail below). The nature of the borrowing requirement related to such schemes may be different from the one related to current budget deficits, but from the viewpoint of enterprises, the bottom lines in both cases are the same, namely that the number of competing needs for available finance, in particular long-term finance, increases significantly.

As Table 6.2 also shows, owing to the rapid decline in the share of household credit, enterprises could for a while increase the size of their slice of the shrinking pie of total domestic credit. However, their share started to decrease rapidly after September 1992. Ironically, this happened exactly when the whole pie, that is domestic credit, started to increase rapidly in real terms, reflecting the loosening of monetary policy in Hungary. The story of investment credit is even more characteristic of economic transformation. As Table 6.2 shows, with the exception of one quarter, the share of investment credit in total domestic credit declined gradually during the period under investigation from 8.5% at the end of 1990 to 6.2% in June 1993. In real terms, the stock of investment credit declined dramatically during the same period (by 45.4%). That is to say, in spite of the increase in household saving and decrease in household borrowing, enterprises had practically no access to banking finance for investment purposes.

The decline of investment credit is one of the most important aspects of economic restructuring (see also Chapter 2 in this volume). This is a very complex issue that can be understood only when one investigates a large number of factors. Dittus (1994) finds the conservative lending policies of commercial banks to be the major factor explaining this development and, at the same time, rejects the crowding-out hypothesis. The introduction of new Western-type prudential regulations has undoubtedly contributed to the decline of lending to enterprises, especially in the longer run. Sudden trade reorientation and a radical liberalization (of goods and financial markets, including imports, though mainly of goods) – leading to fast and substantial changes of relative prices, including that of capital (that is, interest rates) – have indeed increased the risk attached to corporate lending. A sizeable part of large SOEs, the core of the traditional clientele of large state-owned commercial banks (SOCBs), abruptly lost their foreign and domestic markets. This change undermined their creditworthiness and capacity to borrow under market conditions. Under such conditions, a prudent bank management would (or should) indeed radically reduce lending to these firms. On the other hand, the newly emerging private sector, consisting mainly of small and medium-sized firms, though hungry for bank loans, in particular for investment loans, cannot take the place of the ailing SOEs, because it has hardly any proper track record and has very little to offer as collateral. This explanation has undoubtedly pointed to one of the important determining factors in the decline.

Table 6.2 Allocation of Domestic Credit in Hungary, 1989-95

Year	Real DC[a] (1989=100)	Net Credits to Government % of DC	Enterprise Credit % of DC	Investment[b] Credit % of DC	Household Credit % of DC
1989	100	47.7	30.6	8.6	21.4
1990	92.1	43.6	34.3	8.5	21.7
1991	75.6	47.5	37.8	7.9	14.1
1992[c]	75.1	52.2	33.6	7.8	13.9
1993	77.8	56.6	30.3	6.2	12.8
1994	76.7	58.3	28.7	5.9	12.4
1995	67.8	58.2	30.2	N/A	11.1

Notes:
[a] DC = Domestic Credit; deflated by the Producer Price Index.
[b] Represents the component of enterprise credit with a maturity of more than one year.
[c] Includes the impact of the loan consolidation schemes
N/A means not available or insufficient data.
Source: National Bank of Hungary, *Annual Report* (various years) and own calculations.

Another frequently mentioned explanation, especially by bankers, is that demand of enterprises for credit has declined dramatically. This is again undoubtedly an important element of the situation. Real borrowing (lending) rates for enterprises increased enormously during the same period. Figure 6.1 shows, real (*ex post*) lending rates[3] on investment loans increased from -3.1% in 1989 to 16.8% in 1992.[4] It is extremely difficult to believe that any sound business can support such high real rates. That is to say, at these prices enterprises with a reasonably hard budget constraint and a strong interest in maximizing the market value of the firm would undoubtedly decrease their demand for bank finance substantially.

But this is the point where one starts seriously to question the outright rejection of the crowding-out hypothesis. If enterprise demand for bank finance were low and declining, why did prices (interest rates) remain high, or in fact increase rapidly? The only reasonable explanation is the high demand by the government. Government securities, that is, a virtually risk-free form of investment, offered rates of yield for banks comparable to if not higher (at least for certain periods) than corporate loans. In our interpretation of the facts, the crowding-out of corporate borrowers from credit markets by the government was thus indeed an important factor explaining the dramatic decline in investment finance. Though owing to limitations of space we analyse this process in some detail only for Hungary, where this problem is perhaps most acute, available evidence suggests that crowding-out is a very important factor in general, Czechoslovakia (prior to 1992) being the only notable exception.

2.2 Direct (Non-Intermediated) Finance for Investment

Bond and equity finance will perhaps be even more scarce than long-term bank finance. With high and fluctuating rates of inflation characterizing CEE economies (with very few exceptions, see Table 6.1), long-term fixed rate (bond) finance is just too risky for both parties. The lack of institutional investors with long planning horizons and wholesale financial markets (Király, 1993; Székely, 1994) makes this situation even more severe. For small investors, the costs of monitoring enterprises and gathering a reasonably good understanding of future macroeconomic development are just too high. The collapse of the Hungarian bond market in 1988, when inflation started to accelerate and government guarantees on new corporate bonds were terminated, was a clear example of the problems involved (see Székely, 1990).

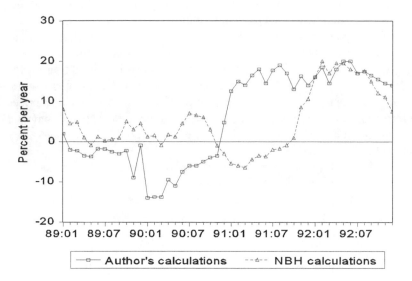

Notes: Average lending rates on bank loans to enterprises with maturity over one year. Real rates are calculated by using PPI inflation rates for the 12-month period ending in the month of observation (NBH's real rates) or beginning in the month of observation (author's own calculations).

Sources: Rates calculated by NBH are from NBH (1992), p.153; rates calculated by the authors are based on nominal interest rates and PPI inflation rates given in NBH (1992) and (1993).

Figure 6.1 Real Long-Term Lending Rates in Hungary, 1989-92

Equity finance faces the same problems. Without Western-type accounting and a proper track record, it is just too risky for private investors to hold equity directly. On the other hand, for the same reason, the supply of tradable shares is also rather limited (Járai, 1993). The underdeveloped financial system is a further stumbling block, because in the absence of industry analysts and finance houses keeping track of industries' performance, it is very expensive to gather information on special firms or industries. Hedging is also very difficult, that is, portfolios are bound to be far from optimal. Though stock exchanges in the Central European transition countries, in particular in Poland, are hot places right now, recording unprecedented increases in stock exchanges indices (see, e.g., Kokoszcyński, 1994) and providing excellent investment opportunities for foreign and domestic portfolio investors, the amounts of fresh capital they have generated for enterprises in these countries have so far been negligible. Most of this boom is related to underpriced shares floated in the course of privatization, rather than to new issues: this boom, at least so far, has generated very little extra (investment) finance for the enterprises whose shares are traded in these stock exchanges.

Foreign direct investment (FDI) is thus a very important source of finance, especially for larger projects. Besides finance, it is also expected to bring in know-how, expertise, and access to distribution networks in the West (market access). The problem is that FDI into the whole region is very limited, and in addition, it is highly concentrated in very few countries where the legal and financial infrastructure is relatively well developed (Gray et al., 1992; Sárközy, 1993), and which enjoy relative economic and social stability (former Czechoslovakia, now the Czech Republic, and Hungary). Even these countries face fierce competition with other very dynamic countries or regions (such as Portugal and Spain, Mexico, South East Asia, China, and Vietnam). Much of the FDI at present is absorbed by the process of privatization, that is, by the purchase of existing capacities. It is hoped that this will generate future investment, but the extent is still rather uncertain.

Domestic direct investment (private placement), though not fully recorded by official statistics, is perhaps the most dynamic source for finance, in spite of the fact that this source has been very much neglected. The advantage of this form, as is the case with any other direct investment, is that moral hazard is less of a problem. However, this process is almost exclusively confined to small private ventures, at least in the first couple of years of economic restructuring. The lack of collateral and track record, as well as that of competition and experience in the financial sector makes it very difficult for these firms to rely on banking finance. New firms created by this process will therefore go through the natural life-cycle of firms mainly relying on retained earnings and direct investment, like many by now large and famous firms in Western Europe after the war. The successful ones will increasingly be able to attract direct equity (including equity holdings by foreign investors and bonds) and banking finance, but this process is bound to be slow, and it is no solution for large existing SOEs in dire need of restructuring.

The most important source of finance for large SOEs during economic transformation will thus be retained earnings (see McKinnon, 1991). Though retained earnings is the major source for corporate finance in market economies as well (Stiglitz, 1992), in CEE countries this will have a rather different impact on the pattern of industrial restructuring. Owing to the lack of other sources of finance and any sort of state assistance in the process (industrial policy or some other less comprehensive schemes), the former (or existing) SOEs which most need restructuring will simply have neither access to the necessary external finance nor the necessary internal funds to do so. While FDI, as pointed out earlier, can be a way out for a handful of large SOEs (for firms like Skoda, or TUNGSRAM), the vast majority are just too risky a venture for foreign investors. Unemployment, especially regionally, may turn out to be a reason for governments to keep some of these enterprises alive in the short to medium term. However, without major restructuring they have very little, if any, hope for survival.

3. CORPORATE GOVERNANCE, INDUSTRIAL RESTRUCTURING, AND FINANCIAL INSTITUTIONS

What one can observe as industrial restructuring at the macro- or mezo- (industry) level can take distinctively different forms at the micro- (enterprise) level. One of these forms, perhaps the one that has attracted the most attention from academics, is the restructuring of existing SOEs. While there is wide agreement that the lack of proper corporate governance is the major factor explaining why the process of restructuring (former) SOEs is (will be) so painfully slow (see, e.g., Dittus, 1994; Mayhew and Seabright, 1992; Phelps et al., 1993; Wijnbergen, 1994), views regarding the question of which of the possible ways to impose a tight corporate governance on large (privatized, or not yet privatized) SOEs are the most efficient and fastest or, put differently, who should be the 'agent of change' (Wijnbergen, 1994), are rather diverse. As Wijnbergen (1994) points out, 'governments throughout Eastern Europe have been singularly unsuccessful in dealing with large loss-making SOEs'. For the very same reason, governments were also unsuccessful in privatizing these enterprises through outright sale: privatization which is thought to be the ultimate solution for the corporate governance problem is hardly a solution for the vast majority of large (loss-making, or low-profit making) SOEs.

As in many other instances, the exception is Czechoslovakia (now only the Czech Republic) where policy makers embarked upon a wholesale voucher privatization of a large number of SOEs at a very early stage, though by construction not choosing from notoriously loss-making SOEs. In the Czech case, the main question is whether the investment funds created in the course of voucher privatization will be successful in imposing tight corporate governance on the privatized enterprises. The other peculiar aspect of the Czech voucher scheme is that the enterprises involved in the scheme were not made subject to any serious bankruptcy regulation prior to privatization. That is, their real financial situations – together with those of the commercial banks also involved in the voucher scheme – might have been left unrevealed. By now, policy makers in Hungary and Poland are also hastily implementing similar schemes to involve small investors in large numbers, but the major difference is that in these countries, with few exceptions, the firms to be involved are chosen among those that were not attractive for large (foreign) investors through most conventional forms of privatization.

Many researchers find the commercial banks are the ones best positioned to impose the needed corporate governance on (large) SOEs (Ábel and Bonin, 1992a; Hrnčíř, 1994a; Wijnbergen, 1994). The main argument is that banks possess the necessary insider information about the enterprises through their previous credit links. But the problem is that these commercial banks themselves lack the necessary corporate governance owing to the sheer fact that they themselves are (again with the exception of the Czech banks) state-owned and loss making. Moreover, they are overburdened with bad loans partly inherited from central planning, partly made by themselves owing to the lack of proper internal organization, corporate governance, and credit appraisal procedures (Golden, 1994; Montias, 1994; Wyczański, 1994). Moreover, as we shall see in more detail below, the privatization of large SOCBs, which still dominate the banking system, is a very slow process. If that is so, why should these state-owned, so far rather poorly performing banks, all of a sudden be able and motivated efficiently to deal with the ailing SOEs? Not surprisingly, some other researchers are rather sceptical as to the capacity and willingness of large, loss-making SOCBs to perform this function (Phelps et al., 1993; Montias, 1994).

The conclusion we can draw in this regard is that even if some of the commercial banks were willing and able to act as 'agent of change', the overall impact of this would be rather limited and delayed.

4. BAD LOANS AND INDUSTRIAL RESTRUCTURING

What is known as the *bad-loans[5] problem* in the literature (Begg and Portes, 1993; Marrese, 1992; Várhegyi, 1993) is in fact a mixture of problems of rather different natures, though with a common origin. The CPEs of CEE were characterized by highly centralized capital allocation mechanisms, coupled with an almost perfect isolation from competitive world markets. Since the price system, as compared to the prevailing prices on competitive world markets, was highly distorted, due to its rigidity, it was not able to establish prices under which a capital allocation system based on expected future profitability could have properly functioned.[6] The necessary corrections had thus to be made by using an enormously complicated system of taxes, subsidies, and exchange rates (multiple exchange rates) lacking any sort of transparency (Newbery, 1990) and finance was allocated directly by the centre. This system rooted out any competitive (market) pressure on firms and made the allocation of production and investment resources rather arbitrary.

When the socio-economic systems of CEE countries collapsed, the quality of the accumulated real and financial assets, not surprisingly, deteriorated rapidly. Economic transformation brought about a large number of changes in the economic environment industrial (and other) enterprises faced. The liberalization of prices, domestic[7] and foreign trade resulted in fast changing relative prices (including the price of labour and foreign exchange). Moreover, the almost inevitable massive budget deficits resulted in high and fluctuating rates of inflation, creating erratic price expectations (including the price of foreign exchange and labour). With a fast changing and rather uncertain economic environment and high nominal interest rates, it is not at all surprising that the quality of loan portfolios, irrespective of who held them,[8] deteriorated rapidly.

In fact, even in a relatively strong and stable market economy, such as the Finnish one, one of the elements listed above, namely the loss of the Soviet market, was enough to produce a large proportion of bad loans in the asset portfolios of commercial banks and create a severe crisis in the financial system (see, e.g., Bordes, 1993; Currie, 1993; Hukkinen and Rautava, 1992; Nyberg and Vihriälä, 1993). Though in principle, with an optimal coordination among the former CPEs, this process could have been kept under some control, and this could have been more gradual and consequently less painful, it is rather unlikely that countries which spectacularly failed in devising coordination to build something up would have been able to do so when dismantling it, even if the political conditions had permitted it and the political will had been there.

Bad loans were difficult to identify because of the lack of proper accounting standards and bankruptcy regulations (see, e.g., Mizsei, 1994). Moreover, banks may have very strong incentives to either overestimate or underestimate the precise amounts of bad loans in their portfolios, depending on which way is more favourable for them given the conditions of the prevailing bad-loan scheme. Thus, it was, and in many countries still is, difficult to estimate the amount of bad loans at any given point in time. Nonetheless, the widely known estimates suggest that at least about 20-30% of loans in the portfolios of the commercial banks may turn out to be bad (problem) loans (see, e.g., Dittus, 1994). Moreover, these loans are highly concentrated mainly in the portfolios of large SOCBs (or their own 'hospital banks').

The literature suggested several different ways to deal with bad loans.[9] Begg and Portes (1993) suggested removing these loans from the portfolios of commercial banks and replacing them at face value with government bonds providing the banks with adequate yield to become (and remain) profitable. The advantage of this scheme is that it lifts the pressure on commercial banks to build up huge amounts of provisions against bad loans financed from wide interest rate spreads. The problem with this scheme is that it ignores the insider information banks possess about the enterprises involved, and thus gives no incentive to the banks to reveal the information they have on the liquidation values or the variability (future financial situations) of the enterprises involved. Székely (1994) suggests a scheme in which loans would be sold in a special type of auctioning process. During this process the sale of the loans would be subsidized in order to bridge the gap between what the banks originally holding the loan could afford to lose on a loan (as compared to the face value) and what the purchaser could afford to pay for it (given its expectation about the actual value of the loan contract). The advantage of this scheme is that it gives some incentive to banks to reveal the information they have on individual loan contracts and enterprises. The disadvantage is that it takes a much longer time than the Begg-Portes scheme and relies on agents and information that may simply not exist in many CEE countries. Gurgenidze (1993), while still opting for a market-based solution, points to the problems involved in trying to market non-standardized individual loan contracts and to the fact that this is very rarely done even in developed market economies. Instead, he suggests a scheme that is based on the securitization of the bad loans involved. The problem of this solution is that it relies on even more sophisticated instruments that do not exist in any of the CEE countries. Ábel and Bonin (1992a) questions the feasibility of a market-based solution and the merits of a wholesale transfer of bad loans to a government-run 'hospital bank' at face value. They suggest a system of incentive contracts for 'lead' banks that would give a strong incentive to the commercial banks to work out the acquired bad loans and collect as much as possible. Finally, Várhegyi (1994) argues in favour of recapitalization of the commercial banks involved.

Naturally, the decision on how to deal with sub-standard loans will have a profound impact on the interest margins of commercial banks (Begg and Portes, 1993; Dittus, 1994) and, through this, on lending rates. However, as pointed out earlier, crowding-out was at least as important as interest spreads charged by commercial banks in producing high lending rates, thus even the most generous solutions will take away only part of the pressure on interest rate spreads. Moreover, if the costs of cleaning up the loan portfolios of banks are assumed by the state budget and not financed by borrowing from capital markets, they result in either a budget deficit monetized by the central bank, or an increase in the tax burden (on successful firms and individuals). In the former case, as pointed out earlier, the impact on portfolio (re)allocation is immediate and unfavourable (a shift towards more liquid short-term assets), again pushing up lending rates. In the latter case, retained earnings are further taxed, reducing the successful enterprises have funds available for new investments.

CEE countries have so far implemented several bad-loans schemes aimed at cleaning up the loan portfolios of commercial banks including certain elements of the solutions mentioned above. However, the results are, at least so far, disappointing (see, e.g., Dobrinsky, 1994; Hrnčíř, 1994b; Várhegyi, 1994). This apparent lack of success was mainly due to the fact that the schemes implemented so far schemes did too little, too late. The solutions were partial and the amounts involved were inadequate. On the other hand, policy makers paid very little attention to the problem of whether the financial institutions involved ('hospital' agency or commercial banks) were able to assume the task of working out the bad loans (see, e.g., Kruse, 1994), and whether the proper incentives had been created for them to do so.

The Hungarian case is rather instructive in this regard. The (too) tough bankruptcy regulation (see, e.g., Mizsei, 1994) made the extent of bad loans, and the real financial situation of SOEs, painfully visible. However, commercial banks, with one exception, made very little effort to impose tight corporate governance and reorganize these firms. They were much more successful in lobbying, together with the SOEs involved, for wholesale rescue operations by the government. As a result, several bad-loan schemes were implemented. The 1992 bad-loan scheme proved that a government-run 'hospital' agency (formerly a properly incorporated and licensed bank) can do little with the acquired loans, giving an obvious, though rather expensive, support to the argument put forward by those who argued against creating such agencies in CEE countries (see, e.g., Ábel and Bonin, 1992a; Székely, 1994; Várhegyi, 1993). The outcome of this scheme also cast doubt on the merits of the scheme suggested by Begg and Portes (1993), at least in the Hungarian case.[10] The only thing the Hungarian 'hospital' agency did was to contract back the management of the acquired loans to the commercial banks where they originally were. This move brought very little success in recovering the loans.

In the 1993 scheme, Hungarian policy makers thus decided not to remove the loans from the portfolios of the commercial banks, but rather to capitalize the banks themselves. Moreover, the government-run 'hospital' agency started to prepare for the selling-off of the previously acquired loans,[11] most likely back either to the borrowers themselves or to the banks from which they came in the first place. The irony of this scheme is that it 'levelled the playing field for banks', that is, it gave vast amounts to those banks that have done very little if anything at all to cope with the bad loans and the enterprises involved, and almost nothing to the ones that made serious efforts and were relatively successful in this regard. This is a typical case of '*ex post*' recapitalization, with an unsurprising outcome. The major problem is that it can (and will) seriously undermine the credibility of the government and can (and will) take away any incentive for the banks to try to collect these loans or take equity stakes in the enterprises involved.

Though the recently implemented Polish scheme may deliver more promising results (see, e.g., Wijnbergen, 1994), the time that has elapsed since its launching in April 1994 is too short to allow us to draw any firm conclusion in this regard.

5. COMPETITION IN THE FINANCIAL SYSTEM: MARKET STRUCTURE, PRIVATIZATION, AND FOREIGN PARTICIPATION

The industry most in need of restructuring was (and still is) the financial services industry (Bonin and Székely, 1994; Brainard, 1991; Calvo and Frenkel, 1991; Kemme and Rudka, 1992; Long and Sagari, 1991). With the exception of Hungary, and to some extent Poland,[12] CEE economies started off with basically a monobank system.[13] That is to say, it is not the case that a relatively well developed financial sector will contribute to, let alone initiate and supervise, industrial restructuring, but rather that these two processes will take place in parallel, interacting with each other. As was already touched upon above, the collapse of many of the large SOEs brought many of the large directly and indirectly state-owned banks to the verge of collapse because of the massive provisioning requirement due to sub-standard loans (Várhegyi, 1993) and also because of their inability to attract more dynamic private firms as clients and to enter relatively dynamic financial markets (Ábel and Székely, 1994).

While in each CEE country there was a spectacular increase in the number of banks and some consequent increase in the degree of competition, the extent of the latter remained limited. The markets for banking products are still highly concentrated and dominated by the large SOCBs.[14] While, this general finding is true for each CEE country, the differences in the extent to which markets are uncompetitive, concentrated, and dominated by large SOCBs are significant, being much lower in the lead countries (Hungary being the leader in this respect) and higher in the late reformers (such as Bulgaria, after the bank consolidation,[15] and Romania). Moreover, there is a wide variation in the extent of the problem across different markets. With very few exceptions, the lower the risk involved (the more short-term the product and the smaller the amount of up-front investment needed to enter that specific market), the lower the degree of concentration (and consequently the more competitive the market).

Thus, in certain groups of fee-based services (related to forex transactions), in (foreign) trade finance for good clients, derivative products related to forex transactions, and in general at the upper ends of markets (that is, in the areas pointed out below when investigating the strategies of foreign banks), the markets are much more competitive. On the other hand, in retail banking, long-term (investment) loans, and in general at the lower ends of markets, there is very little competition, market structures are highly concentrated, and pricing is seriously distorted.[16]

A characteristic example of the differences across markets for banking products is given in the analysis for Hungary by Ábel and Székely (1994). Between 1987 and 1991, the market share of the large SOCBs as measured by the balance sheet total declined from 58.2% in 1987 to 42.4% in 1991. The same pairs of figures for the corporate deposit market were 84% and 54.9%, for the corporate loan market 91.6% and 62.9%, while for the market for discounting of bills of exchange 90.3% and 20.3%. Regarding long-term investment loans, the share of SOCBs in 1991 was around 74%, much higher than for corporate loans in general. Though the new banks (including the newly created SOCBs) did enter the retail market, consumer and housing loans, as well as retail deposit markets, remained much more concentrated, dominated by the National Savings Bank.[17]

The lack of adequate degree of competition is also shown by the wide interest rate spreads mentioned above.[18] More precisely, the indication of the lack of competition is not so much (not necessarily) the fact that spreads are wide in general, but that (new) banks that were free from bad loans, forcing large SOCBs to finance their heavy provisioning needs from wide spreads, gradually started to follow the pricing policies of the large SOCBs by charging similar spreads (see Ábel and Székely, 1994; Dobrinsky, 1994; Daianu, 1994; Hrnčíř, 1994a; Wyczański, 1993). While this process was a very important factor in increasing competition and decreasing market concentration, it also meant that the expansion of the private sector in the financial system was less than sufficient.

With the exception of the Czech Republic where the generally adopted wholesale privatization involved the large SOCBs as well, governments decided to separate the privatization of SOCBs from that of SOEs, and deal with the banks on a case-by-case basis. With the exception of the early sell-off of a few relatively small SOCBs, this resulted in major delays in the privatisation of SOCBs.[19]

Regarding the actually privatized SOCBs, it is important to pay attention to the outcome of the process. Though the Czech voucher privatization led to the sell-off of a major part of the equity shares of the large SOCBs (the Consolidation Bank, which is the Czech 'hospital bank', remaining the only fully state-owned bank), the state retained a substantial equity stake in the large former SOCBs (on the average some 42%). It remains to be seen whether any of the investment funds will be able to impose the much-needed tight corporate governance on these banks and attract foreign strategic partners. These two elements are thought to be vital to the eventual success of these banks.

In Poland, the two privatization deals completed so far raise very similar concerns. While the participation of EBRD is indeed important in attracting (future) foreign strategic partners, in itself it will probably do very little to improve the efficiency of a bank. The example of Wielkopolski Bank Kredytowy, which was publicly offered in the first half of 1993, clearly attests to this suspicion (see, e.g., Kokoszczyński, 1994). The case of Bank Śląski, which was privatized in 1994, is much more exciting and promising, since this is the first case when a relatively large SOCB was privatized with the participation of strategic investors with much-needed expertise, know-how, and access to foreign capital markets. The success or failure of this bank will have a strong bearing on the process of bank privatization in the whole region.

As in other industries, foreign participation is thought to be an important factor in increasing competition in the financial services industry. In the lead countries of CEE, foreign participation became significant in the financial system, in particular in banking.[20] But even in the lead countries, the nature of the business strategies of foreign and joint venture banks turned out to be quite different from what policy makers expected at the beginning of economic transformation. Foreign banks, in particular major international banks with the much desired capital strength, international network, access to international financial markets, and expertise and know-how have showed, at least so far, very moderate interest in exactly those areas where they are most desperately needed. Thus, the interest in buying into large SOCBs or moving into the least competitive (and most costly or risky) segments (such as retail banking or servicing small enterprises) has been, to put it mildly, moderate.

On the other hand, in those segments where foreign banks have huge comparative advantages (such as foreign payment services and related primary and derivative products) and where risk is limited, the capital and staff requirement to efficiently and prudently pursue business is relatively small, and there is no need for a large branch network, foreign and joint venture banks captured significant market shares. Put differently, they concentrated their business activities in areas where the profit-risk ratio is the highest and where activities can be expanded (and contracted) rapidly. Moreover, in each segment where they have significant market share, they concentrate on the upper end of the market, that is, they cream off the market and take only the best clients. Thus, in handling corporate accounts and financing corporate units, they attract the foreign and joint venture firms by offering Western standards of services.

While some researchers (see, e.g., Várhegyi, 1994) and policy makers appear to be somewhat irritated by this attitude of foreign and joint venture banks, from the viewpoint of economic theory it is a very rational approach and not much different from the experiences of some Western countries (see, e.g., Savela and Herrala, 1992 for the Finnish experience). Moreover, it gives a good indication of what business strategy a relatively small bank with proper corporate governance and, consequently, a strong interest in increasing its market value as an enterprise, tends to have in an environment such as the present one in CEE.

Financial markets in CEE are highly volatile and risky for several reasons related to the very nature of economic restructuring. The macroeconomic environment is rather unstable by Western standards, even in the most successful countries. Owing to the rapid changes in relative prices, the sudden trade reorientation, and the consequent massive changes in the market values of enterprise assets, the real financial situations of firms, as well as their economic viability in the future, are extremely difficult to judge. This is made more difficult by the massive and continuous changes in corporate law and other legislation (including such very important areas as accounting and tax regulations). Moreover, regulations regarding financial institutions are new, in many cases as yet untested in courts, and rapidly changing, and supervisory agencies are inexperienced. On the other hand, domestic banks and financial institutions are very inexperienced and ill-equipped to provide certain services and make markets for sophisticated products (such as options or commercial papers). They also lack the necessary infrastructure to meet Western standards in very traditional banking services for foreign and joint venture firms that require this (and are able to pay for it). It is therefore natural for these banks to concentrate their activities and resources on these markets and clients.

With the exception of interbank deposit markets, and some competitive refinance schemes in lead countries, wholesale financial markets are virtually non-existent and the financial system is hardly more than the banking system (Hrnčíř, 1994b; Király, 1993; Kokoszczyński, 1994; Székely, 1994; Wyczański, 1993). There is hardly any external source of competitive pressure on banks (see also the discussion about direct finance previously). As a consequence, the costs of capital and financial services are high, much higher than the ones competing producers in Western Europe face, the quality of services is low, and the necessary products to share or hedge risk are not available. Exporters cannot offer export credits. Export credits are an important tool in market penetration, and the lack of them is a major stumbling block in the process of revitalizing intra-regional trade in CEE.

Future reforms of the financial system, resulting, it is hoped, in higher degrees of competitiveness, more able banks taking part in financing and conducting industrial restructuring, lower costs of capital and financial services, will undoubtedly be important factors in the process of economic transformation, in particular in industrial restructuring, but this will again be a slow and gradual process, where competitive financial firms themselves have to grow up. This is again a factor which supports our general finding that industrial restructuring is more likely to be based on newly emerging and gradually developing and growing enterprises than on existing large SOEs. These producers will no doubt need proper access to high-quality and low-cost financial services and low-cost capital if they are to be competitive in international markets. This gradual process will to a large degree depend on how successful the reform of the financial system in CEE economies is.

6. CONCLUSION

The chapter investigated the role of the financial system in economic transformation, in particular in industrial restructuring, and the likely impact of a more competitive financial system, in particular a more competitive and efficient credit allocation system, on the pattern of industrial restructuring in the short to medium run.

The analysis presented suggests two main conclusions. First, if commercial financing becomes the dominating (or even only) source of external investment finance for enterprises then, with very few exceptions, large SOEs will have very little, if any, chance of finding the necessary internal or external financial sources to embark upon restructuring and new investment projects. On the other hand, emerging new private enterprises, with a few exceptions, will need considerable time before they can rely on banking finance to any extent.

Second, financial institutions will need a considerable time, even in the lead countries, before they will be able to assume the roles that financial institutions, in particular commercial banks, play in developed market economies. In particular, large SOCBs themselves will have to go through substantial restructuring and, eventually, privatization before they will be able to act as the 'agent of change' and impose financial discipline and tight corporate governance over (large, loss-making) SOEs. The degree of competition, though gradually increasing, and the share of the private sector, though again gradually increasing, are just too low at the moment to support a rapid change in this respect.

However, without restructuring and massive new investments, large and inefficient SOEs are bound to suffer and eventually to disappear altogether. If large SOEs are not able to restructure their production, the '*constructive phase*' of industrial restructuring, that is, the process of building up of new, competitive, and export-oriented industrial production capacities will mainly be confined to newly emerging private firms. These firms will however need considerable time to become strong enough to be able to use capital-intensive production technologies. Put differently, the product structures of industrial production and exports for the most part concentrate on products which do not require heavy up-front investments. The process is going to be a slow and gradual *reindustrialization*, based on natural comparative advantages and limited by the capacity of enterprises to assume risk and penetrate markets. Unemployment is then going to be a long-term rather than a short- or medium-term problem.

CEE economies will probably therefore need a long time until they reach the sort of industrial and export structures their potential would suggest. Market concentration (Newbery and Kattuman, 1992) will consequently be less of a problem, once the large SOEs lose their market power.

The goal of the chapter was to argue neither for, nor against, industrial policy or any other less comprehensive form of state assistance to industrial restructuring. The only aim was to point out the likely direction in which commercial finance with gradually strengthening financial systems, without a substantial involvement of the state, will inevitably push this process. The privatization of industrial firms and banks will make this impact even more imminent and pronounced.

POSTSCRIPT

The biggest stumbling block to the maturity of financial systems continues to be the slow and difficult process of privatization of the banking sector. In addition, foreign banks have either shied away from direct competition in many of the transitional economies or have been discouraged from doing so because of dissatisfaction with the privatization process. In addition, there have been problems for both outsiders and insiders in attempting to properly value the assets and liabilities of commercial banks put up for sale. The difficulties which afflict large enterprises and state-owned ones as described in this chapter remain to this day. While they are becoming less acute this represents perhaps one of the slowest aspect of the transition as suggested when this chapter was originally written. Chapter 8 considers the continuing failure of the banking sector to fulfil its intermediation function.

NOTES

*   Originally published under the same title in *Industrial Restructuring and Trade: Reorientation in Eastern Europe*, edited by M.A. Landesmann and I. Székely (Cambridge: Cambridge University Press), pp.337-62, by I. Ábel and I. Székely, reprinted with minor revisions by permission.

1.   The Czech Republic formerly Czechoslovakia) is the only notable exception throughout the whole period. In 1993, Poland also showed a surprisingly low (significantly lower than expected) level of budget deficit (see Table 6.1). This examples shows that strong economic growth can solve this issue even in countries where other factors tend to produce a high level of budget deficit.

2.   The figures in Table 6.1 are expressed as percentages of GDP, but since the denominator is the same for saving and budget deficit, this statement remains valid.

3.   These real interest rates were calculated on the basis of monthly (weighted average) nominal interest rates on loans with maturity over one year deflated by the (*ex post*) rate of PPI inflation for one year ahead. Given that the average maturity was not much longer than one year, this assumes a perfect foresight on the part of lenders and borrowers. Given the very high level of real rates and the sizeable month-to-month fluctuation in this series, one is inclined to question the rationality of price expectations. The NBH calculates real rates (see NBH, 1992, p.153) by deflating nominal rates by

the PPI index for the year preceding the observation period. This implicitly implies naive price expectations. As we have very limited understanding of price expectations in transition economies, it is very difficult to decide which one is the correct way of calculating the real rate expected by lenders and borrowers. For comparison, in Figure 6.1, both series are shown.

4. Average values for the year as a whole, based on monthly figures shown in Figure 6.1 (authors' own calculations). Dittus (1994) reports real lending rates for Czechoslovakia (Czech Republic) and Poland, as well, though figures are average rates for all types of loan, not only longer-term (over one year) loans. Nonetheless, the actual figures for Czechoslovakia are significantly lower, but the tendency is rather similar. For Poland, figures are quite similar to those for Hungary. The Czech figures seem to support our views in that lower budget deficit and public borrowings requirement put less strain on (real) borrowing rates for enterprises.

5. The term 'bad loan' will refer to all kinds of problem loans throughout this section. This is admittedly not a fully precise way of referring to problem loans, but this term is widely used in the literature with such a meaning. Moreover, CEE countries have no uniform classification of problem loans or even the same terms for (the different kinds of) problem loans.

6. 'Properly' in the sense that it would have led to an allocation of capital in line with planners' intentions.

7. The liberalization of foreign trade got much more emphasis in the literature than that of domestic trade, though the latter is perhaps more important in imposing real competitive pressure on domestic producers. One of the main characteristics of CPEs was the almost perfect monopolization of wholesale trade and a large degree of centralization of retail trade. If one forgets about this and carries out the liberalization (privatization) of foreign trade, as was done in many countries in the first phase of reform, the outcome is anything but a competitive system (reflected by distorted pricing behaviour).

8. This refers to the debate as to whether it was wise to transfer the investment portfolio of the previous monobank to the newly created commercial banks. We would like to point out here the simple fact that though this issue is important technically and has some influence on the extent and precise dynamics of the process, the origin of the problem is independent of this choice.

9. Due to the focus of our chapter, we do not attempt to give a complete overview of the existing proposals. We concentrate only on those that have some relevance to our discussion. For a more detailed discussion of the existing proposals, see Dittus (1994).

10. Hrnčíř (1994b) reports on some success of the Consolidation Banks (the Czech 'hospital' agency) to collect impressive proportions of the bad loans in its portfolio in certain cases.

11. That is, the eventual outcome will be what Székely (1994) suggested. The major difference is however that between the two steps (acquiring the loans and selling them) the best part of a year will have elapsed. During this period the market values of the loans involved will most likely have decreased to a considerable extent, resulting in unnecessary loss to the budget.

12. Hungary started to implement financial reforms in 1984 and established a Western-style two-tier banking system in 1987 (see, e.g., Bácskai, 1989). Though, as a result of these reforms, Hungary had a more sophisticated financial system than other CEE countries, the first phase of reforms had very little impact on the behaviour of the financial services industry (Székely, 1990; Blejer and Sagari, 1991). Poland started financial reforms in 1988 and introduced a two-tier banking system in 1989. However, the impact of these reforms was even less significant than that of the Hungarian ones (see Wyczański, 1993). For a general survey on the starting positions of the other CEE countries in this regard, see Kemme and Rudka (1992).

13. For a description of the monobank system which characterized CPEs, see Podolski (1973) and Zwass (1979). For a general overview on the reform of the financial system in CEE, see Bonin and Székely (1994) and Kemme (1992).

14. In the case of the Czech Republic, by the large commercial banks that were privatized via the voucher privatization. These banks, while the majority stakes of their equity shares were floated, remained under the heavy influence of the National Property Fund, which retained 40-45% of the equity shares, while the floated stakes are not necessarily held in one hand.

15. Bulgaria is a very special case in this respect, because in the course of the initial break-up of the monobank system a large number of very small SOCBs were created. Nonetheless, at the local level, this created very little competition, but rather weak banks. This was later realized by policy makers and a bank consolidation scheme was launched. The eventual outcome of this process will determine future market structures. For more details, see Dobrinsky (1994).

16. For detailed information on market structures in Bulgaria, see Dobrinsky (1994), in the Czech Republic, Hrnčíř (1994a), in Hungary, Ábel and Székely (1994), in Poland, Wyczański (1993), in Romania, Daianu (1994), and in general, in CEE, Dittus (1994).

17. The other end of the spectrum is probably occupied by Romania where, as reported by Daianu (1994), the four biggest SOCBs accounted for 94% of total credits in 1991 and for 80% in June 1993. Concurrently, the State Saving Bank (CEC) accounted for 95% of sight deposits and 40% of term deposits by individuals in June 1993.

18. It is again difficult to define and measure precisely interest rate spread, because both the liability and assets structures of banks in CEE are sometimes rather different from those of banks in developed market economies. Sometimes the shares of refinance credit (from the central bank) with very special (non-market) rates, as well as special loans to (mainly) enterprises with again special (non-market) rates might be rather significant. Thus, comparing simply deposit rates to (market) loan rates might be rather misleading. To avoid this, Ábel and Székely (1994) use spreads calculated on the basis of average rates over assets and liabilities. Such figures may however not always be available for other countries. Nonetheless, the typical figures for CEE countries have recently been in the range of 8-15 percentage points and with a tendency to increase. The Czech Republic (formerly Czechoslovakia) occupies probably the low end (rising from 2.8 in the first quarter of 1990 to 6.7 in the last quarter of 1992 in Czechoslovakia, to 7.8 percentage points (see Dobrinsky, 1994). For Hungary and Poland, figures are in the range of 10-20 percentage points (nominal) (see, e.g., Dittus, 1994; Ábel and Székely, 1994).

19. For more details on privatization of SOCBs in CEE, see Ábel and Bonin (1992a); Daianu (1994), Kokoszcyński (1994), Mortimer (1994), and Wyczański (1993).

20. In the Czech Republic in (June) 1993 there were 19 banks with foreign participation and 6 branches of foreign banks (out of 50 banks in total) in Hungary in 1992, 13 banks with foreign participation (out of 38), and in Poland in 1992 11 banks with foreign participation (out of 94). In the other countries, foreign participation is very moderate (see Dobrinsky, 1994; Daianu, 1994).

7. The Gradual Approach to Banking Reform and the Anatomy of the Bad Loans Problem*

PROLOGUE

As pointed out in the previous chapter, while central banks in the transitional economies gave up their role as commercial bankers they could not or would not inherit existing debts. Instead many of these appeared on the balance sheet of the newly created commercial banking sector. While most transitional countries eventually opted to create 'consolidation' banks to sweep up existing 'bad' debts the problem continued to persist and even intensify following the breakup of the Council of Mutual Economic Assistance (CMEA). This chapter explores the bad loans problem by concentrating on the Hungarian experience, although comparisons are also made with other transitional and more advanced industrialized economies.

1. INTRODUCTION

Hungary started to modernize its financial system well ahead of other countries in the region. In 1971, it was the first Eastern European country to issue bonds on the international money markets. In 1981, it gained membership in the IMF and the World Bank. In the early 1980s, Hungarian firms could issue bonds. Since 1987, Hungary changed its one-tier system into a two-tier banking system with distinct central and commercial banks; it also liberalized interest rates and introduced bankruptcy and accounting laws based on Western prototypes. Financial reform has meant that savers can hold their money in domestic (HUF) or foreign currency accounts. Debit cards are becoming available at certain banks. The number of foreign banks operating in Hungary has grown from four in 1987 to eighteen in 1993 (Piper et al., 1994; Székely, 1990, 1994).

Though the amount of qualified debt has increased sharply since 1987 owing to the deep recession and the loss of CMEA markets, the Hungarian bad loans problem is no more serious than that in any transforming country. Rather, as a percentage of GDP in 1993, bad loans in Hungary appear to be a less serious problem than in the Czech Republic and Bulgaria (see Table 7.1). Well-established market economies, such as Finland, Norway, and Sweden, that recently underwent much smaller economic dislocations and a substantial deregulation of the financial sector experienced similar problems: the shares of bad loans reached 12 to 17 percent of total loans at the end of 1992 (BIS, 1993).

Table 7.1 Bad Loans in Four Former Socialist Economies, 1993

	Bulgaria	Czech R.	Poland	Hungary
		(%)		
Enterprise debt to banks/GDP	70	74	21	28
Qualified loans/total loans	40-50	19-24	28	20-25
Qualified loans/GDP	28-35	14-18	5.9	5.6-7

Sources: Dittus (1994); Hrnčíř (1994b); Belka (1995); and Dobrinsky (1995).

In this chapter, we deal with a description of the problem in an attempt to attribute responsibility for it. Although we intentionally avoid any specific policy prescriptions, we characterize the range of options open to policy makers. We believe that attribution is an important consideration for any policy, as it lies at the very core of the issue of corporate governance of the banks. This in turn is a crucial determinant of whether the problem will recur.

2. BAD BANKS VERSUS BAD ENTERPRISES

The problems of bad loans in the banking system are inextricably tied to the prospects of loss-making enterprises. A Ministry of Finance (1993) survey of 1992 tax returns of 57,200 incorporated companies reveals the magnitude of the problem. Nearly half of all Hungarian enterprises are loss-making. These loss-making enterprises hold 59 percent of all bank debt and employ 1.1 million people. The share of these enterprises in sales is 34 percent, in employment 50 percent. Nearly two-thirds of these losses are concentrated in 603 firms (or 1.1 percent of total firms) with 243 billion Hungarian forint (HUF) in outstanding debt (or 35 percent of all enterprise loans) employing 400,000 people (or 18 percent of the labour force). Total losses, HUF 380 billion, equal 13 percent of GDP. The estimated negative operating cash flow of these loss-making enterprises, after allowing for depreciation, amounted to HUF 317 billion or 11 percent of GDP.

How did companies raise the cash needed to make up for this enormous operating cash flow deficiency? They may have sold assets, borrowed from suppliers, left their taxes unpaid, or increased loans from banks.

In the wake of the collapse of traditional markets in the early stages of the transition, assets sale was probably most common, but as companies ran out of valuable assets this source of cash dried out by 1993. Interenterprise debt was an ever increasing phenomenon until the draconian bankruptcy regulation came into force in 1992. Since then companies are more and more reluctant to finance their buyers (Ábel and Siklos (1994), and chapter 2).

Tax arrears continue to increase, but this alone would have been insufficient to make up the difference. The negative operating cash flow provides some of the most convincing evidence that banks continued to extend credit to loss makers through interest capitalization and refinancing.

The root of the problem lies with the legacies of the old system. Financing of enterprises in the old system was almost automatic bank financing. Enterprises did not rely on self-financing, most of them did not have enough of their own funds even to finance their working capital needs. Almost all the enterprises started the transition seriously overleveraged, that is, relying heavily on bank financing even to maintain current activities. But inflation coupled with a credit crunch caused great loss of enterprise profitability. Credit crunch and loss of domestic and export markets are the major causes behind the poor performance of enterprises (Siklos and Ábel (1995) and chapter 3).

3. INHERITED VERSUS NEW BAD LOANS

Initially Hungary's bad loans problem could be traced to the portfolio of loans inherited by the state-owned banks when the one-tier banking system was replaced with separate commercial and central banking functions in 1987. The inherited loans were made under a different economic reality and often irrespective of commercially sound banking practices. The current distribution of problem loans reflects this initial sectoral allocation.

At the time of their creation, the nonperforming part of the loan portfolio of each state-owned commercial bank (SOCB) was identified. In 1987, Magyar Hitel Bank (MHB) held HUF 5 billion, Kereskedelmi Bank (K&H) held HUF 2.5 billion, and Budapest Bank (BB) held HUF 1.9 billion in nonperforming loans. In addition, BB agreed to take on HUF 4.7 billion in government-guaranteed long-term loans to the ailing coal mines, bringing its total of nonperforming loans to HUF 6.6 billion. Clearly this total of HUF 14.1 billion must be considered to be inherited bad debt over which bank management had little or no control. However, banks inherited bad customers along with the stock of bad loans outstanding to these enterprises. Owing to restrictions and market segmentation, the banks were initially constrained in diversifying their activities. The inherited clientele had some influence on the flow of bad debt, that is, the continuing addition of bad loans to the stock of bad debt. By the end of 1990 (before the CMEA shock), the stock of nonperforming loans had grown from HUF 14.1 billion in 1987 to HUF 36.5 billion. From 1987 to

1990, the increase for each of the three SOCBs was as follows: MHB, HUF 11 billion (16 billion from 5 billion); K&H, HUF 7.4 billion (9.9 billion from 2.5 billion); and BB HUF 4 billion (10.6 billion from 6.6 billion). How much of these increases were newly created bad debt attributable to bad bank management, specifically the extension of new credit to nonpaying customers in excess of accrued interest on nonperforming loans, is unknown.

To distinguish between 'inherited' (stock of debt) and 'newly created' (flow of lending) business is crucial to determine whether SOCBs are acting negligently by creating new bad debt through loans to customers known to be bad credit risks. The cross-ownership relationship between the SOCBs and their largest state-owned enterprise (SOE) clients is cited by many observers as leading banks 'to throw good money after bad'. Complicating the issue of attribution are two severe real shocks and a self-induced legislative financial shock. At the beginning of the 1990s, Hungary experienced a sharp drop in real output (from 1989 to 1992, real GDP measured by official statistics dropped 20 percent) owing to a transition-induced recession and a collapse, by 1991, of the CMEA (traditional export) markets. A decline in real output of this magnitude would lead to a sharp decrease in the real value of the loan portfolios of financial institutions in any economy. In Hungary, the real shocks certainly caused new bad bank debt, as companies that may have appeared healthy in the previous environment faced serious financial difficulties and may have become nonviable in the new situation. The extent to which bank management can be held responsible for clairvoyance is problematic.

A further complication in assessing the competence of any bank management involves 'recognized' versus 'unrecognized' bad debt. Given that a bank has a bad debt, knows it, and has decided not to lend any more to the client (not to 'throw good money after bad'), management can choose to recognize the bad debt immediately (classify it and make the appropriate loss provision) or postpone the day of reckoning by capitalizing the interest as it comes due and hiding the fact that the loan is nonperforming. In the face of a significant shock to the real economy, some lag in 'marking to market' the loan portfolio and realizing fully the decrease in asset values would be a natural response in any banking system. The liability side of the bank's balance sheet cannot usually be adjusted immediately to the drop in real value on the asset side because of the lack of sufficient equity capital. If a bank lacks the assets to provide loss reserves for all of its bad debt immediately, the fear of insolvency leads to a gradual recognition of the bad debt with the hope of partially growing out of the problem.

In Hungary, prior to December 1991, accounting practices added a further disincentive for banks to recognize the qualified part of their loan portfolios. The new banking act (officially, Act no. LXIX of 1991 on Financial Institutions and Financial Institutional Activities) was promulgated on 1

December, 1991, but applied retroactively to the balance sheets of the banks for the full year of 1991. The act introduced three qualified categories for rating the loan portfolios of the banks, mandated the accumulation of provisions (loan loss reserves) against loans so qualified, and specified a schedule for meeting capital adequacy targets. According to the banking act and a subsequent decree from the State Banking Supervision (SBS) in March 1992, banks must classify assets in their portfolios as bad if the borrower is in default for more than one year or the claims are held against a company that is in liquidation proceedings. Provisions equal to 100 percent of total 'bad'[1] debt had to be accumulated by the end of a three-year period. The banking act legislates two other categories of qualified loans, namely, substandard and doubtful, with provisions equal to 20 percent of the former and 50 percent of the latter to be accumulated within the same period.

Starting in 1991, the two real shocks were magnified by a self-induced legislated financial shock that made the banks recognize the drop in the real value of their assets over a relatively short period of time. For loans classified as qualified by the end of 1992, banks were required to hold one-third of the prescribed provisions, leaving two-thirds of this amount as a deferred liability. Although these deferred provisions are not subtracted from bank capital by Hungarian accounting procedures, international accounting standards require such deductions. At the end of September 1992, the aggregate stock of qualified loans for the banking sector was reported to be HUF 262 billion. Based on preliminary data for 1992, a joint World Bank/IMF mission estimated full statutory provisions for the banking system to have increased from HUF 83 billion in 1991 to HUF 222.5 billion in 1992.[2] This increment exceeded 1992 profits before tax and provisions by almost 300 percent. The sum of equity plus total provisions for the banking system amounted to HUF 267.9 billion at the end of December 1992. Hence, the banking system itself was virtually insolvent by the end of 1992.

The bulk of the problem lay with the three large SOCBs. Negative capital adequacy ratios (CARs) had been estimated for both MHB and K&H at the end of 1992. Whether the root of the solvency problem for any particular bank was bad management or a combination of inherited factors and real shocks is difficult to disentangle. However, the conventional position attributes the increase in the stock of nonperforming loans during this period to bad bank management at least in these two cases. To avoid incentive problems in the design of government rescue programmes, it is essential that policy makers discern whether bad debts result from bad bank management. How much of the recognized bad debt in Hungary by the end of 1992 was due to poor bank management is a difficult empirical question. However, it does seem clear that the new legislation imposed an immediate flow solution on a partially inherited stock problem.

To illustrate the problem of attributing responsibility for the bad loans problem, we consider the situation of one of the SOCBs in Hungary. The Workout Department of this bank analyzed the structure of the bank's portfolio.[3] At the end of 1992, this bank had a CAR estimated to be positive but a substantial bad loans problem. In Table 7.2, the origin of bad loans outstanding as of 31 December, 1993, is traced. Of the loans originating before 1990, only 12 percent were nonperforming and only 9 percent were classified as 'bad' according to the Hungarian legislation. The situation seems to deteriorate significantly and rapidly with loans originating in 1990, of which 45 percent are 'bad'. Loans originating in 1991 and 1992 during the height of the turbulence caused by the real shocks and the self-induced financial shocks account for 22.8 percent of all loans outstanding as of the end of 1993. Of these loans, only 40 percent qualify as 'pass', while 49 percent are classified as 'bad'. Of the loans originating before 1993, 45 percent are classified as 'qualified' in some way and 38 percent fall into the 'bad' category. That loan portfolios are heavily oriented to short-term debt is evident: 63.9 percent of the loans extant at the end of 1993 were made during 1993.

Table 7.2 Qualified Loans: The Experience of a Hungarian Commercial Bank

Class	Up to 1989	1990	Up to 1990	1991
		(%)		
Pass	8.4 (88)	2.0 (55)	10.5 (79)	2.6 (39)
Qualified	1.1 (12)	1.7 (45)	2.8 (21)	4.1 (61)
Bad	0.8 (9)	1.7 (45)	2.5 (19)	3.9 (59)
Total	9.5	3.8	13.3	6.8

Class	1992	1991-92	Up to 1992	1993	Total
			(%)		
Pass	6.6 (41)	9.2 (40)	19.7 (40)	55.6 (87)	2.6 (39)
Qualified	9.5 (59)	13.6 (60)	16.4 (45)	8.3 (13)	4.1 (61)
Bad	7.2 (45)	11.1 (49)	13.6 (38)	3.8 (6)	3.9 (59)
Total	16.0	22.8	36.1	63.9	6.8

Source: Authors' calculations.

Notes: The table refers to all loans outstanding as of 31 December 1993. The classifications come from the Hungarian Banking Act as amended by the SBS in March 1992 and applied until the end of 1993. Consequently 'bad' is a subset of 'qualified', as the latter includes 'substandard' and 'doubtful' in addition.

The first number in any cell expresses the loans in this cell as a percentage of total loans outstanding as of 31 December 1993. The number in parentheses expresses the loans in that cell as a percentage of total loans originating *in that period*. For example, 12 percent of all loans originating up to 1989 were classified as 'qualified'.

The difference between 'qualified' and 'bad' up to 1989 most likely reflects loans existing in 1987 that were guaranteed by the government and the subsequent accrued interest on these loans.

Regarding the attribution of the bad loans, obviously current bank management must take responsibility for the loans made in 1993 even if some of these were to long-standing clients who have been and continue to be in financial difficulty. For 1993, the percentage of performing (pass) loans is a quite respectable 87 percent. Of the stock of outstanding loans classified as 'bad' at the end of 1993, about 22 percent originated in 1993. Of this same stock, about 14 percent originated prior to 1991. With the exception of loans on the books at the end of 1987 that were qualified but not classified as 'bad' because of government guarantees, all qualified debt outstanding at the end of 1990 was 'bad'. Thus, we regard it as reasonable to consider about 14 percent of 'bad' debt to be clearly inherited. The overwhelming percentage of 'bad' debt, about 64 percent, originated in 1991 and 1992.

A portion of the qualified loans must be attributed to another unfavorable heritage of the large Hungarian banks, namely, their poor financial condition. They were undercapitalized from the beginning, which contributed to the fact that banks preferred to roll over problem loans despite legal and accounting laws that discourage this practice.

In this respect, the financial distress in Hungary was caused by the state's desertion of enterprises and commercial banks. Enterprises formerly financed mainly by state bank credit used self-financing only marginally. As their capital base was very low, when the source of state financing ceased, the whole burden fell on the banks. The low capital base of banks and the inappropriate level of reserves led to a serious credit crunch when regulators introduced Bank for International Settlements (BIS) standards. This was aggravated by the high interest spreads banks had to apply to provide the necessary cash flow to provide against the nonperforming part of their portfolio. This policy has repercussions, causing good clients to turn to cheaper foreign sources and leaving the domestic banks with a risky and weaker clientele. This partly explains the tendency shown in Table 7.2.

Evidently the bad loans are not inherited from the pre-1987 period. The bad loan problem is a result of the combination of the inherited weak capital base of the banks and an induced financial shock that exacerbated the turbulence of the transition environment. Policy makers used a gradual approach on the liability side of the banking sector when they delayed its proper capitalization by collecting profits, taxes, and dividends when these banks posted high profits in 1990 and 1991. But the same policy makers exercised shock therapy on the asset side of the banking system when they introduced the new bankruptcy law and the new banking act in 1992. The bankruptcy law included an automatic trigger that began to have a significant impact in April 1992, when a company with any outstanding debt more than ninety days overdue was required to initiate bankruptcy proceedings. As a consequence, in 1992, 4,231 companies filed for bankruptcy (reorganization), and roughly 10,000 liquidation applications were received (NBH, 1993, p.23). The banking act introduced stringent BIS standards in required provisioning against loan losses. The missed opportunities to accumulate reserves in 1990 and 1991, together with the shock in 1992, led to the unprecedented accumulation of bad loans, as reflected by the figures in our example shown in Table 7.2.

It is hard to detect what role the banks themselves played in the accumulation of bad loans by their poor loan evaluation practices. They share responsibility in what has happened. To solve the bad loans problem, government actions as well as further efforts by the banks themselves are equally required.

4. APPROACHES TO CONCILIATION

Broadly speaking, there are basically two types of approaches to bank conciliation. One is the asset side approach. Here there are also several alternatives, like cleaning up the assets of the banks by taking away bad loans from the banks' books or replacing them with performing assets like government bonds. There are two basic alternatives for taking away bad loans from the books, both of them already applied in one or more of the transforming countries. One alternative is that a separate institution takes over those loans, while the other alternative is that they remain with the banks but as a below-the-line item handled under the auspices of a special contract between the bank and the owner of the claims represented in these loans.

The liability side approach represents the other type of solution. This would basically involve recapitalizing the banks up to a level at which they are able to deal with the problem, that is, accumulate adequate loan loss reserves. The capital increase can be done by shares issues bought by the state or any actor willing to invest in loan losses. It would increase the tier-one capital technically until write-offs consume the capital. A tier-two capital injection would do the same in the short run by replenishing reserves from subordinated debt, or by an actor willing to absorb losses, that is, the state.

Evidently any of these alternatives can be combined, and most of the solutions will affect both sides of the balance sheet.

Whether the state or some other actor should absorb the losses is an issue on which opinions clash. Who will bear the costs of cleaning up? Will equity holders, bank managers, corporate borrowers assume responsibility or absorb part of the cost of resolving the bad loans problem? In our view the loan losses are direct consequences of the losses in state assets that occurred during the transition, so it should be handled basically as an accounting correction in writing off from state assets. This view is best presented by Begg and Portes (1993).

No matter what scheme for bank or debtor conciliation is chosen, several potential problems arise within the procedure. How should the government resources be allocated? Should there be more for the banks with weaker portfolios, or an equal amount for every bank? Any method that does not remove all bad debt and does not effectively recapitalize the bank is bound to have a limited effect.

How will the scheme alter incentives that banks operate under in order to encourage market-oriented bank behaviour? How can the government ensure that bailouts will not be repeated? Changing incentives are vital if we are to put an end to the creation of bad loans.

The clean-up plan should involve not only some changes in incentives and in the governance structure of enterprises and banks, but also revisions to the legal and regulatory environment that contributed to the bad loans problem.

In choosing between bank recapitalization and enterprise recapitalization, bank recapitalization offers more promise. Banks have better information than the government on which companies are likely to succeed. In addition, bank recapitalization has a wider impact on the economy if banks channel funds to the most efficient companies.

5. CURE FOR ALL PROBLEMS: PRIVATIZATION

The main cause of the problem is the collapse of the economy. Therefore, no matter what clean-up scheme is chosen, and no matter how carefully it is carried out, the result of these efforts will ultimately be determined by how they contribute to economic recovery.

As in any other sector of the economy, privatization offers the best hope for Hungarian SOCBs to improve their ability to compete with foreign banks. The clean-up requires a substantial amount of capital, technology, and banking know-how, all of which presuppose foreign participation. The high costs of government bailout, the inadequacy of financing for emerging businesses, and the sharp decline in investment all suggest that the economy would be better off with foreign participation in ownership, at the level accepted in other countries at a comparable stage of development.

Foreign strategic partners are the only ones with access to the capital, low-cost funding and banking expertise needed to improve the competitiveness of Hungarian banks. A foreign strategic partner would provide its Hungarian counterpart with a connection to international banking markets, which offer diversification, higher profits, and strong market position vis-à-vis the small joint venture banks that have been set up over the past few years.

POSTSCRIPT

In all transitional economies the process of privatization remains an arduous one to this day. Nevertheless, if one takes Hungary as an example, there are fewer than a third as many state-owned enterprises by mid-1996 as in 1990. Reductions of this magnitude have been experienced in Poland but not quite as dramatically in the Czech Republic. Also important has been the continued strength and growth in foreign direct investment. While Hungary is the 'champion' in this area, Poland is quickly catching up and the situation has improved for many transitional economies. As has been mentioned on several occasions already, the weakness of the banking sector continues to afflict the emerging private sector.

NOTES

* The first draft of the article was written by István Ábel with the assistance of Pierre Siklos and István Székely. A preliminary version was presented at the Conference on Bad Enterprise Debts in Central and Eastern Europe, Budapest, June 1995.
1. We use 'bad' in quotation marks to refer to the category in the Hungarian legislation, to distinguish the term from the one used to refer to bad (i.e., nonperforming) loans in general.
2. Of the total statutory provisions in 1992, HUF 118 billion was deferable according to Hungarian accounting procedures.
3. For obvious reasons, we do not name this bank. The sole purpose of discussing this example is to illustrate our argument. To make the bank involved and the original data unidentifiable, we use percentages instead of actual values. The analysis of the changes in the structure of the loans portfolio reveals important general characteristics of the problem.

8. The Banking Sector and Macro-economic Performance: A Current Assessment

PROLOGUE

The previous three chapters have explored the role of the banking sector in the early stages of the transition. The present chapter undertakes a current assessment. We examine, for Hungary in particular, but also for Poland and the Czech Republic, whether the banking sector in these countries in the mid to late 1990s are finally performing as true intermediaries as this term is understood in more advanced industrialized countries.

1. INTRODUCTION

When the countries of Central and Eastern Europe undertook the transformation of their economies in the early 1990s, the most pressing problems seemed to be the liberalization of prices and the impact that the sudden move to a decentralized form of decision-making, as opposed to the practice of central planning, would have on overall economic performance. In addition, there was the vital question of how to transfer state-owned assets into private hands. The rest, as they say, is history.

Different countries adopted various strategies for the transition to market, ranging from the shock therapy of Poland and the former Czechoslovakia to the gradualist route taken by Hungarian policy makers. For the most part, there seemed to be few lessons that could be learned from the history of western industrialized economies and so one could not be certain what the optimal road to market looked like at the outset of the transformation process.

Since 1990 at least, a vast literature has emerged which has sought to provide advice to policy makers based on the existing experience of the transformation process. Other studies, by contrast, looked at the comparative performance of economies which opted for different paths along the transition to market. In addition, there have been theoretical analyses of the transition based on frameworks used to previously explain economic performance in other transforming regions of the world, most notably the Southern Cone experience.

The focus on the macroeconomic dimension of the transformation to market was understandable since the speed with which the paradigm of central planning was abandoned in favour of market-driven economics was exceedingly rapid. It is appropriate, however, to begin examining the performance and problems facing some of the key sectors in the transitional or emerging market economies. Given the extant literature, it seems most useful to attempt an assessment of the place of the Hungarian banking sector in the mirror of both overall Hungarian economic performance, and banking developments elsewhere in the world. This is not to say that previous authors have entirely ignored the role of banks, or of other microeconomic factors more generally, in the transition. Quite the contrary. Indeed, there are too many works to cite here which have turned their attention to the great issues facing individual firms, including privatization, corporate governance, ownership and control, to name but a few of the research topics which have been covered by several authors early on in the transition process (e.g., see Blanchard et al. (1992), Sachs (1993), Dornbusch et al. (1993)). However, the general thrust of these studies has been about the *initial choice* of the institutional structure, and the optimal combination of policies which might be expected to minimize the transition costs to a fully functioning market economy, as opposed to the performance of segments of the microeconomy in relation to overall economic performance.

However, it may be now more fruitful for economists interested in the transition process to turn their attention to economic performance at a more disaggregate level.

As will be pointed out in the remainder of this chapter, a deeper exploration of the Hungarian banking sector, for example, reveals that banks in that country have a long way to go if they are to fulfil the same functions as in fully developed financial systems. While the overall prognosis of the situation is one of guarded optimism, the patient is still far from being out of danger. Similar comments can be made about banks in other emerging market economies such as the Czech Republic and Poland.

The following section briefly overviews the transformation process as it has affected the Hungarian banking sector. Section 3 then presents some general evidence about the Hungarian banking sector's performance in the mirror of macroeconomic performance in general, as well in the light of banking sector indicators in a few other key countries. Section 4 elaborates on earlier themes but with a greater focus on the microeconomic dimension of Hungarian banking sector performance. Some international comparative evidence is also presented. Section 5 concludes.

2. LIBERALIZATION, CONSOLIDATION AND PRIVATIZATION[1]

In 1987, the Hungarian government created a two-tiered banking system. While, on the surface, the newly created commercial banks were to operate much like any comparable institution in an industrialized country the newly created banks were, for the most part, saddled with the bad debts accumulated under the previous regime. In addition, the 'rules of the game' did not favour the kind of long-term financing that emerging private enterprises or existing (state-owned) enterprises required for the necessary restructuring. Indeed, there was a built-in bias in favour of lending to the central government (inter alia, see Ábel et al. (1994)). The situation, of course, became unsustainable as the central bank, the National Bank of Hungary (NBH), increasingly came to be relied upon to 'bail-out' banks which were independent in name only. Eventually, as the independence of the NBH was jeopardized, the government began a series of three loan consolidation programmes which began in 1992 (e.g., see Várhegyi (1994, 1995)) and whose cost, at least according to one estimate,[2] amounted to about 10% of Hungary's GDP. Resolution costs such as these are high even by the standards of emerging market economies, though several countries (e.g., Argentina, Chile, Bulgaria) experienced much higher costs in relation to GDP.

Ostensibly, the objective of the consolidation programmes was to 'cleanse' the balance sheets of the banks and move them to a sounder financial footing.[3] As we shall see, however, the Hungarian banking sector is still mired in the problems of the past. This partly explains the difficulties that Hungarian policy makers faced in their attempts both to privatize the largely state-owned banks and to open commercial banking to foreign competition. Complicating the privatization process was the perception of foreign investors that the true financial position of many of the banks up for sale was either being withheld from interested buyers or was was misleading at the very least, prompting them to start up operations as opposed to taking-over existing banks.[4] Adding to these problems has been the role of political factors. The events of the last few years with U-turns in economic policies, and the changing mix of political partners and influence in the coalition-type government set up by the current majority government elected in 1994, have not been conducive to creating stability in the financial sector. This is an extremely pertinent consideration for any assessment of the Hungarian banking sector, since Caprio and Klingebiel (1996) report that political factors played a significant role in stimulating banking crises in approximately one-third of the 29 systemic banking crises they investigated. It is only with the creation of the privatization agency (ÁPV Rt.) that privatization went on to a faster track with the result that a string of privatizations were to be finalized by 1997 (see Bank és Tőzde 1997). These moves were also prompted by hints at conflicts of interest aimed at politicians, in particular at the Finance Ministry which oversaw the work of the ÁPV Rt., and the perception that the government did not want to give up some of the advantages of state-ownership (see section 3 below). As pointed out recently by Mr Zsigmond Jarai, President of the Hungarian Credit Bank (MHB), 'Politicians play games with banks. It's crucial not to put them on the board' (Michaels (1997)).

As a result, Hungary's banking sector reforms are now viewed in a more favourable light. The efforts at privatization were crucial in large part because, freed from the symbiotic connection with the government and its treatment simply as another arm of fiscal policy, banks would be able to pursue more profitable business. This is in contrast to Czech banks which have essentially perpetuated the financial relationships of the past by largely owing the shares of the enterprises to which they also lend. As a result, the Czech experience with the transition, which has been held up as a model for other transitional economies to follow, now showing signs of malaise (e.g., see Boland (1997)).

The transitional experience in Hungary, in particular, suggests that policy makers understood perfectly well the central role that financial intermediation plays in an economy. By contrast, economists and others interested in the analysis of a macroeconomy facing the 'shock' from the transition process were somewhat guilty for failing to incorporate a neglected dimension in their models, namely the key role of the banking sector and of intermediation more generally.[5] Ábel and Siklos (1994) had previously pointed out that the problems facing several of the transitional economies in the early 1990s were reminiscent of the issues faced by the financial sector in the 1950s in the developed world where bank credit was scarce due to a combination of tight central bank monetary policy, the absence of financial innovations, and inadequate reforms putting banks on a sounder financial footing.

3. THE HUNGARIAN BANKING SECTOR IN THE MIRROR OF THE MACROECONOMY

There is little need to dwell on the overall macroeconomic performance of Hungary since, say, 1987, the year the first in a series of major financial reforms were introduced. Suffice it to say that GDP growth has been largely negative (see Siklos and Ábel (1995, Table 13.1))and the budget deficit as a percentage of GDP was considered high by international standards, at least until 1994. In addition, Hungary has experienced for the first time a significant amount of open unemployment culminating in an unemployment rate in double digits, though lower than in several Western European countries. Finally, it is well-known that Hungary was and continues to be saddled by a large foreign debt and, although the fiscal situation has improved dramatically, in part under pressure from the international financial community, Hungary's gross debt to GDP ratio continued to rise into 1995.

A more disaggregated picture is presented in Figure 8.1 which shows the percentage change in 'output' in key sectors of the Hungarian economy. With the exception of the tourism industry, the slump in all of the other major sectors is evident. But the slump continues to this day in the manufacturing sector (with the exception of a one time sharp rise in 1994) while the other sectors appeared to have turned the corner around 1993, and some sectors such as construction and industrial output overall (i.e., industrial production) registered positive growth rates by 1992, that is, two years before Hungary's GDP growth became positive. Interestingly, if one examines the 'investment' loans made by the Hungarian banking sector as a whole, manufacturing's share of these loans has actually risen slightly since 1992[6] while tourism's share has been small and was lower in 1995 than in 1992.[7] Indeed, there has been a remarkable constancy in the share of such loans to the major sectors of the economy. This could be an indication that banks are unwilling to invest in the sectors which appear to be most promising in economic terms or are unable to do so for institutional reasons.

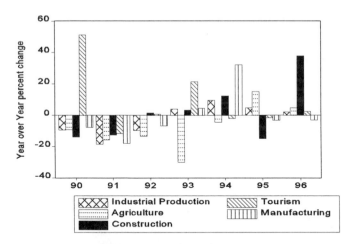

Source: National Bank of Hungary, *Monthly Report* (various issues).

Notes: Data for tourism based on the rate of change of foreign tourists into Hungary. Data for transport based on the rate of change of thousands of tons of goods transported. Other data from seftoral GDP estimates.

Figure 8.1 Output Changes in Selected Economic Sectors

When we turn our attention to the banking sector in general, we immediately get a glimpse how its overall performance has had a potentially negative impact on the speed and intensity of the recovery and has, in effect, acted as a brake on the country's emergence from the transition process. Given the relative performance of each of these sectors, this does not bode well for the overall health of the Hungarian banking industry.

Table 8.1 reveals that domestic credit,[8] in real terms, has actually steadily fallen since 1989. By contrast, capital inflows, in the form of foreign direct investment, have been sizeable. This is true whether the figures are in terms of the size of these inflows as a percentage of GDP, as in Table 8.1, or in US dollar terms, as shown in Table 8.2. Either way, these figures require financial sector intermediation but, unlike the experience of the Southern Cone (e.g., see Edwards and Végh (1997)), the outcome has been a fiscal expansion instead of the consumption boom that afflicted South American countries. The process of intermediating these inflows through an essentially weak banking system also contributed to the real appreciation of the currency which has hurt Hungary's competitiveness (see, inter alia, Siklos and Ábel (1997a, 1997b)).[9]

Table 8.1 Some Macroeconomic Indicators of the Hungarian Banking System

Year	Real Dom. Cr. (1990 PRICES)	Cap./ GDP (%)	Loan/ Dep. (%)	Number of Commercial Banks (of which State-owned)		
				Large	Medium	Small
1989	18.91	NA	228	5 (5)	4 (0)	17 (3)
1990	17.26	NA	169	5 (5)	5 (0)	22 (4)
1991	14.06	4.4	171	6 (5)	9 (0)	20 (5)
1992	13.82	3.9	148	6 (5)	8 (0)	21 (5)
1993	14.47	6.1	148	7 (5)	8 (3)	25 (9)
1994	15.17	2.8	149	7 (4)	11 (3)	25 (11)
1995	13.40	10.1	123	7 (2)	11 (5)	23 (9)
1996	13.31	NA	146	NA	NA	NA

Notes:
a. Domestic credit of the commercial banking system divided by PPI.
b. Direct investment income converted into forint (HUF) at average annual exchange rates divided by GDP at market procurement prices.
c. Enterprise and personal loans to total deposits.
d. Majority interest in the State.

Sources: National Bank of Hungary, *Monthly Report* (various issues) and *Annual Report* (various issues).

Table 8.2 Quality of Loans in the Hungarian Banking System

Year	Classification	
	Problem free (%)	Qualified (%)
1992	88.5	11.5
1993	71.5	28.5
1994	78	22
1995	83.4	16.6

Notes:
a. The sum of loans classified as needing special attention, substandard, doubtful or bad.
b. Since 1992, the data reflect the impact of the loan consolidation programmes.

The loan deposit ratio is also seen to be high, albeit falling, even by the standards of other countries (see the following section), and reflects the bias towards lending to the fiscal authorities, also an indicator of an unhealthy banking sector.

The final set of columns in Table 8.1 show the number of commercial banks by size. While state-ownership of large banks is disappearing quickly, the number of small and medium-sized banks with majority state-ownership has risen since the early 1990s. This reflects the government's focus on privatizing the large banks while lagging behind in its attempts to privatize the rest of the banking system. As noted earlier, however, the government and the ÁPV Rt. have demonstrated a greater urgency in privatizing the remaining state-controlled banks. Unfortunately, in certain other important areas, the banking sector in Hungary reveals exactly in what sense it can be termed to be in a 'weak' state while, in the next section, indicators that are symptomatic of this weakness and which assess the potential implications for the economy as a whole are presented.

An important distinction between the Hungarian experience and that of industrialized countries is that the fraction of the banking system that is foreign-owned has been relatively large and is growing rapidly.[10] Typically, the growth of banking was a domestic affair in most industrialized countries. Indeed, in countries such as the US and Canada there were explicit and implicit barriers to entry. One advantage of the Hungarian approach is that the banking sector can better withstand an adverse economic shock to the domestic economy because foreign banks have ready access to a greater pool of liquidity. In addition, foreign banks have at their immediate disposal a greater stock of expertise about all facets of the banking industry. Disadvantages include a potential bias towards lending to firms based in the home country and a possible negative externality from the effects of the presence of foreign banks on the survivability of domestic banks.

Table 8.3 presents some data showing the overall quality of loans in the banking sector. As noted earlier, the Hungarian government has pushed through three loan consolidation programmes since 1992 (the last ending in 1995). Yet,[11] the percentage of qualified loans is actually higher in 1995 than in 1992 although down considerably from 1993-94 levels. Now, there are two ways of interpreting this piece of evidence. One of the complaints levelled at banks in all the transitional economies is that management had little incentive to run banking operations efficiently as long as the government was likely to bail them out. The fact that there have been three loan consolidation programmes so far certainly raises the spectre that the moral hazard problem inherent with the introduction of such schemes is a significant one. As the president of the MHB pointed out recently, 'Recapitalization saved the bank, but didn't force change' (Michaels (1997)).

Table 8.3 Foreign Direct Investment in Hungary

Year	Millions of US$
1989	187
1990	311
1991	1459
1992	1471
1993	2339
1994	1146
1995	4453

Source: National Bank of Hungary, *Monthly Report* (various issues).

Lax or inadequate banking supervision and regulatory forbearance would also contribute to the relatively high proportion of qualified loans.[12] Alternatively, one could interpret the figure for 1995, in relation to the data for the earlier years, as a reflection of the fact that, unfettered by government involvement, banks are leaning more towards making commercial and personal loans and that, in the present phase of the transition, failure rates are likely to be higher than one would experience in other banking systems. Data to be presented in the following section suggest the latter interpretation has some support though the available data do not point unequivocally in either direction.

More troubling to western eyes is the structure of Hungarian banking assets. Figures 8.2 to 8.4 make the point. Figure 8.2 shows the proportion of total assets which represent credits to the central government for both Hungary and

Poland, another transitional economy much compared to Hungary. While the banking sector in Hungary still devotes almost half of its assets to lending to governments, lending to the fiscal authorities is negligible in Poland. Again these data reflect the poor role of banks as intermediaries in Hungary relative to Poland. In the next section, I show that this state of affairs reflects badly on the Hungarian banking system in comparison with other OECD countries more generally. Not surprisingly then, as revealed in Figure 8.3, Hungary also lags behind in the share of its assets held in the form of non-government securities while Poland's share is more typical of such holdings in more developed banking sectors. Finally, Figure 8.4 shows that while Hungary had caught up with Poland by 1995, in terms of its portfolio allocation towards lending to the non-banking sector, banks in general in the transition behave far less as intermediaries than in countries such as Germany. Hence, if banks are to act

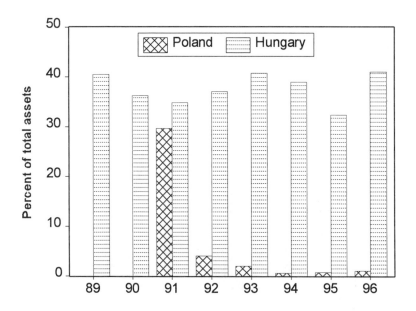

Sources: National Bank of Hungary, Monthly Report (various issues), and National Bank of Poland, Information Bulletin (various issues).

Note: The data represent credits to the central government as a percentage of total assets. There were no data for Poland for 1989 and 1990.

Figure 8.2 Credits to the Central Government in Hungary and Poland

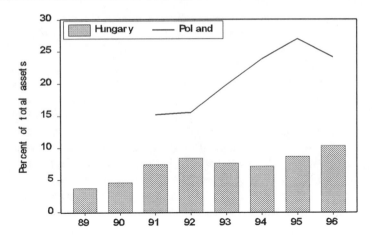

Sources: National Bank of Hungary, *Monthly Report* (various issues) and National Bank of Poland, *Information Bulletin* (various issues).

Note: Holdings of non-government securities as a percentage of total assets. There were no data for Poland for 1989 and 1990.

Figure 8.3   Holdings of Securities by the Banking Sector in Hungary and Poland

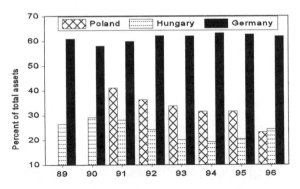

Sources: National Bank of Hungary, *Monthly Report* (various issues), National Bank of Poland, *Information Bulletin* (various issues), Bundesbank, *Monthly Report* (various issues).

Note: For Hungary and Poland, credits to enterprises as a percentage of total assets. For Germany, lending to non-banks (adjusted for Treasury Bill holdings) as a percentage of total assets. There were no data for Poland for 1989 and 1990.

Figure 8.4 Lending to the Private Sector in Hungary, Poland and Germany

as the engine of economic growth, then failure in this respect is most glaring in their timid lending to the non-bank sector. To be sure, there are hopeful signs in this regard, as we shall see in the following section, but banks still fail to meet the essential criteria of intermediation, at least as these are understood in western industrialized economies.

Banks, of course, are not the only institutions to lend funds. In industrialized economies, one of the greatest threats to the traditional intermediation function of banks comes from lending by non-bank institutions. Interestingly, Hungary is experiencing the same phenomenon, as revealed by Table 8.4, which shows a steady rise since 1994 in the share of lending by the non-bank private sector with the result that, in a sense, the banking sector in Hungary is shrinking. By contrast, developments in the Czech Republic and Poland suggest the opposite with the share of lending by the banking sector rising steadily in both countries.

Table 8.4 Share of Lending by Banks and Non-Banking Institutions

Year	Banks			Non-Banks		
	Hungary	Czech R.	Poland	Hungary	Czech R.	Poland
	%			%		
1994	59.2	53.1	28	11.8	34.3	38.2
1995	56.7	61.3	26.1	16.4	29.3	29.6
mid-1996	58.5	60.3	30.7	17.6	31.6	28

Source: 'The Maturity, Sectoral and Nationality Distribution of International Bank Lending', first half of 1996, Basle: BIS, January 1997.

4. THE HUNGARIAN BANKING SECTOR AND THE INTERNATIONAL DIMENSION

In the last section, a general overview of the Hungarian banking sector was provided. The purpose of this section is to explore how the monetary policy of the NBH, as reflected in interest rate and exchange rate developments, have impacted on the banking sector as well as the Hungarian banking sector's performance in the mirror of developments in other countries. Since NBH monetary and exchange rate policies are exogenous factors to the banking sector, but NBH policies are themselves driven by international influences, these are taken as given. Hence, for example, this implies that nominal interest rates and inflationary expectations will be significantly higher in Hungary than in, say, Germany.[13] Moreover, in an era of global banking, it is insufficient to concentrate on the domestic scene alone as Hungarian banks, whether foreign-owned or not, will have to compete with banks worldwide. However, this fact need not prevent the smooth or efficient operation of the intermediation function. In particular, if the costs of banking operations are high, either because the interest rate risks of lending to the emerging private sector are considerable, or owing to the need for high profit margins arising from the costs of restructuring, training of staff, assessment of credit risks, or meeting relatively high reserve requirements, then the ability of intermediaries to perform their functions will be impaired. It is well-known, for example, that reserve requirements in Hungary are high by the standards of most OECD economies (see Kemme (1994) and NBH, *Annual Reports* (various issues) for reserve requirement data). While some authors (e.g., Edwards and Végh (1997)) have argued that reserve requirements can be an effective tool in controlling credit growth, if properly used by policy makers, there are also serious drawbacks with this instrument of policy (also see Loungani and Rush (1995)). First, in a world where capital is highly mobile, it is likely that banks can easily access needed liquidity quickly and at the lowest price although, as far as transitional economies are concerned, the perception of credit risk remains high. This may be largely owing to the failure of supervision and the inability or lack of incentives, until recently, for Hungarian banks to assess credit risk themselves.[14] Second, it is well-known that high reserve requirements have been used as a form of taxation or seigniorage in some countries (e.g., Italy). The introduction of interest payments on balances at the central bank helps mitigate this problem but does not eliminate it entirely since returns on such funds are usually far superior in the marketplace. Moreover, there is the uncertainty associated with frequent changes in the structure and size of the reserve requirements. Again, a look at NBH, *Annual Reports* over the years since 1987 confirms this to be a problem too.[15]

Another contributing factor is the scope of operations permitted by banks. As a former governor of the NBH, Péter Ákos Bod, pointed out not long ago (Bod (1994)) Hungarian policy makers have not yet decided whether to adopt the Anglo-Saxon model (e.g., as in the US) or the universal banking system model (e.g., as in Germany) for the banking system. As we shall see, these features of the structure of the banking system impact on the costs of banking operations.

Figure 8.5 shows, for Hungary and Germany, the average gap between borrowing and lending rates at commercial banks. Interestingly, not only has the gap in both countries fallen, no doubt aided by lower and less volatile interest rates generally, but the differential between Germany's gap and Hungary's gap has also fallen rather dramatically. This is a hopeful sign because the data reflect improved competitiveness in the Hungarian banking sector.

An additional difficulty faced by banks in Hungary is the uncertainty and dispersion in the credit risks of its clients. The spread between highest and lowest lending and deposit rates is significantly higher in Hungary than in Germany, at both short and long maturities. One positive interpretation of this outcome is that it reflects the relatively wider dispersion in the likely economic success of individuals or enterprises who take out loans. Alternatively, improved credit risk assessment might contribute to reducing the spread over time. Also interesting to note is that while lending-borrowing spreads match each other reasonably well at short maturities, the spread is much greater for long-term lending rates than for borrowing rates at Hungarian commercial banks.

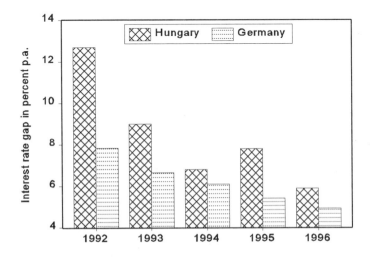

Sources: National Bank of Hungary, *Monthly Report* (various issues), and Bundesbank, *Monthly Report* (various issues).

Note: For Hungary, the difference between average lending rates and deposit rates at commercial banks. For Germany, the difference between current account lending rates and the rate on instalment savings contracts.

Figure 8.5 Interest Rate Gap in Hungary and Germany

Figure 8.6 gives some idea of the real costs of borrowing and lending at German and Hungarian banks. While the real ex post rates are comparable in the two countries, they are clearly more volatile in the Hungarian case. This, of course, reflects the well-known connection between high inflation and inflation volatility but such an outcome also hampers the extent to which intermediation performs its vital functions.[16]

(A)

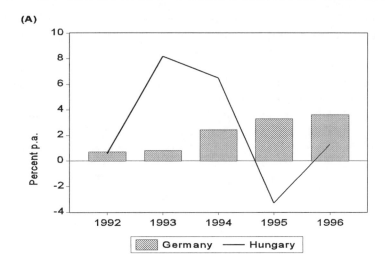

(B)

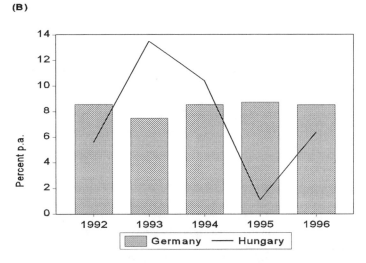

Sources: National Bank of Hungary, *Monthly Reports* (various issues), and Bundesbank, *Monthly Reports* (various issues).

Note to (A): For Hungary, the rate on corproate deposits which mature within a year less inflation in the industrial price index. For Germany, the rate on instalment savings contracts less CPI inflation.
Note to (B): For Hungary, the corporate lending rate by commercial banks less inflation in the industrial price index. For Germany, the current account lending rate by credit institutions less CPI inflation.

Figure 8.6   Real Ex Post Interest Rates in Germany and Hungary

Finally, Figure 8.7 presents some comparative data which includes, in addition to Germany, the US and Greece. Unlike Germany, US banks are more severely restricted in both the scope of their operations and, until recently, their location and, as a consequence, their size too. Greece, on the other hand, could serve as an illustration of another economy with a degree of financial development comparable to that of Hungary. Only data for the period 1991-94 are available while data for 1994 are incomplete in the case of Hungary. The extent to which Hungarian banks generate revenues via interest income is, broadly speaking, comparable to the German and US experiences. As noted earlier, borrowing from the central bank remains a problem for Hungarian banks in relation to, say, German banks.[17]

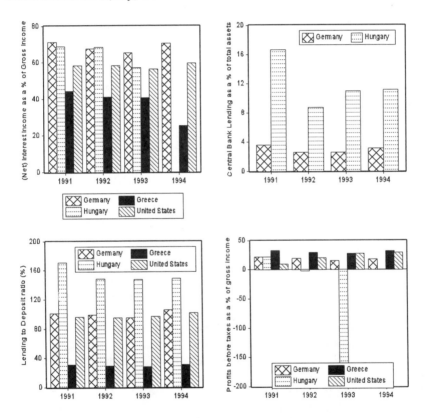

Sources: Bank Profitability (Paris: *OECD*, 1996) and National Bank of Hungary, *Monthly Report* (various issues), *Annual Report* (various issues).

Figure 8.7 Bank Profitability in a Selection of OECD Countries

The loan-deposit ratio which, as noted earlier, is high for Hungary, appears clearly excessive in comparison with the Greek and German experiences. Combined with the high credit risk issue problem discussed earlier, this suggests a relatively higher likelihood of system failure in the Hungarian case. Also, Hungarian banking sector profit performance is, perhaps not surprisingly given the foregoing discussion, substantially inferior to that of other countries with vastly different banking systems. Table 8.5 provides a tentative statistical test which explores some of the potential determinants of bank profitability.

Table 8.5 Panel Regression Estimates of the Determinants of Bank Profits

Variable	Coefficient (Std. Error)
Interest Income ratio	-0.75 (0.709)
Loan-deposit ratio	3.74 (1.90)*
fixed effects	
Germany	-304.28
Hungary	-574.13
Greece	-52.30
United States	-299.03
Adjusted R²	0.29

* signifies statistically significant at the 5% level.
Dependent variable is profits as a percentage of total revenues for the banking sectors in the countries listed above.

Data limitations being rather severe, the results of this exercise can only be viewed as illustrative. A panel regression was run using data for the four countries considered in Figure 8.7. We were interested in whether profit performance across the four banking systems considered could be explained by the fractions of revenues generated via interest as well as the loan-deposit ratio. The latter variable, a rough proxy for leverage, significantly raises the profit rate, as one would expect, while the interest income variable is statistically insignificant. The variable labelled 'fixed effects' gives the country-specific profit rates after allowance for the other factors. Overall, we see from the adjusted coefficient of determination (i.e. the R^2) that profitability remains to be explained by factors other than leverage and sources of income and one can only presume that the structural factors which have and continue to impinge on the Hungarian banking sector are relevant in this connection. Table 8.6 gives some idea of leverage ratios in Hungary relative to the range of ratios in Germany and the USA. Putting aside the difficult issue of measurement errors and differences arising out of evolving accounting standards in these countries, the available data reveal ratios in Hungary to be rather low not only by the standards of more industrialized economies' banking systems better able to weather adverse economic shocks to their financial sectors but also by the capital-adequacy standards of other emerging market economies (Goldstein and Turner (1996, Table 4)).

Table 8.6 Leverage Ratios in Hungary, Germany and the USA

Year	Leverage ratios[1] (%)		
	Hungary	Germany[2]	USA[2]
1996	5		
1995	6		
1994	9.6		
1993	9.8		
1992	4.8		
1991	5.6	1.15-3.98	2.6-8.87
1990	5.6	0.7-60.90	3.3-24.5
1989	6	1.09-19.86	1.12-16.47
1988	6.4	1.17-17.09	2.73-14.93
1987	5	1.43-17.09	1.37-11.65

Sources: Ábel and Szakadát (1997), and *The Banker* (various July issues).
Notes:
[1] Equity divided by assets.
[2] Highest to lowest among banks surveyed. In 1988, *The Banker* expanded its survey from the top 500 to the top 1000 banks.

The final piece of evidence is presented in Table 8.7. Here I consider the evolution of claims outstanding at the six largest banks.[18] There are three noticeable features in the data. First, while the six largest banks have increased loans to households and enterprises and government bond holdings in more or less equal proportions, holdings of government bonds have risen by 324% in the period 1991-95 while total loans have risen by only 142% over the same period in the banking system as a whole.[19] Second, lending to households and enterprises has generally risen faster, at both the short and long ends of the maturity structure, in the banking system as a whole than at the six largest banks. Third, long-term lending has risen faster than short-term lending. Since this is likely to be the type of lending that is most needed to finance long-run economic growth in the fledgling private sector, this is a positive sign which bodes well for the positive intermediary role of the banking system. Nevertheless, the fact that credit has, as noted earlier, fallen in real terms, is hardly conducive to the prospects of strong future economic growth.

Table 8.7   Distribution of Claims of Banks in Hungary
Six largest banks

Year	1991	1992	1993	1994	1995
Total (HUF billion)	1017.8	1081.4	956	1092.5	1250.7
Priv.[1] <1 yr	418.9	400.7	453.7	435.4	448
≥ 1 yr	315.7	361.5	396.5	468.8	470.9
Ent.[2] < 1 yr	123.6	134.4	171.3	163.6	219.1
≥ 1 yr	71.3	56.7	70	100.8	105.1
Govt. Bonds	85.1	82.7	80.8	83.3	95.3

Banking sector total*

Year	1991	1992	1993	1994	1995
Total (HUF billion)	1380.5	1392	1300.4	1706.8	1869.2
Priv. <1 yr	551.7	555	647.3	727.2	737.5
≥1 yr	340.0	394.9	447.7	583.4	570.5
Ent. <1 yr	215.4	213.3	268.5	326.9	350.9
≥ 1 yr	72.5	62.1	80.1	151.7	172.2
Gvt. Bonds	45.1	103.3	137.9	137.8	146.3

* consists of 35 banks.
Source: I. Ábel.

Notes:
[1] Priv. means personal and household loans.
[2] Ent. means loans to companies and enterprises.

5. CONCLUSIONS

This chapter has attempted to assess the performance of the Hungarian banking sector both in relation to the country's overall economic performance as well as in relation to banking sector performance in other countries, including other emerging market economies. While there are several hopeful signs which bode well for the positive future role of banks in Hungary, the current state of affairs leaves much to be desired. Banks, as intermediaries, should be assisting not to hamper the economic growth potential of the country. However, a combination of past policies and practices has fashioned a banking sector still too subservient to the State in a number of ways. While privatization will no doubt change the face of the Hungarian banking sector, the present signs indicate that considerable portfolio reallocation will be required for banks to be able to assume the role of banks elsewhere and the value-added potential that intermediaries fulfil in industrialized countries.

No attempt, however, was made to assess the potential for recurring crises or failures which produced three loan consolidation programmes.[20] Adequate banking supervision, regulation and disclosure are key elements in this respect. It is clear, however, from the data considered in this chapter, that the danger of systemic failure in the Hungarian banking system has subsided for now. Whether this will remain the case if future macroeconomic shocks, especially from abroad, afflict the Hungarian economy, is unclear. Nevertheless, greater availability of banking sector data would be a useful step in the right direction so that interested observers are given the raw materials necessary to warn of future problems.

POSTSCRIPT

It remains to be seen how competitive the banking sector in emerging market economies will become as a result of the important role played by foreign banks. Just as important, it is also unclear whether foreign banks will squeeze domestic firms out of credit markets. As has been emphasized in this chapter, the large role played by foreign banks in emerging market economies is rather unprecedented in the manner in which this has been achieved.

NOTES

*   The original draft of this paper, under the title 'The Neglected Dimension: The Hungarian Banking Sector and Macroeconomic Performance' was prepared by Pierre Siklos. It was an invited address presented at the Conference on Microeconomic Factors of Global Competitiveness, Budapest, Hungary, May 1997. The paper was revised slightly thanks to some useful suggestions made by conference participants.

1.   For more details about this phase of the transition in Hungary and elsewhere in Eastern Europe, see Siklos and Ábel (1995), and Ábel and Szakadát (1997).

2.   See *The Economist*, 12-18 April 1997, p.5, and Goldstein and Turner (1996).

3.   The first consolidation programme was described as a 'bank' centred scheme, the second a 'credit' based programme, while the third was a 'company oriented plan. The first two programmes were deemed failures because none forced change on the banks or in their lending practices. The third programme, by contrast, was aimed at the root cause of one of the weaknesses of the Hungarian economy, namely the poor credit position of enterprises, especially of the large state-owned variety. See 'Consolidation of the Hungarian Banking System', NBH, *Monthly Report,* 10/94, pp.145-57.

4. A common complaint about foreign entrants into the Hungarian banking sector is that they enjoyed an immediate comparative advantage over any fledgling domestic bank, including better access to cheaper sources of funds, tax concessions, and an ability to exploit existing market imperfections.

5. For a recent formal attempt at giving the banking sector a role to play in generating and propagating business cycles, see Edwards and Végh (1997). There is, however, a long tradition of dealing with the role of banks in the macroeconomy often referred to as the credit channel of monetary policy. Until fairly recently, however, this approach had been underemphasized. Also see Ábel and Siklos (1994) who use this approach to explore the links between the banking sector and overall economic performance in the early years of the transition process.

6. The share stood at 32.4% in 1995 and was 31.3% in 1992.

7. 2.5% in 1995 against 2.7% in 1992.

8. As measured on the banking sector's balance sheet. See National Bank of Hungary, *Monthly Report* (various issues).

9. Indeed, Hungary's terms of trade have shown a significant deterioration since at least 1994. Kaminsky and Reinhart (1995) argue that the terms of trade is one of the key indicators leading to a banking crisis in their empirical study of industrial and emerging market economies.

10. Várhegyi (1997, Table 2) calculates that 15.1% of Hungarian banks were foreign-owned in 1994. The same percentage rose to 35.6% in 1995 and is expected to reach 47% in 1996. These percentages would place Hungary in third place in terms of foreign ownership behind Hong Kong and Singapore in a group of 17 emerging market economies surveyed by Goldstein and Turner (1996, Table 6).

11. As will be pointed out in the conclusions of this chapter, it is often difficult to get a complete picture of the true state of the banking sector from NBH monthly and annual reports. This is because either the terminology employed in the report changes over time, or legal changes, and there have been many, imply that the data are not comparable through time. For example, it is not exactly clear how balance sheet figures are adjusted for the effects of the various loan consolidation programmes.

12. This has been a particularly significant problem for the Czech banking system.

13. This aspect is explored in greater detail in Siklos and Ábel (1997b).

14. The costs of performing the necessary risk assessments should fall as software tools, such as, for example, the recently introduced Credit Metrics program by J.P. Morgan, make it simpler for managers to perform the required calculations.

15. And partly explains why they were eventually abandoned in countries such as Canada.

16. The connection between inflation and intermediation is also well-known. See, for example, Siklos (1997, chapter 3) for a textbook discussion of the subject.

17. US banks are prohibited from direct borrowing from the central bank while the figures are negligible for Greece.

18. They are: Magyar Hitel Bank, Magyar Külkereskedelmi Bank, Kereskedelmi Bank, Budapest Bank, Postabank and OTP.

19. The banking system here consists of 35 banks in the sample of available data.

20. See, however, Honohan (1997) and Goldstein and Turner (1996) for a discussion of the relevant issues.

9. Central Bank Independence in the Early Stages of the Transition*

PROLOGUE

In a socialist economy the central bank was an instrument of the state. In a market economy the separation of the Treasury from the printing press is, of course, considered vital. While this much was clearly understood, policy makers could choose from a number of available models in industrialized economies for the actual structure of central bank-government relations.

This chapter considers both the process and problems faced by several former centrally planned economies in ceding control over monetary policy to an independent central bank. The chapter attempts to assess the degree of independence using both a qualitative scale as well as an econometrically based assessment. The overall impression of the transformation process of central banks is that legislative independence generally did not provide comparable effective independence for two reasons: an ineffective capital market and the choice of exchange rate regimes.

1. INTRODUCTION[1]

The notion that central banking authorities should have independent control over monetary policy gained credence during the 1980s, following the severe stagflation faced by industrialized countries during the 1970s and early 1980s. Many came to believe that the primary task of the central bank was to ensure some kind of price stability.[2]

The collapse of central planning toward the end of the 1980s in Central and Eastern Europe, in particular in Bulgaria, Czechoslovakia, Hungary and Poland, meant first the end of the monobank concept of the banking system and the introduction of a two-tier banking system with a central bank and an independent commercial banking sector. Kemme (1992), Calvo and Kumar (1993), and Borensztein and Masson (1993a, 1993b) review the reforms undertaken in this sphere in the transitional economies.

Arguably, the evolution of any transition will be dependent on the model for the central bank chosen by the transitional economies (hereafter TEs). Hence, this chapter provides an assessment of the legal and economic independence of the newly reformed central banks as well as some tentative estimates of central bank reaction functions to economic and political fundamentals.

The chapter is organized as follows. The next section provides a brief overview of existing concepts of central bank independence. Estimates of an index of central bank independence are then constructed for Hungary, Poland, the Czech and Slovak Republics, and Bulgaria, based on the new legislation governing their central banks. These indexes are also compared with the current inflation performance in the same countries as well as in relation to existing indexes based on the legislation under the central planning regime. A separate section presents econometric estimates of selected central bank reaction functions for Hungary and Poland. A concluding section summarizes and suggests the lessons learned so far.

2. THE MEANING OF CENTRAL BANK INDEPENDENCE

While relatively few central banks are mandated to achieve price stability alone, the notion that independent action by central banks in the area of monetary policy can be evaluated via inflation performance has received considerable attention lately. Beginning with the work of Parkin and Bade (1978), with more recent contributions by, among others, Burdekin and Willett (1991), Grilli *et al.* (1991), Cukierman (1992), Alesina and Summers (1993), Banaian *et al.* (1995), qualitative comparisons of central bank legislation and inflation performance suggest that more independent central banks deliver less inflation.[3] Except for Cukierman (1992, pp.427-30), however, these studies tend to assume rather than demonstrate empirically the idea that more central bank independence *causes* lower inflation. Yet, the causal relationship between central bank independence and inflation can easily be reversed. Germany is the archetypical case in this regard because its inflation record has long been associated with a historical aversion to inflation which has, in turn, reinforced central bank independence rather than having been caused by it.[4] As another illustration of this point consider Figures 9.1 and 9.2. Figure 9.1 shows the annual rate of inflation in the G-7 countries. The first vertical bar represents the approximate date of the collapse of Bretton Woods in the early 1970s. The second vertical bar marks the beginning of the European Monetary System (EMS) in 1979. Figure 9.2, by contrast, plots the annual rate of inflation for progressively smaller samples, also for the G-7 countries. The first observation gives the average rate of inflation for the period 1960-1993 based on quarterly data. Every observation thereafter gives the average rate of inflation for samples which omit one year at a time from the beginning of the sample. Thus, the second observation is for the sample 1961-1993, and so on, until the last observation plotted which represents the average inflation rate in 1993 only. Notice that average inflation rates diverge considerably even under

Annual Inflation Rates in Consumer Prices

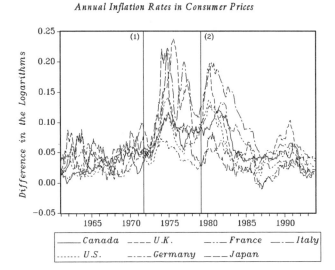

Figure 9.1 Annual Rates of Inflation in the G-7

the Bretton Woods system but divergence is even more apparent following the collapse of the adjustable peg exchange rate system. Convergence in inflation is more apparent during the last few observations which essentially represent the decade of the 1980s, and especially so during the early 1990s.[5] Yet, even according to the most detailed accounts of central bank independence, based on an analysis of the legal provisions governing their behaviour (Cukierman, 1992, Chapter 19, Appendix A), only Canada and Italy among the G-7 countries (see Rymes, 1994, for Canada and Cottarelli, 1993, for Italy) experienced any major changes in central bank legislation since the 1960s. Less significant changes took place in France and the UK during the period under investigation.[6] Notice, for example, that the UK inflation rate is consistently higher than France's and that the gap between their inflation rates widened during the 1980s despite the fact that neither central bank was formally independent of the government in the period considered. Similarly, Italy's inflation rate has been substantially higher than Canada's even though, at least until 1987 in the case of Italy, both central banks have been considered formally dependent.[7] The European exchange rate target zone mechanism may have played a relatively more dominant role in explaining the relative inflation

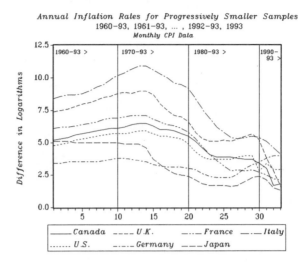

Figure 9.2 Average Annual Rates of Inflation in the G-7

performance of these two countries than central bank behaviour alone. Japan, too, offers a lesson in contrasts between inflation performance and central bank legislation. While the Bank of Japan is not considered to be formally independent of the government and the legislation governing its behaviour has hardly changed over the last thirty years, inflation in Japan has varied considerably since 1960. A low inflation country until the early 1970s, Japan posted the highest inflation rate among the G-7 in the aftermath of the two OPEC oil price shocks. But by the mid-1980s Japan's inflation rate was one of the lowest among the G-7. Thus, Japan has proved to be difficult to classify for some authors who associate the degree of legal independence with inflation performance.[8] Instead, what Figure 9.1 suggests is that one important determinant of central bank independence is the exchange rate regime, about which more is said below.

The most ambitious attempt at providing a numerical measure of legal or statutory independence is in Cukierman (1992, Chapter 19). He constructs an index of central bank independence for 70 countries by deriving numerical values for more than 17 different characteristics of central banking legislation such as term of office, conflict resolution, legislated goals of the central bank, to name but a few of the aspects of the legislation considered. This approach is useful because it allows for a comparison between legislated goals and actual economic performance. At the same time, however, focusing too narrowly on the legislation can lead to a confusion between what a central bank actually does as opposed to what it is legislated to do (see also Mayer, 1976, and Cargill, 1989, in this connection). Famous examples come from the Japanese experience noted previously, as well as the US where the Federal Reserve is guaranteed independence but has often been seen as acting to improve re-election prospects of the President (Woolley, 1988).[9]

More recently, questions have been raised about the connection between inflation and central bank independence because such a relationship fails to hold for developing countries as well as the newly industrialized countries (Siklos, 1995), and because central bank independence appears to be better explained as the result of financial opposition to inflation (Posen, 1995).

A separate strand of the literature estimates, via econometric techniques, central bank reaction functions. This approach seeks to determine how instruments of monetary policy (I) react to aggregate economic information (Z; presumably available with a lag) as well as political factors (P). The equation

$$I_t = B(L)Z_{t-1} + C(L)P_t \qquad (9.1)$$

where $B(L)$ and $C(L)$ are distributed lags, describes the formulation of a typical reaction function. Political factors are ordinarily represented by dummy variables. These are active around election dates or when there are changes in the ideological make-up of government. Johnson and Siklos (1996) provide a brief survey of the literature on central bank reaction functions, while Alesina (1988), Nordhaus (1989), and Cukierman (1992, Chapter 17), review the literature on political and partisan effects on aggregate economic activity. The exact specification of the dummy variables is a function of how economic agents form expectations. However, as these types of political influences are not yet feasibly measured for the transitional economies, we shall instead examine the estimates of reaction functions in light of the role played by economic fundamentals and by introducing a measure of the influence of political events on central bank behaviour.

3. LEGAL AND ECONOMIC INDEPENDENCE IN FIVE TRANSITIONAL ECONOMIES

3.1 Credible Central Bank Reforms?

Several authors (e.g., Jindra, 1992; Boguszewski *et al.*, 1992; Rudka, 1992; Balassa, 1992) have emphasized the fact that the new central bank laws in the FCPEs of Hungary, Poland, the former Czechoslovakia and Bulgaria were modelled after the statutes of the Bundesbank. Presumably, the belief is that the transitional economies can, at least eventually, inherit the enviable inflation record of Germany. In the case of Czechoslovakia this is perhaps no accident. After the end of World War I the newly created Czechoslovakia did not experience hyperinflation unlike Germany, Austria and Hungary. Officials involved in the transition of the Czechoslovak National Bank not only remembered these facts but they also felt an affinity for the importance of price stability as an objective of monetary policy.

Nevertheless, there exists a myth about the Bundesbank whose legal autonomy is, in fact, quite limited. In the first place, there is no legal prescription to maintain price stability unlike the legislation in Austria, the Netherlands or New Zealand. Indeed, the legislation governing the Bundesbank stipulates that it is ultimately required to support the economic policy of the federal government (Article 12, see Aufricht, 1967, p.255).[10] Nor is the Bundesbank absolutely mandated to act independently of the government.[11] Thus, unless the TEs can import the German 'cultural' aversion to inflation, the design of the existing legislation is flawed. Even if one does not believe that Germans are predisposed to desire low inflation, the Bundesbank is a creature of the federal system in which representatives of each Land or regional state generate *de facto* independence for the central bank (Lohmann, 1994).[12] Since neither Bulgaria, Hungary, Poland, the Czech or Slovak Republics are federal states in the German sense it becomes more apparent that the design of central bank laws in the former CPEs may have relied too heavily on an inappropriate model. Indeed, one could argue that the legislation in the transitional economies should be much clearer about the responsibilities of the central bank than in industrialized countries, in view of the concerns expressed by international organizations, such as the IMF, about inflation following the replacement of the central planning model with a market-driven economy. An exception to this interpretation may be the Czech Republic which has adopted a price stability objective, but whether this goal is a credible one is open to question, as we shall see, not least because none of these financial systems in the transitional economies is mature in the western industrialized sense of the term.

3.2 Measurement

Independence is defined in terms of a central bank's ability to use instruments of monetary policy to accomplish primarily an inflation objective. Clearly, central banks may also pursue other objectives in the belief that there exists a short-run trade-off between inflation and output or unemployment. This would produce a broader definition of legal independence. By examining the legislation governing central banks we can provide a sense of notional independence conferred on a central bank by legislators, that is, the degree of independence legislators intended to give the central bank. One difficulty with this approach is that central banking legislation changes very infrequently. Thus, it is possible that subsequent governments or legislators may interpret the meaning of the legislation differently over time even if the central bank laws remain unchanged. Once again this raises the point made earlier about the subtlety of the notion of central bank independence. For example, when the US Congress mandated, under the Humphrey-Hawkins Act of 1978, that the Federal Reserve produce target growth rates for monetary aggregates this was viewed as an attempt to influence the Federal Reserve's independence even though the Federal Reserve Act was not modified. Another example is the so-called Coyne-Rasminsky directive of the early 1960s which arose from a disagreement over monetary policy that ultimately led to the resignation of the Governor of the Bank of Canada, James Coyne. Louis Rasminsky, Coyne's successor, issued a directive to the effect that, in the event of a disagreement between the Governor and the government about monetary policy, the Minister of Finance would be required to issue a directive indicating what policy the Bank should follow. If the Governor disagreed with the directive, resignation would follow, although a version of the directive was later enshrined in the Bank of Canada Act, and unlike the original intent of the directive, it has since been seen as an instrument of more, not less, independence (Rymes, 1994).

Table 9.1 largely follows the indexing system created by Cukierman. The table codifies key elements in the central banking legislation in the five countries considered in this study. The index values range from zero to one, with zero meaning dependence and one signifying complete central bank independence. However, as there are special considerations for the transitional economies, a number of new variables are introduced into the construction of an index of legal and economic central bank independence. Table 9.2 gives the assigned index values as well as a brief definition describing how the values were assigned.

The characteristics of central banking legislation should be broadly interpreted as follows. The longer the term of office of the head of the central bank, the less likely it is that it will overlap with the electoral cycle, reducing the possibility that a government can always appoint the central banker of its choosing, which is interpreted as enhancing central bank independence. Similar observations apply to the other categories under the group heading termed *CEO*. The next set of variables, under the heading *Policy Formulation*, measures the responsibility for monetary policy actions. Thus, for example, if the legislation assigns complete control over monetary policy to the central bank this is taken as a sign that politicians intended to confer independence on the central bank. An important consideration in this respect is whether clear provisions exist for conflict resolution. As noted earlier, the absence of such provisions proved to be critical in Canada's case. Thus, statutes which clearly outline how conflicts between the government and the CEO of the central bank are resolved are assumed to enhance independence.

A third variable, called *CB Objectives*, determines whether the central bank is supposed to satisfy a single and clear objective or a multiplicity of possibly incompatible objectives. For example, specification of the single objective of price stability is an indication that the central bank be permitted to pursue such a goal alone. By contrast, if the legislation specifies several vague objectives, these can be open to government influence thereby eroding central bank independence as defined in this chapter.

A fourth variable, under the heading *Limitations on Lending*, represents a group of variables which evaluate the extent to which the government can borrow freely from the central bank. Clearly, the fewer the limitations on lending to governments, the less room exists for independent central bank action.[13]

As useful as these indicators of central bank independence are, they fail to capture some potential constraints on central bank behaviour which are peculiar, but not exclusive, to economies in the transition to market. One such characteristic is the choice of exchange rate regimes. Table 9.1 suggests that central bank independence is at a minimum under a rigidly fixed exchange rate regime.[14] The reason, of course, is that a rigidly fixed exchange rate implies that inflation would, in equilibrium, be the same as in, say, Germany, the largest trading partner of the countries studied here. While this may be a desirable condition, it nevertheless eliminates any scope for independent monetary policy and, consequently, for the establishment of a credible record on inflation based on central bank action. The greatest scope for central bank action would occur under a pure float which would then permit the monetary authorities to independently influence domestic inflation. The acquisition of credibility by central banks can be important since it is certainly the case, based on the historical record, that governments do change the exchange rate regime over time. Thus, a peg of any kind does not permit the central bank to develop or to demonstrate the credibility of its actions. While the choice of the exchange rate regime would be important in assessing the degree of independence enjoyed by any central bank, this is especially important for the transitional economies since, rather unusually,[15] the central bank laws in *all* the countries considered here have explicit provisions dealing with the fixing of exchange rates. Thus, for example, in the case of Hungary, section 13 of the *Act on the National Bank of Hungary 1991* states:

(1)   NBH (National Bank of Hungary) quotes and publishes the exchange rates serving to convert foreign currencies into forint and the forint into foreign currencies.

(2)   The order of fixing and/or influencing the exchange rates is determined by the government in agreement with NBH.[16]

Table 9.1 Index of Central Bank Independence: Definitions

Variable Definition	Symbol	Hungary	Poland	Czech R.	Slovak R.	Bulgaria
1. CEO						
Term of Office-Head (years)	**too**	6	-[a]	6	6	5
Who Appoints CEO	**app**	PM	PM	Pres.	Pres.	Nat'l assembly
Dismissal of CEO	**diss**	non-political	Par. recall	Pres. recall	Pres. recall	non-political
2. Policy						
Who formulates it?	**monpol**	with gvt	with gvt	Bank alone	with gvt	Bank alone
Conflict Resolution	**conf**	NO	NO	NO	NO	NO
CB active in gvt budget?	**adv**	YES	YES	YES	NO	YES
3. CB Objective						
Single, Multiple?	**obj**	multiple	multiple	price stability	stability of currency	internal/external stability
4. Lending Limitations						
Advances	**lla**	4% of planned revs.[b]	2% of budgeted exp.	5% of previous year's revs.	5% of State Budget revs.	5% of State Budget revs.
Maturity of loans	**lmat**	None	YES	YES	YES	YES
Interest Rate Restrictions	**lint**	YES	YES	YES	YES	NO
5. Transitional Variables						
Exchange Rate Regime	**forex**	adj. peg	adj. peg	adj. peg	adj. peg	float
Enterprise Arrears	**enter**					
BIS standards?		YES	NO	NO	NO	NO
Consolidation Bank?		YES	YES	YES	NO	NO
Foreign Loans Forgiven?		NO	YES	NO	NO	NO
Access to CB funds?		YES	YES	YES	NO	YES

Variable Definition	Symbol	Hungary	Poland	Czech R.	Slovak R.	Bulgaria
Maturity of the Financial System	**mat**					
Limits on Foreign Banks?		NO	YES	YES	YES	YES
Competition in Banking?		NO	NO	NO	NO	NO
Active Stock Market?		YES	NO	YES	NO	NO
Variety of fin. instr.?		YES	NO	YES	NO	NO
Foreign Debt Load?	**debt**	high	high	low	low	moderate
Deposit Insurance?	**depins**	YES	NO	NO	NO	NO
CB Board Structure	**board**					
Who Appoints?		PM	PM	Pres.	Pres.	Pres.
Term		3 years	6 years	6 years	6 or 4 years	5 years
Gvt Representative:						
adv+vote						
adv.		YES	YES	YES	YES	YES
attend only						

Notes: For items 1 to 4, see Cukierman (1992, Chapter 19). For description of items under 5, see text. [a] Unspecified term. [b] No limits were placed in 1992; the limit was 5% in 1993.

Sources: State banking supervision, *New Banking Act in Hungary II*, Budapest, 1 December 1991; Ministry of Finance, *Act on the National Bank of Hungary*, Budapest, 1991; Changes to the Bank Law and Act of the National Bank of Poland, 28 December 1989; Act of 31 January 1989, *The Banking Law* (Poland); *Foreign Exchange Law* of 1 January 1990 (Poland); Act of the Czech National Council No. 61, 1993, *On the Czech National Bank*; The Law of the National Council of the Slovak Republic, 18 November 1992 about *The National Bank of Slovakia*, Hochreiter (1995) and Dittus (1994). Information on Bulgaria kindly provided by Rumen Dobrinsky as well as from documents from the Bulgarian National Bank.

Table 9.2 Indexes of Central Bank Independence

Group/Variables[a]	Numerical Coding				
	Hungary	Poland	Czech R.	Slovak R.	Bulgaria
1. CEO:					
too	.75	0	.75	.75	.50
app	0	.5	0	0	1
diss	.67	.33	.33	.33	.67
2. Policy:					
monpol	.67	.67	1	.67	1
conf	.20	.20	.40	0	.20
adv	.50	.50	.50	0	.05
3. Objectives:					
obj	.4	.4	.8	.4	.80
4. Limitations on Lending:					
lla	.67	.67	.67	.67	.67
lmat	0	.67	.67	.33	.67
lint	0	0	0	0	1
5.Transitional Variables:					
forex	.5	.5	.75	.75	1
enter	.25	.5	.5	.5	.25
mat	.75	0	.5	0	0
debt	0	0	1	1	.5
depins	0	0	0	0	0
board	0	0	.375	.125	.25
gvt	.5	.5	.5	0	0
Aggregate Indexes					
items 1 to 4	.39	.39	.51	.32	.70
Cukierman	.24	.10	NA	NA	NA
policy only	.46	.46	.63	.22	.57
item 5	.36	.21	.52	.34	.29
items 1 to 5	.37	.32	.51	.33	.53
inflation rate[b]	29.2	33.2	18.2	16.4	72.9

Notes to Table 9.2:

[a] For description of variables see Table 9.2 and Section 3.2. Coding for items 1 to 4 is from Cukierman (1992, Chapter 19). The higher the value for the index the more independent the central bank. For items under 5, coding is as follows:

Variable	Codes
forex	fixed=0, adj. peg=0.5, float=1
enter	BIS?: YES=1, NO=0
	Cons. Bank?: YES=1, NO=0
	Loans forg.?: YES=1, NO=0
	CB Borrowing?: YES=1, NO=0
mat	Foreign Banks?: YES=1, NO=0
	Competition?: YES=1, NO=0
	Active Stock Market?: YES=1, NO=0
	Variety of fin. instr?: YES=1, NO=0
debt	low=1, high=0
depins	yes=1, no=0
board	follows **app** and **too** in Cukierman
gvt	advise+vote=0
	advise=0.5
	attend only=1

[b] Annual inflation rate for 1993 in Hungary, November 1992-93 for Poland, inflation for 1993 for the Czech and Slovak Republics, and Bulgaria. Data from the National Bank of Hungary, *Monthly Bulletin* (2/1994), and from IMF, IFS CD-ROM (3/1994). Data for the Czech Republic from *Quarterly Statistical Bulletin* 4/93, *Monitor of the Economy of Slovak Republic*, 8 (1993), Part I. For Bulgaria, the rate of depreciation in the lev (Bulgaria's currency) vis-à-vis the US dollar is used to proxy inflation.

Another characteristic of the Central and Eastern European economies in transition is the role played by enterprise arrears and bad loans, a legacy of the financial structure under central planning and an outcome of the drive to introduce market-driven mechanisms.[17] However, the degree to which the newly reorganized central banks in these countries are affected by this legacy depends in part on the reforms undertaken in the banking sector. If, for example, banks are required to meet Bank for International Settlements (BIS) standards (see Siklos, 1994a, Chapter 11, for the details), this is likely to mean considerable risk of insolvency for the banking system as a whole, especially if the central bank is eventually required to bail out failing institutions either directly or indirectly via the government's budget. Thus, at the outset of the transition, banks which inherit loans with a low probability of repayment, as in Hungary, or who shun commercial lending, thereby exacerbating the financial difficulties experienced especially by the large enterprises, raise the likelihood that liquidity shortages will have to be underwritten by the central bank. This condition is exacerbated by the low capitalization of such banks. It is these conditions rather than the BIS standards themselves which can create difficulties for the banks and, by implication, affect the central banks (see Ábel and Siklos (1994) in this connection). This problem is also likely to be aggravated by the ability of banks to borrow regularly from the central bank under unspecified extraordinary conditions, since this is interpreted as a looser requirement than the expectation that the central bank act as a lender of last resort. Again, conditions under which such loans are advanced exist in the legislation in some of the countries examined in this paper and they clearly impinge on central bank independence.[18] However, the impact of such provisions may be somewhat mitigated by the formation of consolidation banks[19] which manage existing bank loans separately, or foreign loan forgiveness which can increase the ability of the central bank to operate autonomously unless several consolidation schemes are contemplated.

An additional determinant of central bank independence is the maturity of the financial system, that is, the degree to which the financial system is developed. Four characteristics of the maturity of the financial system are considered: whether there are limitations on the operations of foreign banks concerned, that is, whether they can operate legally on an equal footing with domestic banks; whether the financial system is viewed as being competitive; whether an active stock market exists which can generate a significant amount of liquidity; and the variety of financial instruments that the public can hold. More mature financial systems (i.e., ones where the public's share of wealth in financial assets is large) imply that the public has a greater stake in a regime of price stability and this enhances the ability and independence of the central bank to achieve, say, a desirable inflation objective. Put differently, as the fraction of wealth in financial assets rises, the public may become more sensitive to the importance of policies which have an impact on the real interest rate. A central bank which is independent is more likely to attempt to maintain a particular real interest rate level than one which would prevent nominal interest rates from rising when inflationary expectations rise.

A particular concern in some of the TEs continues to be the high level of foreign debts accumulated under the previous economic regime. A high proportion of foreign debt to GDP increases the costs of the transition. If these costs are perceived to be too high, political pressure on the central bank to inflate its way out of the constraints imposed by such debts may grow over time thereby reducing its independence. Alternatively, because high foreign debt, in effect, represents a type of externally imposed constraint, this could be interpreted instead as having a positive influence on central bank independence.[20]

An additional risk facing some former TEs stems from the absence of deposit insurance. Hungary introduced deposit insurance in January 1993 but the shaky nature of the financial sector in that country potentially creates another source of risk that central banks will be called upon to bail-out the commercial banking sector (also see Calvo and Kumar, 1993, and Borensztein and Masson, 1993b, in this connection).[21] This can potentially affect the autonomy of the central bank and it represents a characteristic that needs to be incorporated into an index of central bank independence.[22]

While the newly reformed central banks discussed here have instituted appointment procedures to avoid the overlap of the term of heads of central banks with those of their political masters, the same is not necessarily true of the Board or Council of these central banks where actual monetary policy decisions are made. There is some question about the validity of this point in the initial phases of the transition. Consider the case of Hungary. György Surányi was Governor of the National Bank of Hungary at the time the new law was introduced. When he signed his name to a document criticizing the first democratically elected government, the government did not appoint him as Governor under the new law. The government argued that since a new law was in effect the position of Governor was therefore vacant. The right of centre government proceeded to appoint the former Industry Minister, Péter Ákos Bod. Thus, despite the legislation, the government got the Governor they wanted. This is not to say that the NBH would not act independently, as we shall see.

Indeed, a subsequent election in 1994 returned a left of centre (coalition) government under Gyula Horn. Despite the appointments of a reform minded Finance Minister, László Békesi, and a like-minded head of the privatization programme actual government policy did not heed the warnings of the central bank over its loose fiscal policy (see *Népszabadság,* 30 January 1995). As a result, the head of the privatization programme was fired and the Finance Minister resigned. The Governor of the NBH had previously resigned in December 1994 ostensibly owing to disagreements over fiscal and interest rate policies pursued in 1993 and 1994 described elsewhere in this volume (see, for example, Chapter 3). Yet, however great and successful the political pressures on a central bank are, even if the central bank appears to be dependent, a government which is itself dependent on external financial constraints, as the Hungarian government clearly is, can produce an independent central bank in appearance even if it is not so in fact, thereby reducing considerably the usefulness of legal measures of independence. In fact, subsequent events in Hungary confirmed this to be the case as the Horn government returned György Surányi to the post of Governor of the NBH and appointed Lajos Bokros, himself an independent-minded financial expert, as the Finance Minister.[23]

Moreover, if the Board or Council of the central bank is largely government appointed for terms shorter than the electoral cycle, then this reduces the ability of the central bank to act independently.

Clearly, other issues relevant to the transitional economies could have been brought to bear on the question of central bank independence. Thus, for example, Hochreiter (1995) considers that current account convertibility enhances the commitment to market-driven reform and, by implication, facilitate the tasks of an independent central bank. He also argues that capital account convertibility is not feasible at present, and, indeed, may have a negative impact on a transitional economy because of the currency substitution such a move would engender.

3.3 Indexes of Central Bank Independence

Table 9.2 gives the values assigned to each variable listed in Table 9.1, as well as providing a variety of aggregate index measures of central bank independence. The first aggregate index considers only those variables which also appear in Cukierman's index. The next line gives the aggregate index value as computed by Cukierman (1992, Table 19.3), for Hungary and Poland (Cukierman did not construct an index for Czechoslovakia or Bulgaria). Other indexes were constructed for the newly introduced variables, as well as indexes for the transitional variables alone and all of the variables listed in Table 9.1. To construct the indexes, the mean of the codes assigned within each of the five categories was constructed. Next, each of these mean values was again averaged to produce a mean of means which represents the value of the indexes reported in Table 9.2. It was thought preferable to use an unweighted scheme and instead to present several index calculations since it is unclear, a priori, how one would assign appropriate weights.

On the basis of most of the indexes shown it appears that the Bulgarian National Bank is the most statutorily independent followed by the Czech National Bank, while the Slovak National Bank is the least independent. The National Bank of Poland, by most measures, now rates as slightly less independent than the National Bank of Hungary, although this result is sensitive to the variables included in the index. However, both the National Bank of Hungary and National Bank of Poland appear to be more independent than under central planning. The Slovak National Bank is more independent than the National Bank of Poland when only the transitional variables are considered.

The rise in the index relative to Cukierman's previous estimate is large in both cases, especially in Poland's case, suggesting considerably more legal independence than under central planning.[24] The results are fairly insensitive to the selection of variables included in the index calculations. If we rely on the variables said to be most closely associated with inflation performance, namely the *Policy only* variable, then the central banks of Hungary and Poland are equally independent. Otherwise, the rankings are the same as in the more highly aggregated indexes.

It is also interesting to note that the central banks of Hungary, Poland, Bulgaria, and the Czech Republic all have index values for the broadest index measure above the median of the index values for the 68 countries previously tabulated by Cukierman (1992, Table 19.3). This was not the case for either Hungary or Poland prior to the transition to market. Indeed, the Czech National Bank would now rank as statutorily independent as the US Federal Reserve as if Cukierman's index alone is considered, while Poland's central bank would rank as more independent than the Bank of Canada, according to the same index. Finally, Table 9.2 suggests that the index of central bank independence is not, broadly speaking, inversely related to inflation,[25] as predicted by theory, unless the transitional variables introduced in this study are alone considered.[26] This feature of the data is especially noticeable when the index values for the Czech and Bulgarian National Banks are compared.

4. ESTIMATION OF CENTRAL BANK REACTION FUNCTIONS

Given the availability of data it may be rather precarious to consider econometric estimates of central bank reaction functions, in part because one could argue that it may take some time before the newly reformed central banks can reduce or stabilize inflation. In addition, of course, there are lingering doubts about the quality of the data. In particular, Sachs (1993) argues that in the case of Poland, omission of the emerging private sector from industrial production data overstates the decline of output in the transition phase. This is also likely to be the case for the other countries considered. However, an 'improved' and more reliable measure of output is as yet unavailable. Nevertheless, because legal measures of independence are also fraught with difficulties, as explained above, it would seem useful to consider, in a tentative fashion, how far inflation and economic growth are assumed to be, at least partially, the consequence of central bank actions, as well as how central bank behaviour may have been influenced by political and policy variables since the reform process was introduced in 1987 in Hungary, in 1990 in Poland and 1991 in Czechoslovakia.[27] To accomplish this objective we consider two sets of econometric tests.

4.1 Panel Data Set

In one exercise we consider Czechoslovakia, Hungary and Poland together, for a sample of monthly data which begins in 1987 or later, depending on the country in question and the dating of the beginning of the transition, and ends in 1993 (details are provided in the notes to the Tables). There were too few observations for Bulgaria to include it in the panel data set. Because there are too few elections in the available sample considered to test either electoral or partisan influences on selected macroeconomic aggregates, a political events measure with potential consequences for central bank behaviour is considered.[28] Following the literature on political business cycles the political events variable is a dummy variable active whenever an economic or political event is believed to be likely to influence central bank behaviour or performance. Based on the chronology of events in Siklos and Ábel (1995),[29] two political events dummies were constructed. Economic events which directly influence the countries considered, such as, for example, the suspension of IMF credits, result in an active dummy(=1) for the month in which the event takes place. Political events, such as an election or a change in government, receive a greater weight (dummy is active in the month of the event with a value of 2).

Alternatively, it could be argued that the series of economic and political shocks affecting these countries produces cumulative type pressures on the respective central banks. If this is the case then the value of the political events dummy is a function of whether economic and political events occur in consecutive months or not. For example, if an economic event occurs in February 1990, and then again in April of the same year, the dummy is active in February and April only. If, however, economic and political shocks occur in February and up until April the value of the political stability dummy is cumulated until such shocks disappear, and the political stability dummy eventually becomes inactive the month following the latest economic shock.

The following panel regressions of time series cross-section data on inflation and output growth were estimated (also see Alesina and Roubini, 1992). The general form of the single equation specification is:

$$x_t = \alpha_0 + \alpha_1 x_{t-1} + \ldots + \alpha_n x_{n+1} x_{t-1}^f + \ldots + \alpha_{n+l} x_{t-k}^f + \alpha_{n+k-1} POLEV_t + \epsilon_t \qquad (9.2)$$

where x represents either pooled inflation (*INF* or π) or output growth proxied here by industrial production (*PROD* or y) for the three countries considered and x^f represents foreign inflation or output growth. Standard specification searching is used to select the 'best' lag length in (9.2) subject to data limitations. *POLEV* represents the dummy variable for political events defined in two different ways, as explained previously. Because the economies considered are all small and open, foreign shocks are controlled for by the addition of the German inflation rate or the growth in German industrial by the relevant dependent variable. Tables 9.3 and 9.4 present the regression results based on specification (2). Inflation is proxied by the annualized monthly percentage change in the Consumer Price Index and output growth is proxied by the annualized monthly percentage change in the index of industrial production. Both series were obtained from the International Monetary Fund's *International Financial Statistics* CD-ROM with some observations from country sources (see Siklos and Ábel, 1995). The coefficients in column (2) of Table 9.3 and 9.4 are for the political events dummy active in the months in which some political or economic event is active, while column (4) is for the political events dummy in which economic or political events have a cumulative impact on either inflation or output growth. According to the results in Table 9.3, political events have no statistically significant impact on inflation. When output growth is considered in Table 9.4, political events have a statistically negative influence on output growth when economic and political shocks are permitted to have only a transitory impact on industrial production. This means that these political events have had a negative impact on output growth in the countries considered. Note also that Hungary and Poland had statistically significantly higher inflation rates, while Czechoslovakia's inflation rate is significant only at a higher significance level. This may be taken as some evidence that the Czechoslovak pegged exchange rate had the desired effect on its inflation rate.

4.2 Individual Country Results

There are too few observations available since the start of the transition to estimate separate reaction functions for Czechoslovakia or Bulgaria. Consequently, Tables 9.5 and 9.6 show estimates for Hungary and Poland only. In generating these estimates it was first assumed that a vector autoregression (VAR) consisting in one case of an interest rate,[30] the inflation rate (defined as before) and output growth characterizes the central bank's model of the economy. In a separate VAR, money growth (measured by the narrow aggregate M1, the monetary base being unavailable in the monthly frequency) replaces the interest rate. The interest rate and money growth variables are assumed to proxy the central bank's instrument of monetary policy over which it exerts control.[31] The VARs were estimated recursively to ensure that forecasts of the variables are based only on information that would be available to policy makers. Johnson and Siklos (1996) explain in greater detail the advantages of this procedure for estimating central bank reaction functions. We also generated inflation and output forecasts using a first order

Table 9.3 Pooled Time Series Data Regressions

Dependent Variable: Inflation(*INF*)[a]

Independent Variables	(2) Coefficient	(3) t-stat.	(4) Coefficient	(5) t-stat.
INF(-1)	0.43	6.02*	0.43	6.15*
INF(-3)	0.27	3.84*	0.27	3.88*
German *INF* (-1)	-3.85	-2.21*	-3.91	-2.24*
German *INF*(-2)	-2.93	-1.69[#]	-2.94	-1.69[#]
Dummies				
Czechoslovakia	29.23	1.91[#]	29.24	1.91[#]
Hungary	26.11	2.73*	25.61	2.61*
Poland	52.16	3.62*	49.46	3.60*
POLEV[b]	-0.91	-0.50	-0.95	-0.12
R^2- adj.	0.47		0.47	
S.E.	60.83		60.87	
Observations	161		161	
Dummies=0[c]	3.41 (0.06)		3.39 (0.67)	

Notes: [a]   In column (4), estimates are based on (0,1) political stability dummy. In column (2) estimates are based on cumulative political dummy. The samples are given in Tables 9.5 and 9.6 for Hungary and Poland; for Czechoslovakia the sample is 1990.01 - 1992.12. The pooled data set was created by stacking Hungarian, Polish and Czechoslovak data.

         [b]   Annualized monthly inflation in the Consumer Price Index (International Monetary Fund, *International Financial Statistics* (line 64), calculated as $1200*(\log P_t - \log P_{t-1})$.

         [c]   Test of the null hypothesis that all dummies are jointly equal to zero. Significance level in parenthesis.

         *   Statistically significant at the 5% level.

         #   Statistically significant at the 10% level.

autoregressive model for inflation and the growth industrial production with a dummy variable to capture the break caused by price liberalization in Poland and Hungary. Moreover, allowance was also made for seasonality in January inflation in Hungary owing to its more gradual approach to price liberalization. The forecasts via the above approach yield results which were more satisfactory, in a statistical sense, than those generated by the VAR approach. In particular, the autoregressive scheme worked well for inflation data but more poorly for output growth data though the results still outperformed the forecasts from VARs in the latter case. Since the autoregressive modelling approach is relatively more parsimonious, the results in Table 9.5 and 9.6 are

Table 9.4 Pooled Time Series Data Regressions

Dependent Variable: Rate of growth in industrial production (PROD)[a]

Independent Variables	(2) Coefficient	(3) t-stat.	(4) Coefficient	(5) t-stat.
PROD(-1)	-0.43	-5.00*	-0.42	-5.02*
PROD(-2)	-0.15	-1.60	-0.15	-1.68#
PROD(-3)	0.13	1.58	0.14	1.64#
German PROD (-1)	-0.39	1.18	-0.35	-1.10
German PROD(-2)	-0.59	-1.81*	-0.64	-1.99*
Dummies				
Czechoslovakia	-25.33	-0.80	-25.11	-0.82
Hungary	-5.67	-0.62	-1.67	-0.19
Poland	-3.30	-0.24	9.69	0.77
POLEV	-1.72	-0.72	-30.41	-2.73*
R^2- adj.	0.19		0.23	
S.E.	79.25		77.26	
Observations	142		142	
Dummies=0[b]	0.70 (0.40)		0.72 (0.40)	

Notes: See notes in Table 9.3 for pertinent details. For sample information see the following tables. For Czechoslovakia, the sample is 1991.02 - 1992.12.

[a] Industrial production is an index (1985=100) from International Monetary Fund, *International Financial Statistics* (line 94).
[b] Dummies = 0 tests the joint significiance of the dummy variables, the test is distributed as an F.
*   Statistically significant at the 5% level.
#   Statistically significant at the 10% level.

based on the autoregressive method of forecasting inflation and output growth. Siklos (1994b) reports earlier results based on VAR estimation.

If the central bank targets interest rates or money growth rates independently of political influences then it should react only to unanticipated movements in inflation and/or output growth. Given that central bank reaction is measured via either a change in the interest rate or via money growth this leads to the following two reaction functions.[32] In the case where monetary policy actions are measured via the interest rate we have

$$\Delta R_t = \alpha(L)[\pi_{t-1} - \hat{\pi}_{t-1}] + \beta(L)[y_{t-1} - \hat{y}_{t-1}] + \delta(L)POLEV_t + \zeta(L)\Delta R_t^w + u_t \qquad (9.3)$$

When the stance of monetary policy is measured by money growth the reaction function is written

$$\dot{M}_t = \alpha^*(L)[\pi_{t-1} - \hat{\pi}_{t-1}] + \beta^*(L)[y_{t-1} - \hat{y}_{t-1}] + \delta^*(L)POLEV_t + \zeta^*(L)\dot{M}_t^w + u_t^* \qquad (9.4)$$

where inflation (π) and output (y) growth forecasts are generated in a manner described above. Equations (9.3) and (9.4) specify that interest rate changes (or money growth) react positively (negatively) to greater than expected inflation, and positively (negatively) to higher than forecast output growth. If the central bank is dependent, however, it will respond by reducing interest rates (increasing money growth) when the frequency of political events rises (i.e., political instability rises). Finally, as with the panel data, a small open economy is likely to be influenced by conditions in the rest of world. These are here proxied by German interest rate changes or money growth.[33]

Reaction functions for Hungary are presented in Table 9.5, while those for Poland are reported in Table 9.6. For Hungary interest rate changes are unrelated to unanticipated errors in inflation, while positive output shocks had a negative impact on interest rates. However, the chosen Hungarian interest rate does not react to German interest rate changes. Political events do have a positive impact on interest rates when these types of shocks are allowed to accumulate over time but not when they are transitory. That is to say, political events appear to have permitted the central banks to raise interest rates and demonstrate their independence from government influence.[34] Turning to the reaction functions specified with the money growth policy variable, unanticipated changes in inflation appear to have no cumulative impact (statistically speaking) on current money growth but a positive output shock contributed to lower money growth. Moreover, political events have no statistically significant impact on money growth. The results based on both reaction functions suggest an independent National Bank of Hungary which responds approximately to improved output performance.[35] Anecdotal evidence from Hungary is also suggestive of its independence. Thus, a serious conflict arose in the fall of 1993 between the Minister of Finance and the NBH. Because deficits were higher than legal limits spelled out in the government's budget, the NBH increased its base rate sharply. Moreover, as much of the government's debt is short-term, the rise in interest rates resulted in an even higher budget deficit than originally forecast. Despite complaints from the Finance Ministry, and the fact that the Governor was previously a member of the government, the NBH did not back down. Indeed, the NBH again raised its base rate sharply in June 1994 which produced yet another

Table 9.5 Reaction Functions for Hungary

(Sample: 1988.12-1992.12)

Independent Variables	Dependent Variables					
	ΔR	ΔR	ΔR	M	M	M
Constant	.18	.05	.21	12.36	12.61	12.94
	(.87)	(.23)	(.92)	(3.64)*	(3.24)*	(3.38)*
$\pi_{t-1}-\hat{\pi}_{t-1}$	-.002	-.007	-.001	.10	.02	.04
	(-.13)	(-.45)	(-.05)	(.06)	(.10)	(.19)
$\pi_{t-2}-\hat{\pi}_{t-2}$	.006	-.002	.01	.02	.04	.07
	(.38)	(-.11)	(.47)	(.10)	(.16)	(.78)
$\pi_{t-3}-\hat{\pi}_{t-3}$	-.003	-.007	.002	.20	.21	.24
	(-.02)	(-.47)	(.10)	(.92)	(.93)	(1.05)
$y_{t-1}-\hat{y}_{t-1}$	.08	-.81	.23	.52	.54	.57
	(.02)	(-.22)	(.06)	(.95)	(.96)	(1.02)
$y_{t-2}-\hat{y}_{t-2}$	3.41	3.17	3.25	.09	.10	.05
	(.91)	(.86)	(1.22)	(.16)	(.17)	(.09)
$y_{t-3}-\hat{y}_{t-3}$	-8.54	-8.60	-8.73	-.98	-.98	-1.03
	(-2.25)*	(-2.29)*	(-2.25)*	(1.80)#	(-1.78)#	(-1.85)#
ΔR^{Ger}	.76	.71	.73	-	-	-
	(1.00)	(.95)	(.94)			
$\dot{M}^{Ger}$	-	-	-	.96	.96	.96
				(3.39)*	(3.37)*	(3.36)*
POLEV	-	.18	-.17	-	-.34	-4.18
		(1.65)#	(-.34)		(-.21)	(-.57)
R^2	.12	.16	.12	.23	.23	.24
S.E.	1.66	1.64	1.67	24.17	24.17	24.31
Observations	68	68	67	67	67	67

Notes to Tables 9.5 and 9.6.
Inflation and output are as defined in Tables 9.3 and 9.4. R^{Ger} is the German treasury bill rate. R is the enterprise discount rate for Hungary and the working capital loan rate for Poland. M is $M1$ for both countries. For M^{Ger} a special problem arises because of the effect of German unification in 1990. Since the International Financial Statistics publication makes no adjustment for this shock there is a huge jump in German M1 between 1990.12 and 1991.01 (90.5 billion marks out of an M1 value of 453.1 billion marks in 1990.12). To adjust the figures the growth rate in M1 between 1990.12 and 1991.12, as estimated from the *Monthly Report of the Bundesbank*, vol. 44 (September 1992), Table 2, p.4*, was used to project data from 1990.12 to 1991.12. This resulted in a downward adjustment factor of 0.8308843 from the IFS figures for 1991 and 1992. Growth rates in M1 were thus preserved despite the unification effect.
* Statisitcally significant at the 5% level.
# Statistically significant at the 10% level.

Table 9.6 Reaction Functions for Poland

(Sample: 1989.08-1993.05)

Dependent Variables

Independent Variables	ΔR	ΔR	ΔR	M	M	M
Constant	-10.64	-11.34	-15.64	97.32	128.12	111.90
	(-1.06)	(-.93)	(-1.35)	(5.11)*	(6.11)*	(5.20)*
$\pi_{t-1}-\hat{\pi}_{t-1}$	-.18	-.18	-.19	.17	.15	.18
	(-2.41)*	(-2.38)*	(-2.46)*	(1.22)	(1.13)	(1.29)
$\pi_{t-2}-\hat{\pi}_{t-2}$	-.21	-.21	-.21	-.02	-.06	-.04
	(-2.73)*	(-2.65)*	(-2.64)*	(-.14)	(-.49)	(-.25)
$\pi_{t-3}-\hat{\pi}_{t-3}$	.15	.15	.15	.36	.32	.34
	(1.93)#	(1.91)#	(2.01)*	(2.62)*	(2.50)*	(2.45)*
$y_{t-1}-\hat{y}_{t-1}$	-	-	-	-	-	-
$y_{t-2}-\hat{y}_{t-2}$	-	-	-	-	-	-
POLEV	-	.21	9.24	-	-8.98	-24.93
		(.11)	(.87)		(-2.76)*	(-1.32)
ΔR^{Ger}	.61	-.11	-1.93	-	-	-
	(.02)	(-.003)	(-.05)			
$\dot{M}^{Ger}$	-	-	-	-.47	-.83	-.65
				(-.40)	(-.75)	(-.56)
R^2	.32	.32	.33	.16	.29	.19
S.E.	51.96	52.60	52.11	95.46	88.99	94.66
Observations	46	46	46	49	49	49

Note: See Notes to Table 9.5. To increase the number of observations significantly, output shocks were omitted. Nevertheless, the conclusions reported in this table are unaffected by these changes. See Siklos (1994b).

positive shock to the government's deficit. The NBH successfully argued that it did not wish to monetize any more debt than it had previously agreed to and thereby sent a message to the incoming government, elected in May, that it was up to them to set their fiscal house in order.

The results for Poland (Table 9.6) suggest that the Polish National Bank responds to unanticipated inflation by reducing interest rates and raising money growth. Moreover, money growth is seen to fall in the face of rising political instability when the latter is permitted to have a cumulative impact on monetary policy variables. The econometric evidence suggests then that the Polish National Bank is dependent.[36]

5. CONCLUSIONS

An analysis of the legislation of the reformed central banks in the TEs of Hungary, Poland, the Czech and Slovak Republics suggests, not surprisingly, that they are now clearly less subject to government influence than under central planning. A similar regime change is evident from the available econometric evidence. Nevertheless, to suggest that these central banks are independent because they are modelled after the German Bundesbank ignores the fact that the German central bank is not legislated to guarantee price stability which, if for historical reasons only, is a natural goal for the central banks of TEs to set. The Bundesbank has *de facto* behaved as if it were mandated to guarantee price stability because of its disastrous experience with hyperinflation during the 1920s as well as because of the federal structure of the German state. Poland and Hungary each have experienced hyperinflation this century, twice in the case of Hungary, so perhaps it is sufficient to follow the German model. Yet, there is little evidence that low inflation is seen by the public as a desirable goal in itself, except perhaps in the Czech Republic, which is puzzling. As discussed in the paper, the existing legislation in the countries considered in this study is not sufficiently clear about central bank goals and responsibilities to behave *as if* they were the Bundesbank. Nevertheless, the little econometric and descriptive evidence that is available does point to the conclusion that the Hungarian and Czech central banks appear to act fairly independently of political influences, while the exchange rate policy of the Czech Republic appears to be delivering the desired disinflation. More generally, one has to ask whether price stability or low inflation is a desirable goal in itself. After all, price distortions are still significant as these economies drive toward market-determined prices. Moreover, the financial systems in the transitional economies are rather immature in the sense that relatively few financial instruments are available and liquidity is in short supply. It is particularly important then to be wary of associating measures of statutory independence with the ability of the transitional economies to deliver low or stable inflation.

It will be interesting to consider how well the estimated reaction functions will perform in the future. Given a sufficiently long time horizon, the political events variable could be augmented with electoral variables. It will take a considerable amount of time, however, before distinct partisan influences are detected. Also, a longer sample will enable researchers to delineate the transitional effects from the permanent effects of central bank reforms on inflation in the countries studied here. After all, it is too early to conclusively evaluate the independence of central banks in the transitional economies, faced as they are with a multitude of internal and external economic constraints simultaneously.

POSTSCRIPT

The autonomy of central banks remains under threat in all the transitional economies for at least two reasons. First, as these economies struggle to determine the existing exchange rate regime that should remain, there are inevitably implications for inflation and monetary policy. Second, the desire for lower inflation rates, one of the mechanisms for greater integration into the rest of Europe, implies relatively tight monetary policy with high real interest rates. Obviously, at election times and in an environment where positive economic growth is only a recent occurrence, this puts pressure on central banks to relax monetary policy. However, it is the external constraints which have permitted central banks in the region to successfully fend off attacks on their independence. These external constraints include pressure from international financial organizations as well as international financial investors, both of which continue to demand and expect stable monetary and fiscal policies. In 1997 both Hungary and Poland introduced amendments to the legislation governing their central banks. In the case of Hungary, there is now less scope for the government to borrow from the central bank. In Poland, a new Constitution guarantees the autonomy of the National Bank of Poland.

NOTES

*   Originally appeared under the same title in P.L. Siklos, *The Development and Reform of Financial Systems in Central and Eastern Europe*, edited by J.P. Bonin and I. Székely (Aldershot: Edward Elgar), pp.71-98, and reprinted here with major revisions.
1.   This is a substantially revised version of Chapter 4 in Bonin and Székely (1994) which addresses comments published in that volume and reflects useful conversations with Miroslav Hrnčíř of the Czech National Bank, Werner Riecke of the National Bank of Hungary and Ryszard Kokoszczyński of the National Bank of Poland. We are also grateful to Rumen Dobrinsky for supplying us with the law on the Bulgarian National Bank.

2. While references to price stability exist in the legislation of a few central banks (e.g., Austria; see Aufricht, 1967, p.4, Art. 2(3) and Hochreiter, 1990), it is rare that a precise definition is given to the concept of price stability. An exception is the Reserve Bank of New Zealand Act of 1989 which stipulates the path inflation must take to achieve a target range of 0-2% inflation in the Consumer Price Index by December 1993 (see Dawe, 1992, and Reserve Bank of New Zealand, 1991). The Bank of Canada also has an inflation target to meet but it is part of the Federal Government's 1991 Budget rather than forming an integral part of the legislation governing the Bank's activities. In the 1994 budget the inflation targets agreement was amended so that the target was a 1–3% range in inflation for at least 2 years. The goal of zero inflation was formally put aside and, partly as a consequence, John Crow, the Governor of the Bank of Canada, requested that his term of office not be renewed. It is widely believed, however, that the newly elected Liberal government had no intention of renewing Crow's term.

3. Alesina and Summers (1993), however find that central bank independence does not appear to be associated with real macroeconomic performance.

4. Below, we consider an alternative explanation of the Bundesbank's independence relevant to the transitional economies.

5. Siklos and Wohar (1997) consider a formal test of whether inflation rates have converged among industrialized countries, and find evidence favourable to this hypothesis.

6. In 1994, the Banque de France was made independent in line with the requirements of the Maastricht Treaty. The UK is also considering granting independence to the Bank of England but has not formally done so. There exist, however, formal inflation targets as in Canada and New Zealand.

7. In the sense that qualitative studies of central bank independence have tended to classify the Bank of Canada, for example, as dependent.

8. For additional details on this point, see Johnson and Siklos (1996).

9. Fratianni *et al.* (1993) propose a model which suggests that Japan is the 'odd man' because the qualitative approach to measuring central bank independence ignores the role of political stability. Walsh (1992) posits a model which leads to the interpretation that the relatively superior Japanese inflation performance stems from the fact that the income of its Governor is more closely tied to government action than is the Federal Reserve Chairman's income in the US.

10. Article 3, however, does state that the Bundesbank '... shall regulate the note and coin circulation and the supply of credit to the economy with the aim of safeguarding the currency...' (Aufricht, 1967, p.252).

11. Decisions by the Central Bank Council can be deferred for not more than two weeks (Article 13, see Aufricht, 1967, p. 256). This has generally been interpreted as an independence enhancing device.

12. The Central Bank Council determines the direction of monetary policy. It consists of the President and Vice-President of the Bundesbank, up to eight members of a Directorate, and the Presidents of the Land Central Banks.

13. If, as seems clear, Hungary, Poland and the Czech Republic wish to join the European Community then the Maastricht Treaty will resolve the problem of lending since this is explicitly forbidden under the provisions for the establishment of the European Central Bank.

14. Estonia, for example, has established a currency board arrangement which fixes the value of the kroon to the deutschmark although some fluctuations are permitted. See Hanke *et al.* (1993, Chapter 4). In this case some might argue that lack of independence is a desirable characteristic. What is being discussed is the nominal exchange rate as an anchor. This does not prevent the real exchange rate from being a target of policy makers with consequences for inflation. See Calvo *et al.* (1995) for a description of relevant models. Siklos and Ábel (1995) describe the current real exchange rate policy in Hungary, Poland and Czechoslovakia as resulting in a real appreciation of their respective currencies.

15. Relative to central banking legislation in western industrialized countries. See Aufricht (1967).

16. The Czech National Bank Act (Article 35) stipulates that the Bank 'shall proclaim the exchange rate of the Czech currency vis-à-vis foreign currencies'. This does not preclude the government ultimately determining the exchange rate but officials of the Czech National Bank do not see it this way, according to Miroslav Hrnčíř of the Institute of Economics of the Czech National Bank.

17. For the relevant details, see Siklos and Ábel (1995), and references therein.
18. For example, the legislation governing the Czech National Bank has no specific provisions dealing with the problems arising out of inter-enterprise arrears. The Act on the National Bank of Hungary (para. 17) has explicit provisions regarding credits to financial institutions in emergency situations. However, the modalities of interest and repayment are not clearly spelled out. Maturity, collateral,and related conditions are specific in the case of the National Bank of Slovakia (see the *Law about the National Bank of Slovakia* (1992), part 6, para. 22 to 25). Provisions for credits to banks and other institutions also exist in the case of the National Bank of Poland.
19. Unless such an approach exacerbates difficulties in working out bad loans.
20. To the extent that a high level of foreign debt – which tends to be denominated in foreign currencies – requires an inflow of funds to service it, this may impose discipline on the authorities to ensure low inflation which is assisted by having an independent central bank. The foreign debt situation can also conflict with (real) exchange rate targeting when, say, an appreciation reduces the competitiveness of domestic producers. The resulting deterioration of the current account might result in pressure on the monetary authorities to extend credit thereby exacerbating future inflation.
21. Dittus (1994, Table 12) outlines the basic features of Hungary's deposit insurance scheme.
22. While deposit insurance did not exist in most industrialized countries until after World War II, except in the US, these financial systems were also not jeopardized to the same extent by the prospect of large scale failures or bad loans. Previously, in centrally planned economies, the state could underwrite deposits. The point being made here is that, until formal deposit insurance schemes are implemented, the impression is left that the central bank may be called upon to underwrite losses of the commercial banking sector. Note that this provision is not entirely independent, for example, of the item dealing with competition in the banking system.
23. See 'Hungary picks bank Chief and Finance Minister', *Financial Times*, 8 February 1995, p .1 and 'Uj Pénzügyminiszter és MNB elnök', *Heti Világ Gazdaság*, 10 February 1995.
24. Though one cannot express the 'significance' of the change in statistical terms. One should also ask to what extent it makes sense to regard the operations of 'central banks' in CPEs as resembling anything like the ones in conventional central banks. After all, under the monobank system, national banks were simply passive suppliers of the domestic currency and did not engage in the kind of domestic or foreign currency operations performed by central banks in most other countries. It is thus odd that Cukierman would include these countries or that the value of the independence index would be a number greater than zero.
25. Given that the Slovak crown has been devalued relative to the Czech crown, we are somewhat sceptical of the official Slovak inflation rate figure. Casual evidence suggests that it is considerably higher than in the Czech Republic.
26. With too few observations, it proved not to be possible to conduct a proper pooled cross-section time series test of the statistical link between the rate of depreciation in the real value of money (defined as in Cukierman (1992, p.418), and the major groupings of codes in Table 9.2. Regressions (not reported) suggest that the greater the independence of monetary policy of the central bank, the more specific the central bank objectives, and the less binding the transitional constraints on central bank action, the smaller the depreciation in the real value of money. However, because the regressions could not be run with all the variables jointly these results should be viewed with some caution.
27. In what follows, Czechoslovakia as a whole is examined up to its break-up into the Czech and Slovak Republics at the end of 1992. Separate Czech or Slovak data were available for too short a sample.
28. In earlier drafts, we had called this variable a political stability variable but as the political science literature equates political stability with coups d'états, revolutions and similar events, we preferred to rename it the political events variable.
29. The list of events is contained in a separate appendix available in a working paper version of this study.
30. For Hungary, the enterprise loan rate was used; for Poland, the working capital loan rate; for Germany, the three month Treasury bill rate.

31. The methodology of Johnson and Siklos (1996) is followed except that a monetary aggregate is the objective of monetary policy. Johnson and Siklos (1996) describe the reservations they have about monetary aggregates in reaction functions as well as outlining the arguments for resorting to an interest rate measure even in a world of capital controls. In the context of the FCPEs, however, the major drawback of the interest rate measure of monetary policy actions is that it is not yet clear to what extent movements in it are influenced by the market for debt which is still very much in its infancy in these countries. Moreover, since the currencies considered here are not really convertible on the capital account, the interest rate need not be the chosen instrument of the central bank.

32. See, for example, National Bank of Hungary, *Annual Report* (1992), Chapter 3, for a description of interest rate and credit policies of the National Bank of Hungary. The exchange rate could be an additional policy variable but, as made clear earlier, it is essentially under government control rather than at the discretion of the central bank. This appears to be also true in the other countries considered in this study.

33. A specification more representative of the existing literature on reaction functions, as in Abrams *et al.* (1980), or Woolley (1988), where the monetary policy variable reacts simply to lagged changes in the right hand side variables in (3) or (4) was also considered with no effect on the conclusions reported below.

34. The events considered are typically ones which increase the pressure on governments to inflate or are the result of events which have led to the resignation of governments which attempted to implement or continue to implement inflation stabilization policies, to the extent that pressure on governments to inflate or to go against policies imposed externally, such as those of the IMF, which would translate into pressure on central banks to lower interest rates (or increase money growth), while higher interest rates reflect more independence.

35. The results in Table 9.5 are very similar to those presented in Siklos (1994b) except for the finding that output shocks significantly influence interest rate changes and money growth. This is probably due to the omission of 1993 data in the earlier study, a year when Hungarian industrial production improved.

36. Again, the conclusions are similar to those reported by Siklos (1994b) except that the econometric evidence in favour of National Bank of Poland dependence is now stronger.

10. Stabilization and Convertibility in the Transition: The Legacies of the Twin Deficits*

PROLOGUE

Since budget constraints were essentially meaningless in centrally planned economies, such countries typically experience persistent fiscal deficits as well as deficits on the current account. A crucial decision then on the road to market is the extent to which a transitional economy should liberalize trade and the choice of exchange rate regimes. Unlike well-functioning market-driven economies, typical transitional economies were in a state of severe disequilibrium. This feature has important implications for both macro-economic policies as well as institutional design, as this chapter demonstrates.

1. INTRODUCTION: THE UNCHARTED WATERS

Much has been written concerning the proper approach to the transformation of the formerly centrally planned and bureaucratically managed economies of the now defunct Soviet bloc to market-oriented economies based on private initiative. Some scholars use terms like 'Shock Therapy' and the 'Big Bang' to characterize the urgency and comprehensiveness of the transformation programme (Kornai, 1990, Lipton and Sachs, 1990). Others write of the 'Longest Road' and the need to take a more gradualist approach to economic restructuring (Nordhaus, 1990). Virtually all agree that the most difficult issue in sequencing the steps of the transformation is the privatization of the many large state-owned enterprises. On the other hand, macroeconomic stability is the necessary pre-condition set by most writers for the transformation to proceed successfully.

This transformation of the socialist managed economies of Central East Europe back into capitalist mixed market economies is an event unparalleled in history. A metaphor sometimes used is the unscrambling of an omelette. Throughout the last decade, excess aggregate demand has been ubiquitous in all of the now transforming countries so that balancing the aggregate product market is a crucial first step. To date, little attention has been paid to modelling this transformation process. Because of the importance of macroeconomic stability to the success of the transition, we think that basic macroeconomic balances are a useful place to start. In this chapter, we focus on the macroeconomic framework for the transformation and exclude many important microeconomic issues, such as privatization and restructuring.

Monetary overhang is often cited as the cause of excess aggregate demand in Poland and the Soviet Union so that these two countries are paired in discussing the transformation, while Hungary is often coupled with the former Czechoslovakia. Such a grouping focuses on the macroeconomic problems due to monetary overhang in the first pair and the microeconomic structural problems in the absence of significant monetary overhang in the latter. However, in all of the other formerly socialist economies, financial markets are underdeveloped and a significant cause of inflationary pressure is fiscal deficits. Consequently, as do Cochrane and Ickes (1991), we downplay the importance of monetary overhang and focus directly on aggregate macro-economic flows.

The crucial characteristic separating the transforming countries may not be the presence or absence of pervasive shortages and monetary overhang. Rather fiscal deficits are likely to be a common source of inflationary pressure regardless of the existence of monetary overhang. In Hungary, goods shortages are not prevalent and monetary overhang is not apparent. Yet the fiscal deficit is an important indicator of a macroeconomic disequilibrium that is mirrored in the external accounts by a current account deficit. The twin culprits have been fiscal subsidies for languishing domestic companies and the fiscal servicing of a sovereign debt denominated in foreign currency. If the burden of the foreign debt and the openness of the economy are used as the main characteristics to divide the transforming countries into two camps, Poland and Hungary would be paired while the former Czechoslovakia and the now defunct USSR would fall into a second grouping.

Our intent is to characterize the macroeconomic disequilibrium in a typical European transforming country by considering the domestic investment/ savings imbalance reflecting excess demand in the product market. For this purpose, we construct a simple one-sector open macroeconomic model with restrictions on capital account transactions. The model proves useful for analyzing the medium-term effects of the transformation, for example, the implications of *foreign direct investment* (FDI) on the real exchange rate and the possible incompatibility of trade liberalization and economic stabilization. We focus our attention on the particular problems of the Hungarian economy inherited from the 1980s although macroeconomic models of this type have broad application to the economic transformation of many of the formerly socialist countries.

In the next section, we summarize briefly the salient macroeconomic developments of the past decade in Hungary to motivate the simple integrated macroeconomic framework within which the implications of various broad directives are evaluated. Section 3 presents the one-sector open macroeconomic model based on liberalized external relations; in particular, we assume a flexible (uniform) market exchange rate and full current account convertibility.[1] In the model, we follow the absorption approach in characterizing external transactions and assume that inward FDI is the only allowable private capital account item. In particular, capital flight from the transforming country is effectively prohibited. Two crucial aspects of the transformation from the Hungarian perspective, namely, FDI[2] and the legacy of foreign debt are highlighted. Our concluding section contains some general remarks about the advisability of moving to full trade liberalization and a floating exchange rate regime in the early stages of the transformation.

2. HUNGARY'S TWIN DEFICITS

To motivate the basic framework of our macroeconomic model, we examine the net positions of the four sectors, household, business, government and external in Hungary from 1980 to 1989.[3] In Table 10.1 and Figure 10.1, flows are presented as a percentage of GDP to eliminate inflation. Household savings are defined as disposable income minus consumption. The current account deficit includes all trade both with hard currency areas and within the now-defunct CMEA. The fiscal budget surplus is defined in the conventional way as receipts minus expenditures, which include debt service.[4] Gross business savings are the aggregate net cash flow of companies after taxes and subsidies. In the early 1980s, gross business savings exceeded investment owing mainly to required disbursements to reserve funds. Net business savings, defined as gross business savings minus investment, become negative in 1983, reflecting the increasing role played by the profits tax in the fiscal budget and a decreasing role for direct subsidies. The household savings rate is remarkably low, averaging less than 1% of GDP.[5]

As accounting flows, the four net positions must balance. Consequently, any ex post domestic investment/savings imbalance will be measurable by the current account. The current account is in deficit for all but one year during the 1980s reflecting excess aggregate domestic demand. The central government fiscal budget deficit in Hungary did not rise above 4% of GDP in the 1980s. However, central government expenditures were higher than 55% of GDP throughout the period and the fiscal budget redistributed a large percentage of the national income. Subsidies and other current transfers represented 66.46% of central government expenditures in 1988. A subsidy reduction programme was initiated in 1989 having as its aim the elimination of all price subsidies in four years.

Table 10.1   Net Saving Rates by Sector (Net Saving as a percentage of GDP, Hungary, 1980-1989)

	Business Savings minus Business Investment	Household Savings	Fiscal Budget Surplus	Current Account Deficit
1980	3.27	0.24	-8.38	4.87
1981	1.80	0.90	-6.55	3.86
1982	0.66	0.58	-3.56	2.32
1983	-1.28	0.85	-0.41	0.85
1984	-1.30	0.58	0.92	-0.20
1985	-1.79	0.91	-1.34	2.23
1986	-2.12	1.28	-4.66	5.50
1987	-3.69	-0.17	0.32	3.55
1988	-2.04	0.92	-0.26	1.38
1989	-1.96	0.12	-1.91	3.76

Source: Abel and Bonin (1991).

Another implicit claim on fiscal outlays is the service of the externally held public debt. Per capita foreign debt in Hungary is around $2,000. Foreign debt increased throughout the 1980s as current account deficits accumulated. Excess domestic demand fuelled by fiscal deficits provided the linkage as is evident in Figure 10.1. A strong negative correlation exists between the *fiscal budget surplus* and the *current account deficit*. Hungary exhibits a 'twin deficit' problem in the 1980s.

The legacies of the last decade for Hungary of a large foreign debt denominated in hard currency and an inflationary macroeconomic environment that has discouraged household savings in liquid assets hang like albatrosses on the privatization initiative. Kornai expresses concern that extensive foreign participation in the privatization of Hungarian companies may cause some political difficulties for the newly elected (mainly populist) governments. However, other sources of financing seem inadequate.[6] Furthermore, if FDI is excluded or curtailed significantly, the opportunities available from combining the 'know how' of local business situations provided by current managers and the modern managerial techniques plus the modernized production technology associated with Western companies will be foregone. In Hungary, the additional problem of servicing an already large foreign debt makes it transparent that any meaningful privatization will require new foreign capital.

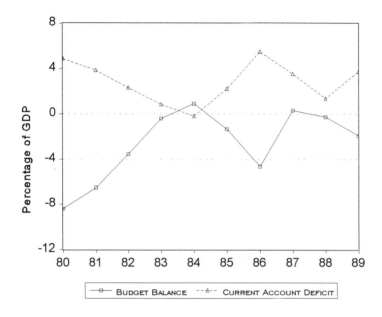

Figure 10.1 Hungary's Twin Deficits (as a percentage of GDP)

In Hungary, FDI measured as cash in the banking system and excluding in-kind contributions increased from $8 million in 1987 to $215 million in 1989; it more than doubled to $569 in 1990 and already equalled $891 million by May of 1991. Indeed, for the first five months of 1991, FDI in cash exceeded the interest payments due on the foreign debt.[7] The importance of both this cash flow and the imported skills and modern technology from in-kind contributions to the success of the transformation is apparent. In the model to follow, the crucial roles of FDI and debt services are highlighted and policy implications are considered in the next two sections.

3. A MACROECONOMIC MODEL OF THE TRANSFORMATION

Our aim is to build a model that focuses on the crucial medium-term interdependencies of the economic system for any transforming country. We begin with a simple one-sector open macroeconomic model of income determination with a flexible exchange rate. In this paper, we concentrate on real effects and leave monetary phenomena to later work. Although we denote the macroeconomic aggregates in monetary terms, the domestic price level is not considered so they may be interpreted as real aggregates.[8] We identify the debt service as a source of potential instability for a country in which the exchange rate is perfectly flexible, trade is fully liberalized, and the capital account is restricted to inward FDI only. The debt service ratio is shown to affect the equilibrium values of income and the exchange rate along with the domestic absorption income multiplier.

Domestic absorption is characterized partially by the following consumption function:

$$C = C_0 + c(1-t)Y \tag{10.1}$$

where C is domestic consumption,

c is the marginal propensity to consume,
t is the *net* personal and business tax rate,
Y is gross domestic product, and
$(1-t)Y$ is disposable income.

For the moment, we assume that domestic investment, I_0, and government expenditure, G_0, are exogenous. However, total investment consists of domestic investment plus FDI (FDI). We specify FDI to be a positive function of gross domestic product (GDP) measured in dollars, i.e.,

$$f(y/e) = fY/e$$

where e is the domestic currency to dollar exchange rate. Since the foreign investor is interested in returns in foreign (rather than domestic) currency, such a specification seems plausible. In a dynamic model, the growth of dollar-valued GDP would play a significant role in the investment equation. Since there are only four data points, we cannot estimate reliably the relationships between GDP and FDI in Hungary. Choosing the simplest form is one thing, but looking at the facts is another. In Figure 10.2 the available data for this short period of time does not seem to be in an unacceptable conflict with our specification.

Given exogenous domestic investment and the assumed relationship between FDI and GDP, investment measured in domestic currency is written as

$$I = I_0 + fY \tag{10.2}$$

Although equation (10.2) is formally equivalent to an induced investment equation in traditional macroeconomic models, the fact that the second term reflects FDI will become important when the external sector is considered.

Following the absorption approach, we assume that exports are exogenous when measured in dollars so that

$$X^\$ = X_0^\$ \qquad (10.3)$$

Imports measured in domestic currency are specified to be a linear function of GDP so that

$$M = mY \qquad (10.4)$$

From (10.3) and (10.4), net exports are a positive function of e so that a stability condition (analogous to the Marshall-Lerner conditions) is satisfied. Specifically, a depreciation of the domestic currency, i.e., an increase in e, leads to an increase in net exports. Finally, debt service measured in dollars is given by

$$\text{debt service} = rD_0^\$ \qquad (10.5)$$

where r is the service rate
and $D_0^\$$ is the initial sovereign debt in dollars.

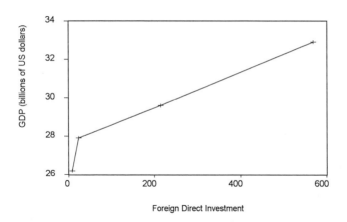

Figure 10.2 GDP and Foreign Direct Investment (Hungary, 1987-90)

Consequently, the external sector balance of payments constraint (BOP) in dollars is written as

$$X_0^\$ - (mY/e) - rD_0^\$ + (fY/e) = 0 \qquad (10.6)$$

Since the debt is sovereign, we assume that it is paid from the fiscal budget so that net government savings in domestic currency given by:

$$S_G = tY - G_0 - erD_0^\$ \tag{10.7}$$

From (10.1), household or personal saving is

$$S_P = -C_0 + (1-c)(1-t)Y \tag{10.8}$$

Total government, private and foreign savings finance total investment. Net foreign savings are:

$$S_F = mY - e(X_0^\$ - rD_0^\$) \tag{10.9}$$

Therefore, total investment (10.2) equals (10.9) plus total domestic savings ((10.7) plus (10.8)).

An investment/savings equilibrium requires:

$$-C_0 + Y - c(1-t)Y - G_0 = I_0 + eX_0^\$ + (f-m)Y$$

from (10.2), (10.7), (10.8) and (10.9). Solving for Y yields

$$Y = (C_0 + I_0 + G_0)\frac{1}{[1-c(1-t)+(m-f)]} + eX_0^\$ \frac{1}{[1-c(1-t)+(m-f)]} \tag{10.10}$$

The equilibrium exchange rate can be determined as a function of GDP from (10.6) as

$$e* = \frac{(m-f)}{(X_0^\$ - rD_0^\$)} Y \tag{10.11}$$

Substituting (10.11) into (10.10) to solve for equilibrium GDP yields

$$Y* = A_0 \left[\frac{1}{\{ 1-c(1-t)+(m-f)(-rD_0^\$/(X_0^\$ - rD_0^\$)) \}} \right] \tag{10.12}$$

where $A_0 \equiv C_0 + I_0 + G_0$. The term in curly brackets in (10.12) is the GDP absorption multiplier. Now (10.12) can be substituted into (10.11) to solve for the equilibrium exchange rate

$$e* = \left[\frac{(m-f)}{(X_0^\$ - rD_0^\$)} \right] A_0 \left[\frac{1}{\{1-c(1-t)+(m-f)(-rD_0^\$)/(X_0^\$-rD_0^\$)\}} \right] \tag{10.13}$$

To present the equilibrium in Figure 10.3, we assume that $(m-f)>0$ and denote

$$\alpha \equiv [1/(1-c(1-t) + m-f)]$$

so that (10.12) may be rewritten as

$$Y* = \alpha A_0 + \alpha X_0^\$ e \tag{10.14}$$

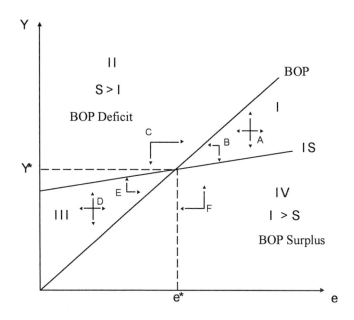

Figure 10.3 GDP-Exchange Rate Equilibrium

Now (10.14) is the investment/savings (IS) balance and (10.11) is the BOP balance in Figure 10.3. The slope of the BOP line is $[X_0^\$ - rD_0^\$/(m-f)]$ and the slope of the IS line is $\alpha X_0^\$$. A necessary and sufficient condition for existence is

$$\frac{(X_0^\$ - rD_0^\$)}{(m-f)} > \alpha X_0^\$ = [\frac{1}{1-c(1-t)+(m-f)}]X_0^\$$$

or

$$[\frac{1-c(1-t)}{1-c(1-t)+(m-f)}] > \frac{rD_0^\$}{X_0^\$} \tag{10.15}$$

Notice that the term in brackets is less than one and smaller the larger is $(m-f)$. Consequently, a high marginal propensity to import relative to the marginal propensity of FDI may lead to non-existence of an equilibrium. Furthermore, the importance of the debt service ratio (to exports) is clear from (10.15). If debt service is too large relative to export earnings, the equilibrium will not exist.

The stability of the equilibrium can be examined from Figure 10.3. The area above/below the IS line represents an imbalance in which savings exceeds (is less than) investment. The area above (below) the BOP line indicates a deficit (surplus) in the balance of payments. The arrows on points C and F in regions II and IV indicate consistent dynamic tendencies. With excess (deficient) savings, a decrease (increase) in income or a depreciation (appreciation) of the exchange rate (i.e., an increase (decrease) in e), reduces (increases) savings. With a deficit (surplus) in the balance of payments, a depreciation (appreciation) of the exchange rate or a decrease (increase) in income leads to a balance of payments equilibrium in the external sector. However, the dynamic adjustments in regions I and III are more complex.

With no further restrictions, or alternatively no precise specifications for dynamic adjustment equations, the dynamics in regions I and III are inconsistent owing to countervailing tendencies as shown by the arrows attached to points A and D. However, it is common in the literature to assume that exchange rate movements are more dominant in restoring BOP equilibrium and spending changes are more dominant in restoring IS balance.[9] In region I, considering only the surplus in the BOP, the exchange rate should appreciate, i.e., e should decrease. Furthermore considering only the fact that savings is greater than investment, income should decline. Thus, if we follow the conventional literature and relate movements in the exchange rate to BOP considerations and movements in income to IS imbalances, the arrows attached to point B give the appropriate dynamics in region I. A similar justification leads to using the arrows attached to point E as representative of the dynamics in region III. Consequently, the apparent instability owing to countervailing tendencies in these two regions is unlikely to cause problems if the usual dominance assumption is imposed.

Table 10.2 presents the comparative statics when the debt service is assumed to be positive. Several of these results are derived algebraically in the Appendix. Since the change in any parameter leads to the same directional change in the exchange rate and GDP, we include a third column in which the combined effects of these two changes on the *dollar* value of GDP, i.e., Y/e, is recorded. The results in this final column are not derived algebraically in the Appendix because they follow directly from considering changes in the slope of the BOP line in Figure 10.3. This slope can be written as export earnings multiplied by (one minus the debt service ratio) and divided by $(m-f)$; furthermore, since the BOP line emanates from the origin, its slope represents Y/e.

Table 10.2 Comparative Statics

	e Exchange Rate	Y GDP	Y/e Dollar GDP
$X^\$_0$ (exports)	-	-	+
m-f [(imports-FDI)/GDP]	+	+	-
C_0, I_0, G_0 (autonomous expenditures)	+	+	None
t (net tax rate)	-	-	None
$rD_0^\$$ (debt service)	+	+	-

Note: Derivations in the Appendix.

Either an increase in the marginal propensity to import or a decrease in the marginal propensity of foreigners to invest resulting in an increase in $(m$-$f)$ leads to a decrease in *dollar-valued* GDP because the slope of the BOP line is flatter. Separated into its two components, an increase in $(m$-$f)$ leads to depreciation in the domestic currency and an *increase* in the forint measure of GDP. In a similar vein, an increase in the debt service or a decrease in exports leads to an increase in the debt service ratio. If the debt service ratio increases, the slope of the BOP line decreases. Consequently, the currency will depreciate, GDP measured in forints will increase, and GDP measured in dollars will decrease. Somewhat surprisingly changes in any component of autonomous domestic spending or in the net tax rate have *no effect* on dollar-valued GDP (Y/e). The expected Keynesian effects are reflected by changes in forint-valued GDP but none of these parameters influences the slope of the BOP line. Hence, the exchange rate moves to countervail exactly the Keynesian effects on GDP and dollar-valued GDP is unchanged.

   That debt service plays a crucial role in our model is obvious from its impact on the BOP line. To derive comparative static results in the absence of any debt service, consider equation (10.12). If debt service is zero, the GDP absorption multiplier is the simple Keynesian multiplier, i.e., the reciprocal of the marginal propensity to save out of disposable income. In this case, forint-valued GDP is unaffected by *any* changes in the external sector, e.g., changes in exogenous export earnings, the marginal propensity to import or the marginal propensity of FDI. From (10.13), the entire brunt of changes in these parameters is borne by fluctuations in the exchange rate. However, separation is not complete because changes in autonomous absorption parameters and changes in the tax rate affect the exchange rate also. In our model, domestic policy and foreign direct investment have significantly different consequences in the presence of positive debt service than in its absence.

In Hungary with its high debt service, an increase in the willingness of foreigners to invest (captured by an increase in f) will increase dollar-valued GDP (Y/e) but it will *decrease* forint-valued GDP. The difference is a result of the appreciation of the forint. In Czechoslovakia, a country with a negligible debt service, the same increase in the willingness of foreigners to invest will not affect GDP measured in domestic currency but will increase dollar-valued GDP because of currency appreciation. Furthermore, a high debt service to export earnings ratio may lead to non-existence of an equilibrium in our model of total external sector liberalization. Finally, from equation (10.12), the GDP absorption multiplier increases with the debt service ratio. As an item of current account, debt service places a wedge between the trade balance and foreign direct investment. The interplay of these three components of the balance of payments is an important consideration in mapping out the journey along the road to transformation in the carriage of liberalized relations with the global economy.

4. CONCLUSION: NAVIGATING IN THE NEW WATERS

During the 1980s, Hungarian macroeconomic policy focused on 'growing out of the debt' under the assumption that exports would increase faster than imports. Advocates for different policies argued that growth in GDP would lead mainly to growth in imports (increased domestic absorption) and, thus, to further indebtedness. During this period, an overvalued fixed exchange rate was maintained as the consensus opinion was that devaluation would not boost net exports because of inelasticities due to trade barriers and direct (exchange) controls. Rather, the likely effect would be a fuelling of inflation, both from the increased costs of imported materials and, more importantly, from the direct monetization of the increased fiscal debt incurred to service the foreign dollar-denominated debt with a devalued domestic currency. Realizing the inflationary danger in continuous devaluation, policy makers were reluctant to pursue a flexible exchange rate policy.

The model presented above has implications for assessing the benefits and pitfalls of moving to full trade liberalization and a freely floating exchange rate at the early stages of the transformation. The existence of an equilibrium is sensitive to the ratio of interest payments on the debt to export earnings and to the difference between the marginal propensity to import and the willingness of foreigners to invest in the country. High interest payments, low export earnings, a high propensity to import, and low propensity to invest by foreigners are likely to be impediments to liberalization. If none of these problems exists, the model indicates that flexible exchange rates and current account liberalization encourage and accommodate FDI.[10]

From the comparative static results, an increase in the marginal propensity of foreigners to invest decreases GDP so that domestic absorption (consumption) falls. However, dollar-valued GDP increases as the currency appreciates and, therefore, FDI increases. These combined changes lead to an increase in the ratio of gross investment to GDP. Thus an initial impetus to investment from an increased desire of foreigners to provide capital will be accommodated rather than crowded out if trade is fully liberalized and the exchange rate is allowed to appreciate to its new equilibrium level.

If encouraging foreign investment is a major objective of the transformation programme, tight fiscal policy can be used to decrease domestic absorption through the decrease in GDP measured in domestic currency. However, the currency will appreciate and dollar-valued GDP will remain unchanged. This resulting appreciation of the currency would help to control domestic inflation and perhaps make the austerity programme and the increased participation of foreign capital somewhat palatable to the populace. However, in such an environment, the potential for virtuous cycles arises. An increase in the willingness of foreigners to invest increases dollar-valued GDP owing to the appreciation of the currency and this leads to more FDI.

On the negative side, lurking in the background is the effect of financing the foreign debt. If either the interest rate charged on the debt or the stock of debt were to increase, the currency would depreciate and dollar-valued GDP would fall. Thus, FDI would be discouraged. On the other hand, debt forgiveness would have stimulating effects in a country with fully liberalized external relations. A decrease in the stock of debt will lead to an appreciation of the exchange rate and an increase in dollar-denominated GDP. The former will dampen inflationary tendencies while the latter will encourage FDI. The comparative statics indicate that debt reduction will lead to a *decrease* in GDP which will again reduce domestic absorption and serve to accommodate the increased FDI.

To the extent that debt service is manageable, full liberalization seems to bring benefits without significant pitfalls. Indeed any appreciation of the currency resulting from additional inflows of FDI reduces the dollar-denominated debt burden. On the other hand, the reefs of instability lurk in the seas and the available navigational instruments may be weak for debt-ridden transforming countries. It may seem unrealistic to suppose that capital inflows will be sufficient to influence significantly the macroeconomy of the transforming countries. Certainly the record to date in Hungary would support such scepticism. However, privatization of the formerly state-protected companies must involve corporate restructuring rather than simple asset redistribution if these transformed companies are to sail successfully in the new waters. Without the 'Big Brother' option available to the now-defunct GDR, countries must look to foreign investment as the most essential component of any privatization programme. Hungary is building the institutional and legal structure to begin to cope with this inevitability.

POSTSCRIPT

The fine balance between real appreciations, and the desire to control inflation, and the need to attract foreign direct investment continues to exist. Since the article was written, Poland has moved to a floating type of exchange rate, Hungary has adopted a crawling peg approach, while the Czech Republic has considerably widened the fluctuation bands for its currency. Foreign debt levels remain a significant problem for Hungary alone, primarily because, unlike Poland, its foreign debt has tended to be acquired from private not public sector sources. The scepticism about the impact of capital inflows on growth continues to be justified as several of the transitional economies have and continue to outperform Hungary.

NOTES

*   Originally published in *Structural Change and Economic Dynamics*, (1992) 3(1), 37-51, with minor revision, by I Ábel and J.P. Bonin, by permission of Oxford University Press. The authors thank the PEW Foundation, MTA-OTKA Research Fund and Wesleyan University for support of this research conducted under the auspices of CEPR's research project on Economic Transformation in Eastern Europe. We are grateful to the referees of this journal who provided extremely helpful comments on an earlier draft. Of course, we are responsible for remaining errors and all omissions.

1.   Williamson (1991) provides an excellent discussion of the issues involved in defining and achieving convertibility in the transforming countries. Kornai (1990) identifies current account convertibility as a crucial element of the transformation.

2.   The Blue Ribbon Commission report stressed the role of foreign direct investment in the Hungarian transformation (Blue Ribbon Commission, 1990). Prior to World War II, foreign ownership of assets in Hungary stood at about 20%; it is currently around 2%. Using the Austrian example as a reference point, the Hungarians advocated a target of 33% foreign ownership within two years.

3.   We exclude 1990 and 1991 because of the disruption caused by external and policy shocks, most importantly the loss of the Soviet market followed by the dissolution of CMEA trade and the stringent restrictions re-imposed by the Hungarian government on households regarding tourist account transactions. See Ábel and Bonin (1991) for a thorough treatment of these issues.

4.   Since our model will have no monetary sector, foreign debt service is considered to be a component of the fiscal budget in the next section. In the earlier part of the period when fiscal and monetary policies were not separated, the flows presented here reflect this accurately. During the later part of the period, the Hungarian National Bank is responsible for servicing the foreign debt. Currently, the fiscal budget contains an internal debt service transfer to the National Bank in forints and at a negotiated below-market interest rate. Now, the burden of obtaining hard currency to service the foreign debt falls on the bank.

5. In 1990, this ratio increases to over 4% of GDP owing mainly to precautionary motives reflected in an attempt to build more liquidity into household portfolios. Chapter 5 documents the illiquidity of household portfolios during this period.
6. As we noted above, household savings increased significantly in 1990 to slightly over 4% of GDP. Early in 1991, the government offered incentives for households to buy back housing mortgages that had been made at subsidized rates. To the extent that households do so, the liquidity of their portfolios will be reduced.
7. Figures are taken from the National Bank of Hungary's 'Market Letter' dated May 1991.
8. A distinction is made between values in the domestic currency and dollar values. To the extent that inflation is captured fully in exchange rate changes, the dollar-valued aggregates could be considered to be real variables and the domestic-currency-valued ones monetary variables.
9. See McKinnon (1981).
10. Of course other conditions like political stability, progress in the privatization programme, and reduced nondiversifiable risks are also crucial for attracting foreign capital.

APPENDIX: COMPARATIVE STATIC DERIVATIONS

Consider (10.12) and (10.13) in the following forms:

$$Y = A_0(X_0^\$ - rD_0^\$)N^{-1} \qquad\qquad (10.12')$$

$$e = A_0(m-f)N^{-1} \qquad\qquad (10.13')$$

where $N \equiv (X_0^\$ - rD_0^\$)[1-c(1-t)] - rD_0^\$(m-f)$

A. (m-f)

$$\frac{dY}{d(m-f)} = \frac{-A_0(X_0^\$ - rD_0^\$)[dN/d(m-f)]}{N^2} = \frac{A_0(X_0^\$ - rD_0^\$)rD_0^\$}{N^2} > 0$$

$$\frac{de}{d(m-f)} = \frac{-A_0(m-f)\dfrac{dN}{d(m-f)} + NA_0}{N^2}$$

$$= \frac{A_0(X_0^\$ - rD_0^\$)[1-c(1-t)]}{N^2} > 0$$

B. A_0

$$\frac{dY}{dA_0} = (X_0^\$ - rD_0^\$)N^{-1} > 0$$

$$\frac{de}{dA_0} = (m-f)N^{-1} > 0$$

C. *t*

$$\frac{dY}{dt} = \frac{-A_0(X_0^\$ - rD_0^\$)dN/dt}{N^2} = \frac{-A_0(X_0^\$ - rD_0^\$)^2 c}{N^2} < 0$$

$$\frac{de}{dt} = \frac{-A_0(m-f)dN/dt}{N^2} = \frac{-A_0(m-f)(X_0^\$ - rD_0^\$)c}{N^2} < 0$$

D. $rD_0^\$$

$$\frac{dY}{d(rD_0^\$)} = \frac{-A_0(X_0^\$ - rD_0^\$)[dN/d(rD_0^\$)] - NA_0}{N^2}$$

$$= \frac{A_0(X_0^\$ - rD_0^\$)[1 - c(1-t) + (m-f)]}{N^2}$$

$$= \frac{A_0(X_0^\$ - rD_0^\$)[1 - c(1-t)] - A_0 rD_0^\$(m-f)}{N^2}$$

$$= \frac{A_0 X_0^\$(m-f)}{N^2} > 0$$

$$\frac{de}{d(rD_0^\$)} = \frac{-A_0(m-f)[dN/d(rD_0)]}{N^2}$$

$$\frac{A_0(m-f)[1 - c(1-t) + (m-f)]}{N^2} > 0.$$

E. X_o

$$\frac{dY}{dX_0^\$} = \frac{-A_0(X_0^\$ - rD_0^\$)[dN/dX_0^\$] + NA_0}{N^2}$$

$$= \frac{-A_0 rD_0(m-f)}{N^2} < 0$$

$$\frac{de}{dX_0^\$} = \frac{A_0(m-f)[dN/dX_0^\$]}{N^2} = \frac{-A_0(m-f)[1-c(1-t)]}{N^2} < 0$$

F. Proof that $\left| \dfrac{dY}{dX_0^\$} \cdot \dfrac{X_0^\$}{Y} \right| < \left| \dfrac{de}{dX_0^\$} \cdot \dfrac{X_0^\$}{e} \right|$

From (10.12'), (10.13') and (E) above

$$\left| \frac{dY}{dX_0^\$} \cdot \frac{X_0^\$}{Y} \right| = \frac{X_0^\$ rD_0^\$(m-f)}{X_0^\$(X_0^\$ - rD_0^\$)N} \quad and$$

$$\left| \frac{de}{dX_0^\$} \cdot \frac{X_0^\$}{e} \right| = \frac{X_0^\$(m-f)[1-c(1-t)]}{(m-f)N}$$

Algebraic manipulation indicates that the result follows if and only if

$$rD_0^\$(m-f) < (X_0^\$ - rD_0^\$)[1-c(1-t)].$$

However, the condition is necessary for N as defined above to be positive.

References

Ábel, I. and J.P. Bonin (1992a), 'Hungary's Loan Consolidation Program: Is It A Step Backward?' unpublished manuscript.

Ábel, I. and J.P. Bonin (1992b), 'Stabilization and Convertibility in the Transition: The Legacies of the Twin Deficits,' *Structural Change and Economic Dynamics*, 3(1): 37-51. *A revised version appears as chapter 9 in this volume.*

Ábel, I. and J.P. Bonin (1992b), 'Capital Markets in Eastern Europe: The Financial Black Hole', *Connecticut Journal of International Law*, 8 (Fall), 1-17.

Ábel I. and J.P. Bonin (1991), 'Közvetlen külföldi beruházás és az adósságszolgálat' [Foreign Direct Investment and Debt Service], *Közgazdasági Szemle*, Nos. 7-8.

Ábel, I. and I.P. Székely (1994), 'Market Structures and Competition in the Hungarian Banking System', in J.P. Bonin and I.P. Székely (eds.), *The Development and Reform of Financial Systems in Central and Eastern Europe*, Aldershot: Edward Elgar, 272-92.

Ábel, I. and I.P. Székely (1993), 'Changing Structure of Household Portfolios in Emerging Market Economies: The Case of Hungary, 1970-1989,' in I.P. Székely and D.M.G. Newbery (eds.), *Hungary: An Economy in Transition*, Cambridge: Cambridge University Press, 163-80. *A revised version appears as chapter 5 in this volume.*

Ábel, I. and I.P. Székely (1990), 'Credit, Imports and Inventories', *Engineering Costs and Production Economics*, 11-17.

Ábel, I., J.P. Bonin and P.L. Siklos (1994), 'Crippled Monetary Policy in Transitional Economies: Why Central Bank Independence Does Not Restore Control', in P.L. Siklos (ed.), *Varieties of Monetary Reforms: Lessons and Experiences on the Road to Monetary Union*. Boston, MA: Kluwer Academic Publishers, 367-82.

Ábel, I. and P.L. Siklos (1994), 'Constraints on Enterprise Liquidity and its Impact on the Monetary Sector in Hungary', *Comparative Economic Studies*, 13-32. *A revised version appears as chapter 2 in this volume.*

Ábel, I. and I.P. Székely (1992a), 'The Conditions for Competition and Innovation in the Hungarian Banking System', unpublished manuscript.

Ábel, I. and I.P. Székely (1992b), 'Monetary Policy And Separated Monetary Circuits In A Modified Centrally Planned Economy: The Case Of Hungary', *Acta Oeconomica*, 44(3-4), 393-428.

Ábel, I., and L. Szakadát (1997), "Bank Restructuring in Hungary", CERT/Phare ACE Conference paper, May.

Abrams, R.K., R. Froyen and R. Waud (1980), 'Monetary Policy Reaction Functions, Consistent Expectations And The Burns Era', *Journal of Money, Credit and Banking*, 12, 30-42.

Act on the National Bank of Hungary (1991), Budapest: Ministry of Finance.

Aghlevi, B.B., E. Borensztein and T. van der Willigen (1992), 'Stabilization and Structural Reform in Czechoslovakia: An Assessment of the First Stage', IMF Working Paper, 92/2 (January).

Alesina, A. (1988), 'Macroeconomics and Politics', *NBER Macroeconomics Annual*. Cambridge: The MIT Press.

Alesina, A. and N. Roubini (1992), 'Political Cycles In OECD Economies', *Review of Economic Studies*, 59, 663-688.

Alesina, A. and L.H. Summers (1993), 'Central Bank Independence And Macroeconomic Performance', *Journal of Money, Credit and Banking*, 25, 151-162.

Aufricht, H. (1967), *Central Banking Legislation, Volume II: Europe*. Washington, D.C.: International Monetary Fund.

Bácskai, T. (1989), 'The Reorganization of the Banking System in Hungary,' in C. Kessides, T. King, M. Nuti and C. Sokil (eds.), *Financial Reform in Socialist Economies*, Washington, D.C.: World Bank.

Baird, D.G. (1986), 'A World Without Bankruptcy', *Law and Contemporary Problems*, 50 (Spring), 173-93.

Balassa, Á. (1992), 'The Transformation And Development Of The Hungarian Banking System', in D.M. Kemme and A. Rudka, A. (eds.), *Monetary and Banking Reform in the Postcommunist Economies*, New York: Institute for EastWest Studies.

Balcerowicz, L. (1994), 'Common Fallacies In The Debate On The Transition To A Market Economy', *Economic Policy*, 19, 16-50.

Banarian, K., R.C.K. Burdekin, and T.D. Willett (1995), 'On the Political Economy of Central Bank Independence', in K.D. Hoover and S.M. Sheffrin (eds.), *Monetarism and the Methodology of Economics: Essays in Honour of Thomas Mayer* (Aldershot: Edward Elgar), 178-97.

Bank és Tőzde (1997), 'Bank Privátizáció: Itt a Vége?', 21 February.

Bank for International Settlements (1997), *International Banking and Financial Market Development*, February.

Bank for International Settlements (BIS) (1993), *Annual Reports*, 1992-1993, BIS: Basle.

Bank Profitability (1996), Paris: OECD.

Bank Research - Eastern Europe (1991), Budapest Bank Rt. Hungary.

Blejer, M.I. and S.B. Sagari (1991), 'Hungary: Financial Sector Reform in a Socialist Economy', Working Paper, WPS 595, Washington, D.C.: World

Bank.

Begg, D. and R. Portes (1993), 'Enterprise Debt and Economic Transformation: Financial Restructuring in Central and Eastern Europe', in C. Mayer and X. Vives (eds.), *Capital Markets and Financial Intermediation*, Cambridge: Cambridge University Press, 230–55.

Belka, M. (1995), 'Financial Restructuring Of Banks And Enterprises: The Polish Solution', in K. Mizsei and I.P. Székely (eds.), Bad Enterprise Debts in Central and Eastern Europe. New York:Institute for EastWest Studies.

Bernanke, B.S. and C.S. Lown (1991), 'The Credit Crunch', *Brookings Papers on Economic Activity,*(2), 205-39.

Bernanke, R. and A.S. Blinder (1988), 'Credit, Money, and Aggregate Demand', *American Economic Review Papers and Proceedings*, 78 (May), 435-39.

Bianchi, B., F.M. Frasca and S. Micossi, S. (1979), 'Trade Credit in the Theory of the Firm: Relevance For Monetary Policy', Economic Papers 2 (July), Bank of Italy Research Department, 7-68.

Blanchard, O., R. Dornbusch, P. Krugman, R. Layard, L. Summers (1992), Reform in Eastern Europe, Cambridge: The MIT Press.

Blommenstein, H.J. and M.G. Spencer (1993), 'The Role of Financial Institutions in the Transition To A Market Economy', Working Paper, 93/75 (October), Washington, D.C.: International Monetary Fund.

Blue Ribbon Commission (1990), *Hungary in Transformation to Freedom and Prosperity*. Indianapolis: Hudson Institute.

Bod, P.Á. (1994), "Rebirth of the Hungarian Banking System", National Bank of Hungary, *Monthly Report,* 11, 147-51.

Boguszewski, P., W. Czulno and W. Prokop (1992), 'Monetary And Credit Policy Of The National Bank Of Poland', in D.M. Kemme and A. Rudka (eds.), *Monetary and Banking Reform in the Postcommunist Economies*, New York: Institute for EastWest Studies.

Boland, V. (1997), 'Czechs Find Transition Harder than they Thought', *Financial Times,* 3 (April), p. 2.

Bonin, J. and J. Mitchell (1992), 'Creating Efficient Banks During the Transition: Do Bad Loans Lead to Bad Policy?', paper presented at the American Economics Association Meetings, Anaheim, CA, January 1993.

Bonin, J.P. and I.P. Székely (1994), *The Development and Reform of Financial Systems in Central and Eastern Europe*, Aldershot: Edward Elgar.

Bordes, C. (1993), 'The Finnish Economy: The Boom, The Debt, The Crisis and the Prospects,' in *Three Assessments of Finland's Economic Crisis and Economic Policy*, Series C:9, Helsinki: Bank of Finland.

Bordo, M.D. and L. Jonung (1987), *The Long-Run Behavior of the Velocity of Circulation: The International Evidence*, Cambridge: Cambridge University Press.

Borensztein, E., and P.R. Masson (1993a), 'Financial Sector Reform And Exchange Arrangements in Eastern Europe. Part II', Occasional Paper No. 102, Washington, D.C.: International Monetary Fund.

Borensztein, E. and P.R. Masson (1993b), 'Exchange Arrangements of Previously Centrally Planned Economies', Part II of *Financial Sector Reforms and Exchange Arrangements in Eastern Europe*, Occasional Paper No. 102, February.

Brada, J.C. and A.E. King (1992), 'Central Planners as Market Stabilizers: Evidence from Poland and The Soviet Union', *Review of Economics and Statistics* 74(1), 1–13.

Brainard, L. (1991), 'Strategies for Economic Transformation in Central and Eastern Europe: The Role of Financial Market Reform', in H. Blommenstein and M. Marrese (eds.), *Transformation of Planned Economies: Property Rights Reform and Macroeconomic Stability*, Paris: OECD.

Brechling, F.P.R. and R.G. Lipsey (1966), 'A Rejoinder', *The Economic Journal,* 76 (March), 165–167.

Brechling, F.P.R. and R.G. Lipsey (1963), 'Trade Credit And Monetary Policy', *The Economic Journal*, 73(December), 618–641.

Bruno, M. (1992), 'Stabilization and Reform in Eastern Europe: Preliminary Evaluation', IMF Working Paper, 92/30 (May).

Burdekin, R.C.K. and T.D. Willett (1991), 'Central Bank Reform: The Federal Reserve In International Perspective', *Public Budgeting and Financial Management* 3, 619–650.

Calvo, G., C. Reinhart, and C. Végh (1995), 'Targeting the Real Exchange Rate: Theory and Evidence', *Journal of Development Economics,* 47 (June), 97-133.

Calvo, G.A. and F. Coricelli (1993), 'Credit Market Imperfections And Output Response in Previously Centrally Planned Economies', unpublished manuscript, Washington, D.C.: International Monetary Fund, May.

Calvo, G.A. and F. Coricelli (1992), 'Stagflationary Effects of Stabilization Programs in Reforming Socialist Countries: Enterprise-Side and Household-Side Factors', *The World Bank Economic Review,* 6 (1), 71-90.

Calvo, G.A. and J.A. Frenkel (1991), 'Obstacles to Transforming Centrally-Planned Economies: The Role of the Capital Markets', Working Paper Series 3776, Cambridge, MA: NBER.

Calvo, G.A. and M.S. Kumar. (1993), 'Financial Markets and Intermediation', Part I of *Financial Sector Reforms And Exchange Arrangements In Eastern Europe*, Occasional Paper No. 102, Washington, D.C.: International Monetary Fund.

Caprio, G., and D. Klingebiel (1996), 'Bank Insolvencies: Cross-Country Experiences', unpublished, Washington: The World Bank.

Caprio, G. Jr. and R. Levine (1992), 'Reforming Finance in Transitional Socialist Economies: Avoiding the Path from Shell Money to Shell Games', *World Bank Policy Research Working Paper Series*, No. 898.

Cargill, T.F. (1989), 'Central Bank Independence and Regulatory Responsibilities: The Bank of Japan and the Federal Reserve', Solomon Brothers Center for the Study of Financial Institutions Monograph Series in Finance and Economics No. 1989-2.

Chang, H. and R. Rawthorn (1994), 'Role of the State in Economic Change: Entrepreneurship and Conflict Management', paper presented at the WIDER Conference, Cambridge, UK.

Charemza, W.W. and J. Király (1988), 'Plans and Exogeneity: The Generic-Teleological Dispute Revisited', University of Leicester Department of Economics, Working paper, 71.

Coates, J.B. (1967), 'Trade Credit And Monetary Policy: A Study of the Accounts Of 50 Companies', *Oxford Economic Papers*, 19(March), 116-32.

Cochrane, J. and B.W. Ickes (1991), 'Inflation Stabilization in Reforming Socialist Economies: The Myth of the Monetary Overhang', *Comparative Economic Studies*, 2 (Summer), 97-122.

Cohen, D. (1991), 'The Solvency of Eastern Europe', *European Economy*, Special Edition No. 2, 263-303.

Commission of the European Communities, *European Economy*, Special Edition No. 2, 1991.

Cottarelli, C. (1993), 'Divorce: The Theory and Practice of Limiting Central Bank Credit to the Government', Working Paper, International Monetary Fund.

Csunderlik, C. (1985), 'The Interrelationship of Private Housing and Personal Savings: An Economic Disequilibrium Analysis of the Hungarian Housing Market, 1960-1983', paper presented at the Fifth World Congress of the Econometric Society, Boston (August).

Cukierman, A. (1992), *Central Bank Strategy, Credibility and Independence*. Cambridge: The MIT Press.

Cukierman, A., S. Edwards, and G. Tabellini (1992), 'Seigniorage and Political Instability', *American Economic Review*, 82 (June), 537-55.

Currie, D. (1993), 'The Finnish Economic Crisis: Analysis and Prescription', in *Three Assessments of Finland's Economic Crisis and Economic Policy*, Series C:9, Helsinki: Bank of Finland.

Daianu, D. (1994), 'Banks in Romania Today', paper presented at the conference on 'Banking Reform in the FSU and Eastern Europe: Lessons from Central Europe', Budapest (14-15 January).

Dawe. S. (1992), 'Reserve Bank of New Zealand Act, 1989', in *Monetary Policy and the New Zealand Financial System*, Third Edition, Wellington: Reserve Bank of New Zealand, 31-40.

Dittus, P. (1994), 'Corporate Governance in Central Europe: The Role of Banks', BIS Economic Papers No. 42, Basle: Bank Of International Settlements.

Dobrinsky, R. (1995), 'Enterprise Arrears And Bad Loans In Bulgaria', in K. Mizsei and I.P. Székely (eds.), *Bad Enterprise Debts in Central and Eastern Europe*, New York: Institute for EastWest Studies.

Dobrinksy, R. (1994), 'Reform of the Financial System in Bulgaria', in J. Bonin and I.P. Székely (eds.), *The Development and Reform of Financial Systems in Central and Eastern Europe*, Aldershot: Edward Elgar, 317-45.

Dornbusch, R. W. Nölling, and R. Layard (1993), *Postwar Economic Reconstruction and Lessons for the East Today*, Cambridge: The MIT Press.

Duchatczek, W. and A. Schubert (1992), 'Monetary Policy Issues in Selected Eastern European Economies', SUERF Papers on Monetary Policy and Financial Systems No. 11, Tilburg.

Edwards, S., and C. Végh (1997), 'Banks and Macroeconomic Disturbances Under Predetermined Exchange Rates', Working Paper, UCLA, March.

Fischer, S. (1991), 'Privatization in East European Transformation', National Bureau of Economic Research Working Paper No. 3703 (May).

Fratianni, M., J. von Hagen and C. Waller (1993), 'Central Banking as a Political Principal-Agent Problem', Discussion Paper No. 752, London: Centre for Economic Policy Research.

Friedman, B. (1983), 'The Roles of Money and Credit in Macroeconomic Analysis', in J. Tobin (ed.), *Macroeconomics, Prices and Quantities*, Washington, D.C.: Brookings Institution, 161-88.

Gazdaságkutató Intézet (Economic Research Ltd.)(1990),'A Magyar vállalatok finanszírozási szerkezetének főbb jellegzetességei' [Characteristics of the structure of financing hungarian enterprises], GKI Tanulmányok.

Glück, H. (1994), 'The Austrian Experience with Financial Liberalization', in I. Székely and J.P. Bonin (eds.), *Development and Reform of Financial Systems in Central and Eastern Europe*, Aldershot: Edward Elgar, 179-95.

Golden, R.A. (1994), 'Discussion of Chapter 5', in J. Bonin and I.P. Székely (eds.), *The Development and Reform of Financial Systems in Central and Eastern Europe*, Aldershot: Edward Elgar, 127-29.

Goldstein, M., and P. Turner (1996), 'Banking Crises in Emerging Economies: Origins and Policy Options', *BIS Economic Papers*, No. 46, October.

Gordon, R.H. (1982), 'Interest Rates, Inflation And Corporate Financial Policy', *Brookings Papers on Economic Activity*, 12(2), 461-91.

Gray, C.W., Hanson, R. and M. Heller (1992), 'Legal Reform for Hungary's Private Sector,' *Working Papers*, WPS 983, Washington, D.C.: The World Bank.

Grilli, V., D. Masciandro and G. Tabellini (1991), 'Political And Monetary Institutions And Public Financial Policies In The Industrial Countries',

Economic Policy, 13, 342–92.

Gurgenidze, L. (1993), 'Securitisation of Non-Performing Loans in Transitional Economies', New York: Institute for the EastWest Studies (December), mimeo.

Hanke, S., L. Jonung and K. Schuler (1993), *Russian Currency and Finance: A Currency Board Approach to Reform*, London: Routledge.

Hardy, D.C. and A.K. Lahiri (1992), 'Bank Insolvency and Stabilization in Eastern Europe', IMF Working Paper 92/9 (January).

Hare, P. and T. Révész (1992), 'Hungary's Transition to the Market: The Case Against a "Big Bang"', *Economic Policy* (April), 228-64.

Henderson, R.F. (1959), 'Trade Credit', in B. Tew and R.F. Henderson (eds.), *Studies in Comparative Finance*, Cambridge: Cambridge University Press, 92-107.

Herbst, A.F. (1974), 'A Factor Analysis Approach to Determining The Relative Endogeniety of Trade Credit', *The Journal of Finance*, 29 (Sept.), 1087-103.

Hilbers, P. (1993), 'Monetary Instruments And Their Use During The Transition From A Centrally Planned To A Market Economy', Working Paper 93/87, Washington, D.C.: International Monetary Fund (November).

Hochreiter, E. (1995), 'Central Banking In Economies In Transition', in T.D. Willett and R.C.K. Burdekin, R.J. Sweeney and C. Wihlborg (eds.), *Establishing Monetary Stability in Emerging Market Economies*, Boulder, Col.: The Westview Press, 127-44.

Hochreiter, E. (1990), 'The Austrian National Bank Act: What Does it Say About Monetary Policy?', *Konjunkturpohtik*, 36(4), 246-56.

Honohan, P. (1997), "Banking System Failure in Developing and Transition Countries: Diagnosis and Prediction", Bank for International Settlements Working Paper No. 39, January.

Hrnčíř, M. (1994a), 'Reform of the Banking Sector in the Czech Republic', in I. Székely and J.P. Bonin (eds.), *Development and Reform of Financial Systems in Central and Eastern Europe*, Aldershot: Edward Elgar, 221-56.

Hrnčíř, M. (1994b), 'Banks And Bad Loans In The Czech Republic', paper presented at the International Conference on 'Bad Eenterprise Debts in Central and Eastern Europe', 6-8 June 1994, Budapest.

Hrnčíř, M. (1993), 'Financial Intermediation in Former Czechoslovakia [Lessons and Progress Evaluation], presented at the Conference on Company Management and Capital Markets, Prague (April).

Hrnčíř, M. (1991), 'Money and Credit in the Transition of the Czechoslovak Economy', in H. Siebert (ed.), *The Transformation of Socialist Economies*, Tübigen: J.C.B. Mohr (Paul Siebeck), 307-25.

Hrnčíř, M. and J. Klacek (1991), 'Stabilization Policies and Currency Convertibility in Czechoslovakia', *European Economy*, Special Edition No.

2, 17-40.

Hukkinen, J. and J. Rautava (1992), 'Russia's Economic Reform and Trade between Finland and Russia', *Bank of Finland Bulletin* 4.

Hulyák, K. (1983), 'Disequilibrium in Consumption,' (Egyensúlyhiányok a lakosság fogyasztásában I. II), *Statisztikai Szemle*, 61(3), 229-43; 61(4), 369-80.

Jaksity, G. (1993), 'Egy Nem Hàtékony Piac Alkimiàja [The Alcheny of an Inefficient Market]', Budapest: Lupis Bròkerhàz (January).

Járai, Zs. (1993), 'Ten Per Cent Already Sold, Privatisation in Hungary,' in I.P. Székely and D.M.G. Newbery (eds.), *Hungary: An Economy in Transition*, Cambridge: Cambridge University Press, 77-83.

Jindra, V. (1992), 'Problems in Czechoslovak Banking Reform', in D.M. Kemme and A. Rudka (eds.), *Monetary and Banking Reform in the Post-Communist Economies*, New York: Institute for EastWest Studies.

Johnson, D. and P.L. Siklos (1996), 'Political and Economic Determinants of Interest Rate Behaviour: Are Central Banks Different?', *Economic Inquiry*, 34 (October), 708-29.

Junk, P. (1964), 'Monetary Policy And The Extension of Trade Credit', *Southern Economic Journal*, 30 (January), 274-77.

Kalocsay, T., G. Papp and W. Riecke (1988), 'Household Saving and Accumulation of Financial Assets in Hungary,' (A magánháztartások megtakaritásai és pénzvagyonképzése Magyarországon) (in Hungarian), mimeo.

Kaminsky, G. and C. Reinhart (1995), 'The Twin Crises: The Causes of Banking and Balance of Payments Problems', unpublished, Washington: Board of Governors of the Federal Reserve System.

Kapitány, Z. (1989), 'Kereslet és kínálat a 80-as évak autopicán', *Közgazdasági Szemle* 36(6), 592-611.

Kaser, M.C. (1990), 'The Technology of Decontrol: Some Macroeconomic Issues', *Economic Journal*, 100 (June), 596-615.

Kashyap, A.K., J.D. Stein and D.W. Wilcox (1993), 'Monetary Policy And Credit Conditions: Evidence From the Composition of External Finance', *American Economic Review*, 83 (March), 78-98.

Kemme, D.M. (1994), 'Banking in Central Europe During the Protomarket Period: Development and Emerging Issues', in I. Székely and J.P. Bonin (eds.), *Development and Reform of the Financial System in Central and Eastern Europe*, Aldershot: Edward Elgar, 41-60.

Kemme, D.M. (1992), 'The Reform of The System of Money, Banking and Credit in Central Europe', (unpublished manuscript), The Wichita State University.

Kemme, D. and A. Rudka (eds.) (1992), *Monetary and Banking Reform in Postcommunist Economies*, New York: Westview Press.

Király, J. (1993), 'A Short Run Money Market Model of Hungary,' in I.P. Székely and D.M.G. Newbery (eds.), *Hungary: An Economy in Transition*, Cambridge: Cambridge University Press, 137-48.

Király, J. and G. Kőrösi (1990), 'Consumption, Housing, and Money Demand in Hungary,' paper presented at the World Congress of the Econometric Society, Barcelona (August).

Klasmeyer, B. and B. Kubler (1983), 'Bankruptcy and Insolvency', in R. Ruster (ed.), *Business Transactions in Germany*, New York: M. Bender.

Kliesen, K.L. and J.A. Tatom (1992), 'The Recent Credit Crunch: The Neglected Dimensions', *Review of the Federal Reserve Bank of St. Louis*, 74 (September/October), 18-36.

Kokoszczyski, R. (1994), 'Money and Capital Market Reform in Poland', in I. Székely and J.P. Bonin (eds.), *Development and Reform of the Financial System in Central and Eastern Europe*, Aldershot: Edward Elgar, 257-67.

Kolodko, G.W., D. Gotz-Kozierkiewicz and E. Skreszewska-Paczik (1992), *Hyperinflation and Stabilization in Postsocialist Economies*, Boston, MA.: Kluwer Academic Publisher.

Kornai, J. (1992), 'The Postsocialist Transition and the State: Reflections in the Light of Hungarian Fiscal Problems', *American Economic Review*, Papers and Proceedings, 82 (2), 1-21.

Kornai J. (1990), *The Road to a Free Economy - Shifting from a Socialist System: The Example of Hungary*, New York, London: W.W. Norton.

Kruse, D. (1994), 'Discussion of Part One,' in J.Bonin and I.P. Székely (eds.), *The Development and Reform of Financial Systems in Central and Eastern Europe*, Aldershot: Edward Elgar, 61-7.

Kuti, A. and M. Móra (1989), 'A vállalati válság kezelése a nyolcvanas évek végén - avagy az új csődtörvény (nem-) alkalmazásának tapasztalatai' [Handling the Enterprise Crisis of the 1980s - Experiences with the New Bankruptcy Law], unpublished manuscript.

Laffer, A.B. (1970), 'Trade Credit And The Money Market', *Journal of Political Economy*, 78(March/April), 239-67.

Laki, M. (1983), *Vállalatok megszűnése és összevonása*, [The Dissolution and Merging of Enterprises], Budapest: Közgazdasági és Jogi Könyvkiadó.

Lane, T.D. (1992), 'Inflation Stabilization and Economic Transformation in Poland: The First Year', *Carnegie-Rochester Conference Series on Public Policy*, 36 (July), 105-56.

László, G. and L. Szakadát (1992), 'Money, Banking, and Capital Markets in Hungary: Recent Developments', mimeo, Budapest: Budapest Bank.

Li, C. and M. Pradhan (1990), 'Inflation, Financial Liberalization And Bankruptcies In Argentina', in K. Phylaktis and M. Pradhan (eds.), *International Finance in Less Developed Countries*, New York: St. Martin's Press, 98-113.

Lipton, D. and J. Sachs (1990), 'Creating a Market Economy in Eastern Europe: The Case of Poland', *Brookings Papers on Economic Activity,* 1, 75-133.

Lipton, D. and J. Sachs (1991), 'Privatization in Eastern Europe: The Case of Poland', in V. Crobo, F. Coricelli and J. Bossak (eds.), *Reforming Central and Eastern European Economies: Initial Results and Challenges,* Washington, D.C.: The World Bank, 231-52.

Lipton, D. and J. Sachs (1990), 'Creating a Market Economy in Eastern Europe: The Case of Poland', *Brookings Papers on Economic Activity,* 1, 75-147.

Lohmann, S. (1994), 'Designing A Central Bank In A Federal System: The Deutsche Bundesbank, 1957–1992,' in P.L. Siklos (ed.), *Varieties of Monetary Reforms: Lessons and Experiences on the Road to Monetary Union,* Dordrecht: Kluwer Academic Publishers, 247-77.

Long, M. and S. Sagari (1991), 'Financial Reforms in Socialist Economies in Transition,' *PRE Working Paper,* 711, Washington, D.C.: The World Bank.

Loungani, P. and M. Rush (1995), 'The Effects of Changes in Reserve Requirements on Investment and GNP', *Journal of Money, Credit and Banking,* 27(May), 511-26.

Marrese, M. (1992), 'Solving the Bad-Debt Problem of Central and Eastern European Banks: An Overview', Evanston, IL.: Northwestern University, unpublished manuscript.

Mayer, T. (1976), 'Structure And Operations Of The Federal Reserve System', in *Compendium of Papers Prepared for the Financial Institutions and Nation's Economy Study,* Committee on Banking, Currency and Housing, 94th Congress, Second Sess., Washington, D.C.: General Printing Office.

Mayhew, K. and P. Seabright (1992), 'Incentives and the Management of Enterprises in Economic Transition: Capital Markets Are Not Enough,' *Oxford Review of Economic Policy,* 8, 26-34.

McKinnon, R.I. (1991), *The Order of Economic Liberalisation,* Baltimore: Johns Hopkins University Press.

McKinnon, R.I. (1981), 'The Exchange Rate and Macroeconomic Policy: Changing Postwar Perceptions', *Journal of Economic Literature,* No. 2 (June), 531-58.

Meckling, W.H. (1977), 'Financial Markets, Default, and Bankruptcy: The Role of the State', *Law and Contemporary Problems,* 41(4), 13-37.

Mellár, T. (1990), 'Disequilibrium and Spill Over', (Egyensúlytalanság és a piacok közötti kapcsolatok) (in Hungarian), *Közgazdasági Szemle,* 37(12), 1333-50.

Meltzer, A. (1964), 'Monetary Policy And The Trade Credit Practices of Business Firms', in Commission on Money and Credit, *Stabilization Policies,* Englewood Cliffs, NJ: Prentice Hall, 471-97.

Meltzer, A. (1960), 'Mercantile Credit, Monetary Policy, and Size of Firms', *Review of Economics and Statistics,* 42 (November), 429-37.

Mérő, K. (1990), 'Vállalatfinanszírozás Magyarországon', *Gazdaságkutató Intézet,* 38-151.

Michaels, D. (1997), 'East Europe's Banks Show How Success Hinges on Reform', *Wall Street Journal Interactive Edition,* Business and Finance - Europe, 11 April.

Miller, M.H. (1977), 'The Wealth Transfers of Bankruptcy: Some Illustrative Examples', *Law and Contemporary Problems,* 41(4), 38-46.

Ministry of Finance (1993), 'Tasks of the Implementation of the Bank and Debtor Consolidation', Budapest, mimeo.

Mitchell, J. (1990), 'Managerial Discipline, Productivity, and Bankruptcy in Capitalist and Socialist Economies', *Comparative Economic Studies,* 32(3), 93-137.

Mizsei, K. (1994), 'Bankruptcy and Banking Reform in the Transition Economies of Central and Eastern Europe', in J.P. Bonin and I.P. Székely (eds.), *The Development and Reform of Financial Systems in Central and Eastern Europe,* Aldershot: Edward Elgar, 132-51.

Mizsei, K. (1993), 'Bankruptcy and the Post Communist Economies of East Central Europe', New York: Institute for EastWest Studies.

Montias, J.M. (1994), 'Financial and Fiscal Aspects of System Change in Eartern Europe', in I. Székely and J.P. Bonin (eds.), *Development and Reform of Financial Systems in Central and Eastern Europe,* Aldershot: Edward Elgar, 9-40.

Mortimer, K. (1994), 'Banking Privatisation Policy in Poland and Czechoslovakia,' paper presented at the conference on 'Banking Reform in the FSU and Eastern Europe: Lessons from Central Europe', Budapest (14-15 January).

Muraközi, L. (1992), 'Államháztartás a kilencvenes évek Magyarországán' (Government Finances in Hungary in the Nineties), *Közgazdasági Szemle,* 39(11), 1050-66.

Nadiri, M.I. (1969), 'The Determinants of Trade Credit in the U.S. Total Manufacturing Sector', *Econometrica,* 37 (July), 408-23.

Nadrai, L., I. Szalkai and J. Száz (1985), 'Credit Policy and the Balance of Payment Position,' (A hitelpolitika és a fizetési mérleg egyensúlya) (in Hungarian), *Szigma,* 18, 69-88.

Nagy, M. (1992), 'Nagybankok a hazai bankrendszerban', Budapest Bank Tanulmanyok No. 8.

Narodowy Bank Polski [National Bank of Poland] (1993), *Information Bulletin,* 5/1993.

National Bank of Hungary (1993), *Monthly Reports,* various issues, Budapest.

National Bank of Hungary (1992), *Annual Report,* Budapest.

National Bank of Slovakia (1992), _The Law of the National Council of the Slovak Republic_ (November).

New Banking Act in Hungary I and II (1991), Budapest: State Banking Supervision, 1 December.

Newbery, D.M. (1990), 'Tax Reform, Trade Liberalisation and Industrial Restructuring', _European Economy_, 32, 67-95.

Newbery, D.M. and P. Kattuman (1992), 'Market Concentration and Competition in Eastern Europe', _World Economy_, 515-34.

Nordhaus, W.D. (1990), 'Soviet Economic Reform: The Longest Road', _Brookings Papers on Economic Activity_, 1, 287-318.

Nordhaus, W.D. (1989), 'Alternative Approaches to the Political Business Cycle', _Brookings Papers on Economic Activity_, 2, 1-68.

Nyberg, P. and V. Vihriälä (1993), 'The Finnish Banking Crisis and its Handling', Discussion Papers, 8, Helsinki: Bank of Finland.

Nyers, R. and G. Lutz (1992), 'A Nagybankok Portfòliòjànak Javitàsa [Correction of Large Banks' Portfolios]', _Bankszemle_ (1-2), 34-43.

OECD (1992), _Financial Market Trends_, 51 (February), 15-30.

Owens, R.E. and S.L. Schreft (1992), 'Identifying Credit Crunches', Working Paper, Federal Reserve Bank of Richmond (August).

Papanek, G. (1986), 'Hungarian Enterprises Surviving Critical Financial Situations', _Acta Oeconomica_, 37(3-4), 305-23.

Parkin, M. and R. Bade (1978), 'Central Bank Laws And Monetary Policies: A Preliminary Investigation', in M.G. Porter (ed.), _The Australian Monetary System in the 1970s_, Clayton: Monash University.

Peek, J. and E. Rosengren (1993), 'Bank Regulation and the Credit Crunch', Working Paper 93-2 (February), Federal Reserve Bank of Boston.

Phelps, E.S., R. Frydman, A. Rapaczynski, and A. Schleifer (1993), 'Needed Mechanisms of Corporate Governance and Finance in Eastern Europe', Working Paper No.1, European Bank for Reconstruction and Development, (March).

Pinto, B., M. Belka and S. Krajewski (1993), 'Transforming State Enterprises In Poland: Microeconomic Evidence on Adjustment', Policy Research Paper WPS1101, Washington, D.C.: The World Bank.

Piper, R.P., I. Ábel and J. Király (1994), 'Transformation at a Cross-roads: Financial Sector Reform In Hungary', Policy Study No. 5, The Joint Hungarian-International Blue Ribbon Commission.

Podolski, T.M. (1973), _Socialist Banking and Monetary Control_, Cambridge: Cambridge University Press.

Portes, R. (1993), 'EMS and EMU After the Fall', _World Economy_, 16 (January), 1-15.

Portes, R. (1991), 'The Path Of Reform In Central And Eastern Europe: An Introduction', _European Economy_ Special Edition No. 2, 1991, 1-16.

Portes, R. (1983), 'Central Planning And Monetarism: Fellow Travelers?', in P. Desai (ed.), *Marxism, Central Planning, and the Soviet Economy: Essays in Honour of Alexander Erlich*, Cambridge: The MIT Press, 149-65.

Portes, R. (1978), 'Inflation Under Central Planning', in F. Hirsch and J.H. Goldthorpe (eds.), *The Political Economy of Inflation*, London: Martin Robertson, 73-87.

Portes, R. (1977), 'The Control of Inflation: Lessons From East European Experience', *Economica*, 44(May), 109-30.

Portes, R. and A. Santorum (1987), 'Money and Consumption Goods Market in China', *Journal of Comparative Economics*, 11(3), 354-71.

Portes, R. and D. Winter (1978), 'The Demand for Money and for Consumption Goods in Centrally Planned Economies', *Review of Economics and Statistics*, 60, 8-18.

Posen, A. (1995), 'Is Central Bank Independence (and Low Inflation) The Result of Financial Opposition to Inflation?', *NBER Macroeconomics Annual 1995*, Cambridge: The MIT Press, 253-74.

Pruist, J. And I.M.F. Team (1990), *The Czech and Slovak Federal Republics: An Economy in Transition*, IMF Occasional Paper 72, October, Washington, D.C.: International Monetary Fund.

Rădulescu, E. (1995), 'Interenterprise Arrears: The Romanian Type of Bad Enterprise Debts', in K. Mizsei and I.P. Székely (eds.), *Bad Enterprise Debts in Central and Eastern Europe*, New York: Institute for EastWest Studies.

Rappai, G. (1990), 'A Disequilibrium Model of the Consumption Goods Market,' (A fogyasztási javak piacának nem egyensúlyi modellje) (in Hungarian), *Statisztikai Szemle*, 68, 663-77.

Reserve Bank of New Zealand (1991), *Monetary Policy Statement*.

Riecke, W. (1985), 'About the Money Saving of Households,' (A lakóssági pénzmegtakarításról), *Szigma*, 18, 9-26.

Rudka, A. (1992), 'Reform of The Banking System In Poland', in D.M. Kemme and A. Rudka (eds.), *Monetary and Banking Reform in the Post-communist Economies*, New York: Institute for EastWest Studies, 72-153.

Rymes, T.K. (1994), 'On The Coyne-Rasminsky Directive And Responsibility For Monetary Policy', in P.L. Siklos (ed.), *Varieties of Monetary Reforms: Lessons and Experiences on the Road to Monetary Union*, Dordrecht: Kluwer Academic Publishers, 351-66.

Sachs, J. (1993), *Poland's Jump to the Market Economy*, Cambridge, Mass: The MIT Press.

Sanford, G. and M. Myant (1991), 'Poland', in S. White (ed.), *Handbook of Reconstruction in Eastern Europe and the Soviet Union*, London: Longman Current Affairs, 167-82.

Sánta, L. (1992), 'Sorbanálás Magyarországon', [Queing in Hungary] National

Bank of Hungary, mimeo.

Santorum, A. (1987), 'Expenditure and Portfolio Behaviour in China', London: Birbeck College, mimeo.

Sárközy, T. (1993), 'Legal Framework for the Hungarian Transition 1989-1991', in I.P. Székely and D.M.G. Newbery (eds.), *Hungary: An Economy in Transition*, Cambridge: Cambridge University Press, 239-48.

Savela, J. and R. Herrala (1992), 'Foreign-Owned Banks in Finland', *Bank of Finland Bulletin*, 66(4), 8-12.

Schaffer, M.E. (1992), 'The Polish State-Owned Enterprise Sector and the Recession in 1990', *Comparative Economic Studies*, 34 (Spring), 58-85.

Schwartz, R.A. (1974), 'An Economic Model Of Trade Credit', *Journal of Financial and Quantitative Analysis*, 9 (September), 643-57.

Schwartz, R.A. and D.K. Whitcomb (1979), 'The Trade Credit Decision', in J.L. Bickseler (ed.), *Handbook of Financial Economics*, Amsterdam: North-Holland, 257-73.

Scott, D., and R. Levine (1992), 'Old Debts and New Beginnings: A Policy Choice in Transitional Socialist Economies', *World Bank Policy Research Working Paper Series*, No. 876.

Scott, J.A. and T.C. Smith (1986), 'The Effect of the Bankruptcy Reform Act of 1978 on Small Business Loan Pricing', *Journal of Financial Economics*, 16(1), 119-40.

Siklos, P.L. (1997), *Money, Banking and Financial Institutions: Canada in the Global Environment*, Second Edition, Toronto: McGraw-Hill Ryerson Ltd.

Siklos, P.L. (1995), 'Establishing Central Bank Independence: Recent Experiences in Developing Countries', *Journal of International Trade and Economic Development*, 4 (November), 351-84.

Siklos, P.L. (1993), 'Income Velocity And Institutional Change: Some New Time Series Evidence, 1870–1986', *Journal of Money, Credit and Banking*, 26 (August), 377-92.

Siklos, P.L. (1994b), 'Central Bank Independence in The Transitional Economies: A Preliminary Investigation of Hungary, Poland, The Czech And Slovak Republics', in J.P. Bonin and I.P. Székely (eds.), *The Development and Reform of Financial Systems in Central and Eastern Europe*, Aldershot: Edward Elgar, 71-98. An updated version appears as chapter 8 in this volume.

Siklos, P.L. (1990), 'Hyperinflations: Their Origins, Development and Termination', *Journal of Economic Surveys* 3: 225-48.

Siklos, P.L. and I. Ábel (1997), 'Real Exchange Rate Targeting in a Transitional Economy and the Stabilisation Problem: The Hungarian Experience', in T.D. Willett, R.-D. Sweeney and C. Wihlborg (eds.), *Trade and Currency Policies for Emerging Market Economies*, Boulder, Col.: The Westview Press, chapter 11.

Siklos, P.L., and I. Ábel (1997a), "Monetary Policies in Transition: An Evaluation of the Hungarian and Czech Experiences", in P. Gáspár (ed.), *Macroeconomics of recovery in Central and Eastern Europe* (Budapest: Magyar Tudományos Akadémia), 111-30.

Siklos, P.L. and I. Ábel (1995b), 'Fiscal and Monetary Policy In The Transition: Searching for the Credit Crunch', in T.D. Willett, R.C.K. Burdekin, R.J. Sweeney and C. Wihlborg (eds.), *Establishing Monetary Stability in Emerging Market Economies*, Boulder, Col.: The Westview Press, 237-68. A revised version appears as chapter 3 in this volume.

Siklos, P.L. and K. Eckhold (1997), 'Income Velocity In Turbulent Times: The Role Of Institutional Factors In The New Zealand Experience', *Journal of Macroeconomics*, 19 (Winter), 31-52.

Siklos, P.L. and M.E. Wohar (1997), 'Convergence in Interest Rates and Inflation Rates Across Countries and Over Time', *Review of International Economics*, 5 (February), 129-41.

Simeon, K. et al. (1987), *Doing Business in France*, New York: M. Bender.

Stanczak, K. (1992), 'Inflation Stabilization and Economic Transformation in Poland: The First-Year - A Comment', *Carnegie-Rochester Conference Series on Public Policy*, 36 (July), 157-62.

Stiglitz, J.E. (1992), 'Interest Rate Puzzles, Competitive Theory, and Capital Constraints', invited paper presented at the tenth World Congress of the International Economic Association, Moscow (August).

Stiglitz, J.E. (1972), 'Some Aspects of the Pure Theory of Corporate Finance: Bankruptcies and Takeovers', *The Bell Journal of Economics and Management Science*, 3(2), 458-82.

Sundararajan, V. and T.J. Baliño (1991), 'Issues in Recent Banking Crises', in *Banking Crises: Cases and Issues,* Washington, D.C.: International Monetary Fund, 1-57.

Szabó, L. (1991), 'A Pénzintézetek Gazdálkodása 1987 és 1990 között a Mérlegadatok Alapján', [Activities of Financial Institutions Between 1987 and 1990 on the Basis of Balance Sheet Performance], *Bankszemle*, 29-46.

Székely, I.P. (1994), 'Economic Transformation and The Reform of The Financial System In Central And Eastern Europe', in A. Aganbegjan and E. Bogomolov (eds.), *Economics in a Changing World*, 1, London: MacMillan, 260-91.

Székely, I.P., (1990), 'The Reform of The Hungarian Financial System', *European Economy*, No. 43 (March), 107-23.

Székely, I.P. and J.P. Bonin (1996), *The Development and Reform of Financial Systems in Central and Eastern Europe*, Aldershot: Edward Elgar.

Székely, I.P. and D.M.G. Newberry (1993), *Hungary: An Economy in Transition*, Cambridge: Cambridge University Press).

Tardos, M. (1988), 'How to Create Markets in Eastern Europe: The Hungarian Case', in J. Brada, E. Hewett and T.A. Wold (eds.), *Economic Adjustment and Reform*, Durham and London: Duke University Press, 259-84.

Thorne, A. (1992), 'The Role of Banks in the Transition: Lessons from Eastern European Countries' Experience', *The World Bank ECA/MENA Technical Department*, mimeo.

Várhegyi, É. (1997), 'A Magyar Bankrendszer Privatizálása', *Külgazdaság*.

Várhegyi, É. (1995), *Bankok a Versenyben*, Budapest: Pénz. Rt.

Várhegyi, É. (1994), 'The 'Second' Reform of The Hungarian Banking System', in J.P. Bonin and I.P. Székely (eds.), *The Development and Reform of Financial Systems in Central and Eastern Europe*, Aldershot: Edward Elgar, 293-308.

Várhegyi, É. (1993), 'Key Elements of the Reform of the Hungarian Banking System: Privatisation and Portfolio Cleaning', *CEPR Discussion Paper Series*, 826, London: CEPR.

Voszka, É. (1986), 'Company Liquidation without a Legal Successor', *Acta Oeconomica* (Budapest), 37 (1-2), 59-71.

Wadhwani, S.B. (1986), 'Inflation, Bankruptcy, Default Premia And The Stock Market', *The Economic Journal*, 96(March), 120-38.

Walsh, C. (1992), 'Incentive Contracts For Central Bankers And The Inflationary Bias Of Discretionary Monetary Policy', Working Paper, University of California, Santa Cruz. [A related paper entitled 'Optimal Contracts for Central Bankers' appears in *American Economic Review*, 85 (March 1995), 150-67.]

Weston, F.J. (1977), 'Some Economic Fundamentals for an Analysis of Bankruptcy', *Law and Contemporary Problems*, 41(4), 47-65.

White, M.J. (1989), 'The Corporate Bankrtupcy Decision', *Journal of Economic Perspectives*, 3 (2), 129-51.

White, M.J. (1984), 'Bankruptcy, Liquidation and Reorganization', Chapter 35 in D. Logue (ed.), *Handbook of Modern Finance*, Boston: Warren, Gorham and Lamont.

White, W.H. (1964), 'Trade Credit And Monetary Policy: A Reconciliation', *The Economic Journal*, 74(December), 935-45.

Wijnbergen, S. van (1994), 'On the Role of Banks in Enterprise Restructuring: The Polish Example,' *Discussion Paper Series*, 898, London: CEPR.

Williamson, J. (1991), *The Economic Opening of Eastern Europe*, Washington, D.C.: Institute for International Economics.

Woolley, J.T. (1988), 'Partisan Manipulation of The Economy: Another Look at Monetary Policy with Moving Regressions', *Journal of Politics*, 50, 335-60.

World Bank (1989), World Development Report, Oxford: Oxford University Press.

Wrightman, G. and P. Rutland (1991), 'Czechoslovakia', in S. White (ed.), *Handbook of Reconstruction in Eastern Europe and the Soviet Union,* London: Longman Current Affairs, 29-58.

Wrightsman, D. (1969), 'Optimal Credit For Accounts Receivable', *The Quarterly Review of Economics and Business,* 9, 59–66.

Wyczański, P. (1994), 'Discussion of Chapter 5', in J. Bonin and I.P. Székely (eds.), *The Development and Reform of Financial Systems in Central and Eastern Europe,* Aldershot: Edward Elgar, 130-31.

Wyczański, P. (1993), 'Polish Banking System', Economic and Social Policy Series No. 32, Warsaw: Friedrich-Ebert Foundation.

Zwass, A. (1979), *Money, Banking and Credit in the Soviet Union and Eastern Europe,* New York: M.E. Sharpe.

Index